T0065770

## MISERABLE AND GUILT-RIDDEN, TINA STUMBLED OFF TO HER BEDROOM AFTER THE ARGUMENT. . . .

She hated being sent to bed at the same time as the foster kids, but she also hated the way she fought with her parents all the time. She didn't like yelling, she didn't like always being unhappy and wishing her life could change. Why didn't her parents try to understand this?

Tina undressed and crawled under the covers. She looked at her digital clock radio, and the figures started racing, just like they did when she set the time. But she wasn't pushing any buttons. She wasn't even touching the clock. In front of her eyes the clock seemed to say it was becoming later and later, closer to the appropriate bedtime for a teenager like herself.

Suddenly, music blared; the radio had come on by itself. Tina turned it off, but it came back on. Weird, she thought. She unplugged the clock, and the music stopped. Tina was not concerned; she had another clock radio.

The next morning passed without incident. Tina hadn't told anyone about her clock radio, and by the following afternoon the incident seemed minor compared to what was to follow. . . .

# UNLEASHED

*Of Poltergeists*
*and Murder:*
*The Curious Story of*
**TINA RESCH**

WILLIAM ROLL, Ph.D, AND VALERIE STOREY

PARAVIEW POCKET BOOKS
New York   London   Toronto   Sydney

PARAVIEW
191 Seventh Avenue, New York, NY 10011

POCKET BOOKS, a division of Simon & Schuster, Inc.
1230 Avenue of the Americas, New York, NY 10020

ISBN: 978-0-7434-8294-3

First Paraview Pocket Books trade paperback edition May 2004

10  9  8  7  6  5  4  3  2  1

POCKET and colophon are registered trademarks of
Simon & Schuster, Inc.

Manufactured in the United States of America

For information regarding special discounts for bulk purchases,
please contact Simon & Schuster Special Sales at 1-800-456-6798
or business@simonandschuster.com

To my grandchildren,
David, Martin, Jensen, Giles, Annika, Georgi, and Anders.
—William Roll

# CONTENTS

# UNLEASHED

# PROLOGUE

I watched in disbelief as four burly officers from the Carroll County sheriff's department took their seats behind the small, white casket covered with flowers, a toy rabbit perched on top. It was the Saturday before Easter, 1992. The open casket showed a pretty little girl wearing her pink Easter dress. Even with the heavy makeup that hid the autopsy sutures, you could see Amber had been a beautiful child.

The Almon Funeral Home chapel was filled to overflowing, but there was no sign of the child's mother. I assumed she was sitting in the private, screened section reserved for family members. Charged with Amber's murder, her mother, Tina Resch, now using her married name of Christina Boyer, had sat in jail for the past three days while the media vilified her. Almost without exception, it seemed the entire town of Carrollton, Georgia, had banded against her, the Northern outsider; a woman so out of control she could kill her three-year-old daughter. In a show of solidarity, the outraged community had taken Amber as one of their own; Almon donated the casket; local florists sent sprays of flowers; police officers provided the burial plot. The only thing from Tina was the pink Easter dress.

My mind was a blur of shock and distress. All I could think was, How? How had this happened? It was impossible. I had known Tina since she was fourteen years old. In an ironic twist, she had been the center of a media blitz then, too; the wild child who could move objects with the power of her mind. The reports hadn't been off base. Much of my research and writing of the previous eight years had focused on Tina's impressive abilities, one of the most convincing cases of poltergeist activity I had ever witnessed. Now a tall, lively, and volatile young woman in her early twenties, Tina could still be that troubled teen desperate for affection and dreaming of happy endings. Abandoned by her mother at the age of ten months and adopted into a rigid, unforgiving household, Tina had not been ready for single parenthood at eighteen, and she often found the role difficult and irritating. But she could never have killed Amber. Amber was her one real hope for a family of her own and a better future. Somehow this message had to get through to the authorities. Tina was innocent.

Pastor Geron Crawford delivered the sermon. When he finished, the officers behind the casket slowly advanced, stationed themselves at each corner of the coffin, and then carried it out, their large bodies almost concealing their tiny charge. Along with a mass of mourners, I followed the procession outside. I was oblivious to my surroundings: the weather, the people beside me—I couldn't register anything. The words of the sermon stayed with me: "We have been left in a thick darkness." A darkness had indeed descended, and Tina needed my help perhaps more than at any other time in her life.

# A CALL FOR HELP

**"I**'m seeing something I can't understand." Mike Harden, a reporter for the *Columbus Dispatch*, had just called Duke University, famous for their Parapsychology Laboratory, and asked for someone who knew about objects that moved by themselves. As was their usual practice, Duke forwarded the call to my office in Chapel Hill, North Carolina, where I was the director of the Psychical Research Foundation. Over the years our office had heard from many worried people, frightened that their homes harbored evil spirits or that their encounters with the unknown would be branded "crazy." Mike's call was more down-to-earth. Describing himself as "the ultimate skeptic of the paranormal," Mike was looking for someone to help him with the strangest news story of his career.

To all appearances, the suburban home of Joan and John Resch, Tina, their adopted fourteen-year-old daughter, and four foster children currently living with the family had developed a mind of its own. Electric lights and household appliances were turning themselves off and on, and bottles and glasses were flying and crashing without visible cause.

The household was in chaos. No one could guess what would happen next. Mike knew the story sounded incredible, straight out of *The Twilight Zone,* but other visitors had seen the bizarre events as well and had been astonished. Because the chaos swirled around Tina, the Resches suspected the girl was responsible. After visiting the house himself, Mike didn't know what to think.

"I had just arrived at the house and was standing in the kitchen, looking into the family room," he said. "There were papers and things on the end table. They just kind of shot out from the table. Tina was nowhere near them." The magazines and newspapers had fallen to the floor two or three feet away. "My first thought was, 'What the hell was that?' "

Mike went into the family room and sat down on a large couch across from where Tina sat in a recliner. As he talked with the girl and her mother, "A small toy cradle near the fireplace flipped into the air, perhaps two feet, and dropped to the carpeting." Tina was about six feet away. A little girl, one of the Resches' foster children, was also in the room playing with her dolls, her back to the adults. She went over to the cradle, picked it up, and announced, "It's broke!" This type of thing had been happening all weekend. Just as Mike was trying to make sense of that episode, a full cup of coffee on a table beside Tina flipped through the air, landed on her lap, spilling coffee, then crashed into the fireplace. "She was in my line of vision when it happened. Again, I did not see her aid its movement in any way."

Listening to Mike, my first thought was that when a fourteen-year-old is the center of flying objects, the most likely explanation is a teen who is venting her frustration. Mike didn't think this could explain what he had seen, but he had no experience in such matters; he could be mistaken, he said.

I asked Mike what else he could tell me about the family. He explained that the previous October he had written a column for the *Dispatch* about Joan's outstanding work as a foster mother. She and her husband, John, had taken care of some 250 children over the years. Joan and John were highly regarded members of the community and had received numerous awards for their work. But the call Mike had received from Joan this March morning of 1984 had nothing to do with awards or foster children. "If I hadn't known Joan," he said, "I would have dismissed the whole thing as a crank call."

Joan told Mike that things were happening that she couldn't understand and asked if he knew someone who might help. Mike didn't think she was looking for publicity. The Resches sounded desperate for a solution. Their belongings were being ruined and they just couldn't figure out what was going on. Worse, Joan was worried about the safety of the four foster children in the house. Things were flying about and she was afraid one of them might get hurt. "She was asking for help—really crying out," Mike said. It was the strangest call he had ever received.

Mike asked Joan if he could come out to the house and see for himself. Joan said he would be welcome, and he arrived about ten-thirty that morning. "Even though I knew the family," he said, "I did go in very skeptically." But after a few minutes in the house, Mike knew he was seeing something real. He just couldn't reconcile it with his worldview: "It seemed to me that I was witnessing something which defied both my skeptical instincts as a journalist as well as all of the traditional laws of physics."

Knowing that the Resches were becoming edgier and more anxious by the day, Mike asked if he could write a story about what he had seen. Perhaps one of the readers of the *Dispatch* would know about this type of trouble and how to make it stop. This was the reason for Mike's call to my office. He wanted me to fly up to Columbus and determine if the incidents were real. And maybe I knew a way to put an end to the turmoil.

The case, as interesting as it sounded, was not really one I wanted to pursue. The foundation was not well endowed and I wasn't in a position to just take off and investigate every claim that came my way, even if it was backed by a sane and serious witness like Harden. One more case would probably not add anything new.

"You know," I said, "a number of people are going to say, 'These people are mad,' " speaking of the Resches. Harden knew. He had phoned a psychology professor at Ohio State University for someone to call. The professor told Harden to phone Duke, saying he might do so without dialing.

I laughed, but as much as I sympathized with Mike's dilemma, I had to decline his request that I come to Columbus. It was just too expensive and time-consuming. Besides, I had investigated enough poltergeist cases, which this seemed to be, to have a rough idea of what was going on. Mike wasn't so easily dissuaded: "The newspaper has its own plane. We will fly you and an assistant up at our expense."

This put a new spin on things. Offers for free air travel, and an executive jet at that, were something I couldn't just turn down.

I didn't become a parapsychologist by accident. I was born in 1926, in Germany, where my father was American vice-consul. He was of Norwegian descent, my mother Danish. Norwegians and Danes usually get on well with each other, but not my parents. They divorced when I was three, and I went with my mother to Denmark. I visited my father in Norway and once, for several months, at his home in Oakland, California. Otherwise I was a Danish schoolboy in the town of Birkerød, north of Copenhagen. Then, April 9, 1940, on our way to school, my friend Klaus and I found green slips of paper on the road. They had been dropped by planes from the German air force and announced, in broken Danish, that we had been occupied "for our own protection." Normal life was a thing of the past, and I lost all contact with my father. Two years later my mother died suddenly, and I became the ward of a guardian who disliked me. I didn't do well in school.

In September 1944, the leader of the resistance in Birkerød, Peter Tegner, a former navy commander and our neighbor, asked me to join the resistance movement. I was to be a courier between him and the group leaders. I was short and looked more like fourteen than eighteen; I wouldn't arouse suspicion. Tegner had gone underground to avoid arrest, and only I knew where he was staying at any one time. After a while Tegner told me to go underground as well. If I had been caught and tortured, the resistance in Birkerød might have unraveled.

The nine months I was in the resistance, until the liberation on May 5, 1945, were the best in my life. My duties as a courier and learning to handle weapons were exciting. Tegner and the group leaders respected me, and I was working for a good cause, the best under the circumstances, freedom from barbarians. The self-confidence my guardian had sucked away was restored.

The Germans capitulated to the Allied forces and the resistance in Birkerød came out in the open. We stopped and checked traffic on Kongevejen, the King's Road, which connects Copenhagen and Elsinore, and arrested the few Nazi collaborators in town. The German soldiers and a large group of noncombat Germans were ensconced in two army camps where we became the guards.

One day after returning from guard duty, I received a phone call from Norway. It was my father, now a major colonel with SHAEF, the army's intelligence unit. I was elated and astonished that he was so close. He was restoring the American embassy in Oslo and would soon do the same in Copenhagen. When he arrived, he was driving a convertible Mercedes he had commandeered from a group of German officers. Our reunion was joyful and I learned to drive the car.

Sometime after my mother's death, I began having out-of-body experiences, perhaps because of the shock. I didn't know about such things, but a neighbor, Jacob Paludan, a fiction writer and reviewer of books about parapsychology and Eastern religion, befriended me and lent me his books. The books said that an invisible web connects people regardless of national or racial differences. If this web could be shown to actually exist, I thought, wars and conflicts would surely end. I am no longer that naive, but this was my main motive for turning to parapsychology.

In 1947 with the war behind us, I went to the University of California, Berkeley, because it was close to my father's home. I expected to study parapsychology, but there were no such courses so I settled for psychology and philosophy. Neither told me anything meaningful. After graduation I turned to sociology. I would surely learn about the web of connections I had read about, but sociology was as irrelevant to my concerns as the others.

I was still committed to parapsychology and came across the parapsychological writings of H. H. Price, a renowned philosophy professor at Oxford University. Price accepted me as a special student. I married a girl I had met from New York, Muriel, and we went to Oxford expecting to stay for a year. It stretched to seven.

In 1957, after finishing my studies in England, I received an invitation from J. B. Rhine, the founder of modern parapsychology, to join his staff at Duke University. I had met Rhine while still in England shortly after my daughter, Lise, was born. A photo of Rhine shows him holding Lise in his arms.

My office at Duke was on the second floor of the West Duke Building, over the main entrance. It had the largest window in the building. If you looked up from the street, you would think I had the largest office. It was the smallest. The end of the upstairs corridor had been cut off to make a room.

My office may also have been the hottest because of the large window. In 1957 there was no air-conditioning, only fans. My papers would glue themselves to my arms or fly like leaves in a storm. This was a change from England, where the problem was lack of heating. The excitement of being at the Parapsychology Laboratory of Duke University easily made up for these discomforts.

There was a problem though. I had gone to Oxford to investigate extrasensory perception and I expected to continue the work at Duke, but my tests weren't going anywhere. My fellow students at Oxford showed some evidence of ESP, but the tests I conduced at Duke didn't rise above chance.

Then in early 1958, we heard about a house of "flying objects" in Seaford, Long Island. Rhine asked Gaither Pratt, assistant director of the lab, and me to take a look. The occupants, James and Lucille Herrmann, had complained to the police that their porcelain figurines and other belongings were flying through the air and breaking against the walls and furniture. They first thought that their twelve-year-old son, Jimmy, was throwing things because they only moved when he was home. But when the Herrmanns and the police witnessed movements of objects away from the boy, the family thought that an evil spirit had invaded their home. They were Catholic and put out bottles of holy water to discourage the demon, but the bottles spilled with an explosive sound when no one was in the room. The bottles that were affected all had screw caps. Gaither and I tried to duplicate the phenomenon by filling containers with dry ice, but the gas escaped along the threads or the bottles exploded.

After visiting the home and speaking to the family and the police, Gaither and I thought that the occurrences were probably real. Our impression was confirmed when a bottle in the basement fell over with a bang and spilled while we were upstairs with the family. We coined a term, *recurrent spontaneous psychokinesis* or *RSPK*, for the occurrences. In earlier ages, and in modern movies, the phenomena have been attributed to *poltergeists*, which is a German word for "rowdy ghosts." The occurrences were rowdy, but there was no evidence of ghosts in the Herrmann home. We attributed the occurrences to unconscious psychokinesis by Jimmy.

The following years my colleagues and I investigated other homes and businesses where things moved when no one was in a position to throw them. This was a whole lot more interesting than my ESP tests, and more convincing that something real was happening. I wrote a book, *The Poltergeist*, about my investigations and published articles about historical cases. I then turned to other matters until I received the call from Mike Harden.

\*         \*         \*

I told Mike that I would need to speak to the Resches myself. I wanted to be sure that my presence wouldn't be just one more disruption in a household already under siege.

In the meantime I suggested that Mike advise the Resches to take Tina to a neurologist. I wanted to know if she had any brain anomalies that might be associated with the occurrences. If she wasn't just a mischievous child staging stunts to gain attention, there might possibly be a biological aspect, such as epilepsy, behind the occurrences.

Two days later I called Joan Resch to introduce myself and to ask if she wanted me to investigate. Joan sounded relieved by the offer and said that not only was I welcome, but that I and an assistant could stay in the house. Things had become so unmanageable that she had had to send their four foster children away to temporary shelters, leaving an empty bedroom.

Expanding on Mike's story, Joan told me the disturbances had begun over the weekend. But Monday morning was quiet and she hoped there would be no need to involve anyone else. She had let Tina sleep late because the activity had kept everyone up Sunday night. The girl was taught at home so there was no need to get up for school.

After Tina had come down for breakfast, Joan heard knocking from the front door. Before she could answer, she saw it was the candleholder on the wall in the hallway that was banging against the wall by itself. The six candles had already been broken or stored away, leaving the empty holder and the chain that held it in place. As Joan watched from the kitchen, she said the holder "banged on the wall till it broke its chain."

Then a carton of apple juice on the counter by the sink sailed into the family room, smashing against the door to the garage. Juice spilled out everywhere. A picture in the hallway and a large picture over the couch in the living room swung back and forth on their nails. She and Tina held them in place, but when they let go, Joan said, the pictures went back to swinging. "We would stop them and they'd begin again."

Next the lamp on the end table by the couch in the living room fell to the floor. It didn't break and they put it back, but it fell again. This happened about four more times, Joan said, until they left it on the floor. That's when she thought of calling Mike Harden.

We finished speaking and I considered my next move. To make the trip worthwhile, I needed to accomplish three things. First, I wanted to see for myself whether the incidents were genuine or fraudulent. If things started moving on their own, the way Mike Harden said they did, I would try to film them with my camcorder. Second, I wanted to find out as much as I could about the things that had happened in the past by speaking to witnesses, especially to people from outside the home. Visitors may have less reason to perpetrate a fraud than the family. Third, with the assistance of a psychologist and depending on what we found, I hoped to help the family understand what was going on and counsel them about how to deal with the situation. An assistant would also be useful for keeping an eye on Tina while I did my interviews.

My choice of assistant was a young man named Kelly Powers. Kelly had an MA in clinical psychology from Florida State University; if Tina needed counseling, his training could be useful. He was also young enough at twenty-four to develop a friendly rapport with Tina that might encourage her to be open and frank with us. I had met Kelly at the Patricia Hayes School for Inner Sense Development just outside Durham, North Carolina. Slim with finely chiseled features and curly, brown hair, Kelly was intelligent and humorous, with a caustic compassion for his fellow beings. He seemed quick at grasping psychological problems and finding solutions. I had watched him at the Patricia Hayes School and been impressed with his empathetic manner in dealing with difficult people. There was one hitch. I was unable to pay an assistant. Fortunately, Kelly was willing to donate his time; another example of his good nature. With no further obstacles to keep me home, I was ready to confront the situation in Columbus. I just hoped it wasn't going to be a waste of time.

# 2

# THE HOUSE ON BLUE ASH ROAD

**S**unday, March 11, 1984. Just as Mike Harden had promised, Kelly and I flew into Columbus on a plane sent by the *Dispatch*. The plane taxied to a stop at the airport's section for private aircraft. It was shortly after noon, and Kelly and I felt like celebrities as we stepped out onto the runway, Mike waiting to greet us. His friendly face was familiar to *Dispatch* readers. They would see it above his column, brown hair parted on the left and covering the tops of his ears, a neatly trimmed beard framing a smile.

When we left North Carolina, it was spring; the best time of year, not too cold and not too hot. The whites of dogwoods lit the woods round my house, and the reds of azaleas warmed the yard. When we reached Columbus, it was winter and snow. I was glad Mike was there to drive us to the house.

During the trip, Mike filled us in with some of the news from the past week. His story "Strange Happenings Unnerve

Family" had been printed not only in the *Dispatch*, but had also been picked up by wire services all over the country and the world. The media attention was almost as wild as the events themselves. Some papers reported just the bare facts, others took a more speculative approach. The New Jersey *Trenton Times*, for one, wondered if the Resches were living in "another Amityville."

The response from the public had been overwhelming, even if none of it was helpful. Every day letters and calls poured into the *Dispatch* offices with suggestions for the Resches. They should pray more, they should avoid tarot cards and Ouija boards, and they should place dimes above the doorway—a surefire way to get rid of demons. One woman claimed to have seen UFOs in the sky as she was hanging out her laundry; could they be coming from the Resch home? But the family found no workable answers in any of the offerings.

Mike said that the occurrences were as frequent and as disruptive as ever, but he had some discouraging news. A few days earlier, a press conference had been held at the Resch home. "The force," as everyone was calling whatever was behind the occurrences, was not in a cooperative mood and had refused to perform for the news-hungry reporters. After nearly nine hours of waiting for something to happen, Tina had been caught on film pulling down a lamp with her hand. She didn't succeed on her first try, misjudging the distance between her hand and the lampshade, but a second attempt brought the lamp to the floor. Great, I thought. Just what I needed to hear.

My first impression of 5242 Blue Ash Road was of a well-kept house on a quiet street on the north side of Columbus, one of several brick-and-stucco homes. Joan Resch met us at the door. In her midfifties, carefully dressed and not a blond hair out of place despite the ruckus she had been living through, Joan was welcoming and easygoing as she led us into the spacious living room to meet her husband, John, and their daughter, Tina. We were also introduced to the family pet, Pete, a huge brown-and-white Siberian husky with mismatched eyes, one brown and the other blue. The neurologist Tina had been visiting at my suggestion, John Corrigan, was also waiting to talk with us. As soon as possible, John Resch excused himself to continue his ongoing repair work. A heavyset, silent man who seemed more comfortable working with his hands than making small talk, he had a basement full of broken household items—thanks to the force—that needed his attention.

Tina was a tall, bright-eyed, and vivacious girl excited at the prospect of having visitors. She took to Kelly and me right away. Spirited and shy at the same time, she soon warmed, especially to Kelly. He later described her as "kinetic, frenetic, bright-eyed and bushy-tailed and darting all over." We liked the girl and could sense that some of her difficulties probably stemmed from being a growing teenager in a crowded house. Tina seemed to need a lot of space and outlet for her energy. For the time being, though, she was simply happy to take us upstairs to show us her room, which was to be ours for the next few days.

The room was large and light with two beds and two dressers. A bookcase and a set of shelves held Tina's collection of odds and ends, including her collection of perfume bottles. I put my bags on the bed by the window and Kelly took the other. Then I noticed something suspicious. On the bedside table was a child's paperback of magical tricks. Tina was apparently interested in magic. I was surprised she would leave the book where Kelly and I couldn't help seeing it. Perhaps she wanted to be found out, like the perpetrator who leaves a clue at the scene. I decided not to ask Tina about the book, and to wait and see what tricks she might come up with during our stay.

Before leaving us to unpack, Tina showed us the adjoining room where she would be sleeping. With its beds and crib, it had been used by the foster children until "the force" had sent them away. Her older brother Craig, now spending the day at his job in JAYS, a convenience store, had the adjacent room. The rest of the upstairs consisted of the master bedroom and bathroom on the opposite side of the hallway. A second bathroom, used by the children, was there as well.

As Tina gave us the guided tour, I couldn't help but notice her propensity for colliding with the walls and furniture. She was like a bumper car, except that her movements were fluid, even graceful. Walking like this seemed to be her usual way. Regardless of the book on magic, Tina didn't strike me as someone who would be good at sleight of hand. It had taken her two tries to pull down the lamp for the reporters, and the lamp was right next to her. If the force turned out to be just a troublesome child playing games, Kelly and I would soon expose the situation.

When we got back downstairs, Mike was leaving. I arranged to meet him later in the week so I could make a tape recording of his experiences. Once he left, Tina went back upstairs. That's when the first incident took place. As Tina was walking up the stairs, a framed photograph of her nephews Jim and Eric came off the wall. The glass had cracked but was still in the frame. We didn't know how this had happened, but it told us that the occurrences, real or contrived, were still going on.

Kelly went upstairs to join Tina, and I went into the living room to talk with John Corrigan. He told me he had spent fifteen hours in the home talking with Tina and her parents. He and George Paulson, chairman of the Department of Neurology at Ohio State University, had interviewed and tested Tina there. They had not found any abnormalities. Everything was within normal range. The girl did, however, have a history of dizziness and poor coordination, and her temper was a problem, often turning into tantrums where she had to be restrained in her room. Relations with her parents were at an all-time low, especially with her father. Corrigan believed John Resch was partly responsible for this as he blamed the girl for the disturbances. For the last two months she had suffered from headaches, complaining of a dull pain at the back of her head, which Corrigan attributed to tension.

I asked Corrigan if there had been any occurrences in the house while he was there. There had, Corrigan said, and in his opinion, Tina had done them all in a perfectly normal manner; no psychokinesis that he could tell.

We had come too late, I thought; the time for genuine phenomena, if there had been any, had gone. Corrigan said that he believed the incidents witnessed by Mike Harden were probably real, and I agreed. We had both been impressed by Harden's account, and I didn't think an experienced reporter like Harden could have been hoodwinked by a fourteen-year-old. In any case, a few days in the house should tell us whether the occurrences were genuine psychokinesis.

As I talked with Corrigan, Kelly was upstairs witnessing a few incidents on his own. A table lamp in Joan and John's bedroom fell to the floor when Tina was near enough to have pushed it, but then something happened that Tina apparently could not have done. She was in the master bathroom telling Kelly about an incident that had happened there when they heard a sound from Joan and John's bedroom. When Kelly looked in, he found a perfume bottle on the floor. He thought it might have been there all along and that he had missed seeing it, but in that case, he couldn't explain the sound. No one else was upstairs.

Tina and Kelly came downstairs, he to the living room to describe the occurrences to me and Corrigan, while Tina went to the family room to tell Joan. Suddenly there was a crash and a cry. I rushed into the kitchen and found Tina crying and holding her left arm. She said that she and Joan had been walking out of the family room when the phone from the table between the two recliners had come out and struck her. She had been downstairs ten minutes when this happened. Because she had been behind her mother when the phone flew out, I thought she could have staged the event, but I kept my thoughts to myself.

With Kelly's and my arrival, Joan felt hopeful that we would find a solution to rid the house of its scourge, and she wanted to celebrate. She proposed we go out for dinner. After the force had taken up residence, she no longer cooked. Preparing a family meal in the midst of flying food and broken glass had become impossible.

I told Joan and John to go on ahead; Kelly and I would stay in the house with Tina. Joan said to help ourselves from the refrigerator. Corrigan had to be home for dinner, and he left at the same time as the Resches.

With her parents gone, Tina took over the role of hostess and set out paper plates, Styrofoam cups, and plastic utensils; glasses and china had long been replaced by nonbreakable items. Kelly and I discovered that a meal in the Resch home was like a picnic threatened by a shower. You wanted to eat as fast as you could. Tina seemed to enjoy the relaxed ease of our do-it-yourself dinner, made even easier when we finished and threw our tableware in the garbage can. The force may have destroyed Joan's domestic routine, but for Tina life had become pleasantly simplified with no need to stack and empty the dishwasher. There were also no foster children to diaper and look after, and her household chores had vanished.

We were sitting around the kitchen table with our Styrofoam coffee cups when Tina asked if we knew aggravation. Here it comes, I thought, she is going to tell us about life with Joan and John, and sooner than I expected. We encouraged her to go on, but, no, what she meant, she said in an exasperated voice, was did we know the *game* Aggravation, and did we want to play?

Tina explained the rules. "You throw a pair of dice, aiming for doubles. When you score a hit, you get an extra throw to your advantage and the aggravation of the other players."

Kelly and I agreed to play. The game would break the ice, and it appealed to us for another reason. If Tina could influence the fall of the dice, this might indicate she had psychokinetic abilities. It would not be a conclusive PK test, however. For that we would have needed automated equipment and a way to keep Tina from any contact with the dice. But we reduced the possibility of cheating by using one of the Styrofoam cups for shaking and throwing the dice.

Tina gave herself to the game with enthusiasm and jumped with glee whenever she scored a hit. She also jumped whenever the phone rang or Pete barked. Under the lightheartedness of the game was a current of tension. Tina made frequent trips to the bathroom, another indication of stress.

After an hour, Tina had enough Aggravation. She got ten doubles for her thirty-five throws, which is somewhat better than chance. Seven of the ten doubles were in the first twelve throws. This suggested beginner's luck, often seen in PK experiments. Perhaps, I thought, Tina did have some PK ability. Kelly's and my scores were flat chance.

Tina then lost momentum and became quiet. For a while she stayed in the kitchen with Kelly and me, then she went and sat at the bottom of the stairs. She tried watching television, but came back to the kitchen a moment later. Something was on her mind, and this time it was not her parents or the flying objects. Tina was developing a crush on Kelly.

We had not prepared for this possibility. To conduct an effective investigation we had to fit into the household as unobtrusively as possible. I needed everything to be as normal and ordinary as could be, given the circumstances. Both of us liked the girl, and she returned our attention tenfold, but I didn't want her to feel she had to demonstrate her abilities in order to attract Kelly's attention. We knew that there had been four foster children in the home prior to our arrival, one with severe brain impairment. That couldn't have left much time for Tina, and her emotional neediness showed; she seemed starved of affection.

Joan and John returned a little while later. The evening out had put Joan in a relaxed mood, but John seemed even more silent and withdrawn than he had been earlier in the day. The Resch marriage was the proverbial meeting of opposites. She was blond, he was dark; she wore a constant smile, he a perpetual frown; she was sociable and talkative, he was introverted and taciturn. They got on well together. Before the disturbances, they had spruced up their home with new candleholders and pictures for the walls from Sears, a silk lemon tree for the hallway, six hanging baskets with live plants for the dining room, and a large terrarium for the living room.

Joan suggested we go into the family room, a comfortably furnished, homey place. The couches were covered with a pattern of light brown, and the wall-to-wall carpeting was mottled orange, practical colors for a home with small children. The walls were protected from little hands by wood paneling, three feet high. But something wasn't right. Behind John's brown recliner, one of a pair matching Joan's, the leaves of an artificial philodendron plant poked out from a stack of toys. The small space also contained a lamp and other items that obviously didn't belong. Joan told me they had been stacked there for safekeeping. Otherwise the room was bare of pictures or knick-knacks you'd expect in a family room. Joan explained that everything had either been broken or put away to keep from damage or from flying out and hitting people.

Joan told us about some of the things that had happened in the family room. The lamp that used to be on the side table by the large couch, "that's completely busted," Joan said, "after it hit the floor seven times or so." The other lamp, the one on Joan's filing cabinet between the two recliners, had fallen three or four times and was still fairly intact. The filing cabinet itself had only moved once. John said he saw it scoot sideways fifteen inches. The side table in front of the filing cabinet and between the two chairs had moved three or four times.

"It jerks in one direction or another," Joan said. This partic-ular table had been the launching pad for at least twenty flights of their telephones and an equal number of flights of Joan's mail caddy.

The side table by the large couch, Joan said, "that always comes out." Earlier that day before Kelly and I had arrived, it had scooted out once and flipped over another time.

Some objects and areas were singled out by the force, while others nearby were spared. The space behind John's chair where errant objects were now together with the children's toys was off-limits to the force. So were the bookcases on either side of the television, as well as the top of the set, though all held potential missiles. Joan took advantage of the safety zones. When an object had flown, she often stuck it behind John's chair so it would stay put. This was the explanation for the philodendron and other items I had noticed there. Joan couldn't figure out why this area was safe. The master bedroom had also been left nearly unscathed, and again she wondered why. In this home, where unexplained occurrences were the order of the day, the places with few incidents stood out. Moving objects had become normal; objects that stayed in place were paranormal.

Over the past week, Joan had become accustomed to the turbulence that swept through her house like the gusts of a storm. It was destructive and annoying, but she had learned to protect her valuables by stowing them away. John was less accepting. Like the eye of a hurricane, their storm had a center, and John knew it was Tina. How or why, he couldn't explain, but she was the cause of the trouble. Except for one Sunday when the furniture moved while Tina was in church, she was smack in the middle of the tempest.

What to do? Send Tina away? John had hinted to Joan that it was her or him. He had already told Joan not to be surprised if he was gone one day; he just could not take it any longer.

"Wednesday, everything is moving," Joan said, "and I'm thinking, we can't send her away for the rest of her life." Joan's main concerns were not her belongings but her family.

"I'm not so much worried about the breakage as to what's happening to the family," she told me. "I think it's going to take a while to get the family back." John was her main worry; she was afraid that the tension was becoming too much for him. Although he was only fifty-seven, John had retired the previous October. He had been the general superintendent at

Vorys Brothers, a sheet-metal warehouse. John was a perfectionist, and the work had been too stressful. He had high blood pressure and then a heart attack. The doctor told him to quit smoking, cut down on drinking, and lose weight. He had managed the first two, but was still overweight. His new lifestyle, helping Joan around the house, agreed with him. He didn't feel he'd retired when he'd left Voreys Brothers, he'd changed jobs. Instead of trying to make a bunch of bullheads do the work they were supposed to do, he helped Joan take care of the foster children. He liked being home. Joan had a bad back from lifting children for so many years and could use the help, especially when it was the children's bathtime. Now he was watching everything he had worked and saved for collapse in ruins, and for no visible reason. This was the most maddening part of all. The things that were happening were simply impossible.

Whatever the case, Joan did not believe any evil presence was in her home. No one who visited felt it, she said, including her good friends the Hughes family, and they were born-again Christians. Joan was not a believer in the supernatural, which made my role as investigator easier for the family to accept. This had not been true for the family of a twelve-year-old boy, Roger Callihan, I had visited some years before. Things had been flying and breaking in the home of his grandparents where Roger was helping with chores. The incidents spread to Roger's own home when I visited, and Mrs. Callihan, convinced that a demon was responsible, asked me to leave. She thought that I had brought the demon from the grandparents' house into her own home and hoped the demon would follow me back to Duke University. This did not happen.

I assured Joan that rather than seeking the supernatural, Kelly and I were looking for a natural cause for the disturbances. But before we could give the family any advice, we needed to know the full story: when the disturbances had started, and how they had occurred. We would also need to talk with witnesses and have them describe what they had seen in their own words. I did not say so, but if Tina was playing games, our suggestion on how to deal with the situation would obviously be different than if the phenomena were real. Aloud I said it was important for us to be present when things happened. Joan replied that she did not think this was going to be a problem.

"The stuff can fly like magic, but to lift a dustcloth—" she said, describing life with Tina.

# 3

# SOMETHING ABOUT TINA

"Today, after Tina got home from church, it was terrible," Joan told me. She thought back over the past week and a half. "Some days she was only home two hours, and those two hours seemed like a year."

Tina spoke up, "When I'm busy, usually nothing happens. When I sit down and I'm doing nothing, that's when it happens." The storm also subsided when she was asleep.

I wondered if we were not simply dealing with a rambunctious teenager. Hardly anything had happened after Kelly and I had arrived.

Tina was a mixture of adult and child. She immediately called Kelly and me by our first names, and her vocabulary was that of an adult. At the same time she enjoyed childish horseplay. Her favorite was standing behind a door and emitting a loud "Boo!" when I walked by. She was quick to laugh, but her anger could be explosive if things did not go her way.

The talk got around to the foster children, with Joan remarking that Tina was jealous of them. "Why don't we get rid of them?" Tina piped up, only half-jokingly. "I just like to be an only child, I just like to be spoiled."

Craig came home from work shortly after ten and joined us in the family room. Seeing the four of them together, Joan, John, Craig, and Tina, I saw what looked like a normal American family. Something was clearly wrong in the house, but was anything wrong with the Resches? John seemed to be under a black cloud, but that could be the result of ten days of turmoil. Joan and Tina carried lesser weights, and Craig none at all. To him, the disturbances had been entertaining rather than frightening; he was having the time of his life.

It was late, about ten-thirty, but Joan wanted to talk. Tina was upstairs with Kelly, and John had gone to bed. The house was quiet.

Since Tina was about four, Joan recalled, people had said she was "different."

"It's nothing anybody has been able to put their finger on, but we've heard it a lot. I guess kindergarten went pretty good, but by first grade she was having problems."

Joan had enrolled her daughter in Parkmoor Elementary School, which was just across the street. The difficulties were minor, but they snowballed and overpowered Tina and eventually Joan, too. It began with crafts. Tina lacked depth perception and couldn't glue things together the right way. Her teacher made fun of her and held up her work for the class as examples of how not to do the projects. Tina would become frustrated with her failure and angrily smear glue on her desk.

"Tina," Joan said, "can go to church, recreation centers, Scouts, and she doesn't have any trouble getting along. But from the first grade on her teachers made an example of her."

Joan told the school that Tina might have a learning disability, but this fell on deaf ears.

Parents in Columbus had a choice. They could send their children to a traditional school or to a liberal, alternative school. Parkmoor belonged in the second category. Thinking Tina needed a stricter environment, Joan sent her to the traditional school for second grade. This was a mistake. One of the rules in the new school was that children must not touch the walls. Tina, poorly coordinated as she was, could not help bumping into the walls as she walked along.

"And so she was always getting into trouble for things like that," Joan said.

I had noticed that Tina was still bumping into walls. It was not an awkward clumsiness; her unwieldiness had a certain grace, and it was not in evidence when she was walking fast or running. Joan said Tina's poor coordination had led to many injuries, including a broken nose, arm, and leg.

But Tina saw herself as a ballerina. From the time she was little she loved to dance and had persuaded Joan to take her to ballet lessons. But her poor balance always cut the classes short. Now at age fourteen and standing five feet eight inches tall, Tina still dreamed of becoming a dancer. Inside the girl there was another, lighter self; nimble and able to leap over any obstacle.

Bad though Parkmoor had been, the second school was worse. The stress caused stomach upsets, and Tina's doctor had her transferred to Oakland Park for the third grade. The old wounds were reopened.

"That teacher had us in every week for a conference," Joan said. "They couldn't put their hands on what was wrong. We started having psychologicals done, but nothing ever really came out or showed anything that we were made aware of."

After a pause, Joan continued in a weary voice, "It just

seemed we were called in for more school conferences probably than anybody in the city of Columbus." Tina did have a
real problem, Joan said, she was hyperactive. She suffered
from attention deficit disorder. To make her easier to handle,
the school asked Joan to put her on Ritalin.

"They had her on so much Ritalin at one time, I said I
didn't want it. And then the teachers were mad because I
didn't load her up on Ritalin."

Joan thought the teachers took the position that if she,
Joan, was not going to make things easier for them by giving
Tina the drug, then they were not going to help Tina.

Joan gave in and agreed to put Tina back on Ritalin. "Then
the teacher would say, 'Did you remember to take your pill
this afternoon, Tina, so you're quiet?' The kids picked up that
she was taking pills for that.

"And this all by third grade; that's a lot to handle," Joan
added.

The damage done at school was more than Joan could repair at home. There just weren't enough hours in the day to
make up for all the difficulties Tina was going through.

The teachers set Tina up as a failure, and the kids followed
suit. She became a victim of playground torture.

"She had clothes ripped off of her," Joan said. Whenever
she asked the school authorities, "What did Tina do?" they'd
say, "'Nothing, she's an easy target.' And I'll bet I've heard that
'easy target' a thousand times as an excuse for things that have
happened.

"One time the kids tied her up and left her out on the playground. They knew the teacher was going to stick up for them
no matter what they did to Tina. From early times, what she
did was wrong, and the kids, well, it doesn't take long to pick
up on that."

The middle school in their district, Woodward Park, was only a year old, and Joan hoped things would improve when Tina got to a new and different school. "She was really looking forward to starting middle school at Woodward Park," Joan said.

Yet when Tina was ready to attend Woodward, the other children had been there a year and already had their circle of friends. Again she was excluded and was targeted by the other kids. The teachers soon joined in.

"Why don't you comb your hair before you come to class?" the teacher would say right in front of all the others. Tina would try to find time to stop in the rest room and fix her hair between classes, but then she'd be in trouble for stopping in the rest room. Tina came home crying, "No matter what I do, it's wrong."

Joan added, "I'm not saying she didn't do things to egg it along. But the kids would follow her home, step on her heels so her shoes would come off, anything they could do." Joan complained to the school, but that only made matters worse.

Joan remembered a school conference she had with a new vice principal because the principal was not in that day. The vice principal could not believe what Joan told him. "He said, 'This type of thing doesn't happen at schools in this end of town, that's why I asked for a transfer up here.'

"So we kept working," Joan said, "trying to meet with the school, see what could be worked out, but these girls would come over, come right up to our door and harass us." The boys, too, hounded Tina. They once pushed her out on the street into traffic with her books. Joan called the school, and this time the boys were punished. But they got their revenge.

The next time they rode in the bus with Tina, they yelled to the driver, "Tina's having a seizure!" The bus driver pulled over and called for security. The driver did not see any seizure; security did not see any seizure. All the same, they brought Tina home. The boys bragged at school about how they had been able to get back at Tina and Joan for complaining. The boys had to do a detention, and the school left it at that.

Tina's adoption became another source of ridicule for her. Years earlier, her older brother Jack had written a theme for school where he mentioned that he was adopted. "Everyone thought he was special," Joan said, "so when Tina was having a rough time dealing with kids making fun, Jack said, 'This is what I did, it came out great.' Tina tried it, and it went the other way. Kids thought she was some kind of freak: 'Well, your mother didn't really want you.' So everything she tried, it seemed like it always bombed."

Unwilling to mend the harm they had done, the school passed it on to the Resch family. "They really gave me a rough time," Joan said. She decided that the only solution was to take Tina out of the school and apply for home tutoring.

Tina came to see her parents, in the place of her teachers, as jailers and her home as a prison. Instead of the other kids who were always favored by the teachers at school, life at home seemed to center around the foster children and their needs. And when John retired, there were two disciplinarians around the clock. Tina felt constricted, physically and emotionally, and socially deprived.

She was not completely cooped up. There were weekly visits to church and Girl Scouts. Tina got on well at both places. She won the Wider Opportunities prize at Scouts, a weeklong trip she had yet to take.

Joan was proud of her daughter. "That's supposed to be quite an honor. They said very few make it, and she did make it. She's the only one in her troop going."

Tina also belonged to a youth group at church, and to a recreation center. "We can let her do those things with no problems," Joan said.

The brightest light in Tina's life had been Craig's former girlfriend, a petite, pretty girl with brown eyes and short, dark hair, who was also named Tina, Tina Scott. Eleven years older, Scott had been Tina's confidante, counselor, and best friend, and the Resches regarded her as a member of the family. For a while she had even lived with the Resches, sharing a room with Tina.

"She was very close to the family," Joan told me. "I don't think she ever left without kissing and hugging me."

On one of the last days of February 1983, Tina Scott went to a party with her friend Helen. Scott didn't have a car, so Helen drove. On the way home, Helen went too fast, swerved, and plowed into a guardrail, bashing in the passenger side of the car. Scott died instantly. Helen escaped with cuts and bruises.

With Tina Scott's death, Tina's sense of abandonment deepened. She began to fantasize a reunion with her birth mother and a life as an only child. This much Tina knew about her history: on an August day in 1970 when Tina was ten months old, her mother brought her into a hospital emergency room, saying the child was sick. Dressed in a frilly, lace-trimmed, pink dress and white, patent leather shoes, Tina had with her only an immunization card and birth certificate, both simply listing her name as Tina Davis. Neither of the items mentioned Tina's father. Under the pretext of needing to make a phone call, Tina's mother slipped out of the examination room and never returned. No one saw her leave, no one knew where she had gone.

When it became apparent that Tina's mother wasn't coming back, a caseworker from Franklin County Children's Services brought Tina to the Resches. For the next year, assisted by a local newspaper, the authorities attempted to find Tina's mother. Nothing turned up, and finally at the age of two and a half, Tina was adopted by Joan and John, becoming the youngest of six children. She was renamed Christina Elaine Resch, and following Ohio state law, any records of her life prior to this time were forever sealed.

Tina had asked Joan for the name of her mother, also saying that as soon as she found out, she was going to call all the people in the phone book with that name until she reached her mother. Fearing that Tina was far too immature to handle the information, Joan refused to give Tina her birth certificate, and the issue came to epitomize everything Tina perceived as unjust throughout her life. Tina had been abandoned by her mother as an infant and abandoned by her teachers at school. With the foster children vying for Joan's attention, she felt neglected at home as well. Then her best friend died, and she was isolated anew.

Whatever Joan did, she was unable to reach Tina. "I've taken every course I know in helping kids—and nothing worked—there was just something there that you just couldn't put your finger on. She was getting very frustrated, very angry, cursing a lot, just really uptight. She's very mouthy. She's always had a mind of her own. She never held back. She wasn't as bad as she is now, but she was always almost like an adult talking to you; she would say exactly her feelings or what was going on."

Being a child had been a disaster for Tina. If she acted like an adult, perhaps she would be accepted as one and life would be better. Things had been like that for more than a year. Joan could not understand how Tina could be so contrary at home when she was so helpful at church and Girl Scouts. "Her Scout leader thinks she's great," said Joan, adding wistfully, "so I'm sure when they talk, it's not the same things that she'd be talking with someone else," meaning herself.

"Here she does not like to accept responsibility. I have trouble even getting her to do things like getting her shower, things that should be done, brushing her teeth, and you know she just resents anytime you say anything. She comes back verbally abusive. I do feel she's had probably ten times more attention than any of the other kids we've had—doing for her, telling her we love her, and it always seems like there's always something else right there.

"She's a very complicated kid," Joan said. "I think she needs help."

By the time Joan finished talking, it was early Monday morning. We said good night, and before turning in, I discussed my first impressions with Kelly. Uppermost in my mind was the question whether there were any authentic psychokinetic occurrences, whatever had happened in the past. Kelly was skeptical because the incidents had just about stopped by the time we came to the house. This didn't bother me. The same had happened in other cases where I later witnessed genuine phenomena. Anybody who changed the routine in the home, such as scientific investigators and television crews, usually inhibited the phenomena, at least at first. I had found that I needed to stay two or three days to see anything myself. By then I would no longer be a stranger and my presence would be less intrusive.

It bothered me more that Tina had been in close proximity to the objects that had moved. With the exception of the bottle that had apparently fallen in the master bedroom when

Kelly and Tina were in the adjacent bathroom, she could easily have picked up the things and thrown them herself.

I checked the time on the clock on the nightstand between
Kelly's bed and mine. The figures were racing. I supposed it
was a simple malfunction and showed the clock to Kelly. He
punched the buttons and shook the clock until it went back to
normal. I would have paid more attention if I had known that
the same thing had happened the night it all began.

# 4

# HEART MONITOR

From what I have been able to gather, the first signs of trouble started with a clash of wills. On Thursday night, March 1, Tina and her father had a confrontation that would change their lives forever.

At around nine o'clock that night, Tina fell into an argument with her mother. They were well used to the pattern: Joan would find something to criticize or nag Tina about, Tina would respond by shouting and cursing. Joan would begin to yell; Tina would yell louder. When Joan had had enough, she would do as she always did, tell John to give Tina something to really cry about. Tonight the argument was over bedtimes. Joan had gone into the family room to gather the children for bed. Tina didn't want to go.

"I'm fourteen and I'm older than the other kids. I should be able to stay up a *little* bit later and not be treated like a two- or three-year-old." One of the reasons Tina wanted to stay up was to spend some time with her mother. In spite of their frequent battles, Tina craved her mother's affection. But Joan was adamant; nine o'clock, final decision. Bedtime justice aside, she needed a few hours' rest from Tina, who seemed to take up more space than her growing frame occupied. Tina became enraged—Joan never understood her, never wanted her around, never let her do anything but what Joan wanted. Furious with Tina for talking back, Joan went to get John.

The Resches believed children should be "seen and not heard." They also believed in corporal punishment, especially when it came to Tina. They way they saw it, Tina was loud, mouthy, lazy, and ungrateful for all the care she had been given. As an adopted child, things could have been a lot worse for her if it weren't for the Resches, and Tina needed to show more respect and consideration. If she didn't, she knew what to expect, and plenty of it. But Tina was a big girl, too big for Joan to spank. That was John's job. As Tina grew more and more difficult to control, the spankings turned into outright beatings. John was loyal to his wife and systematic in his methods. If Joan said Tina needed a whipping, that's what she got, no questions asked. It happened so routinely there wasn't even any need to speak to the girl.

This particular night, as John lunged toward her, Tina turned the tables. Instead of submitting as she usually did, she fled into another room. John followed and Tina ran into the next one with her father in hot pursuit. The downstairs floor plan connected most of the rooms together in a circle, so that when Tina ran from the hallway to the living room, she could run from there to the dining room and the kitchen and back to the hallway. As she and John went round and round, Tina found herself almost choking back laughter; it seemed so stupid to have her big, lumbering father chase after her like a figure from a Bugs Bunny cartoon. But after they had traversed the circuit a couple of times, Tina was just plain mad. She was far too old for this kind of punishment and she was sick of her father hitting her. Running into the kitchen, Tina took a large knife from a drawer and told John she would stab him if he came any closer. Tina was terrified of knives, but she couldn't think of anything else to do.

John stopped in his tracks, his expression registering complete disgust. There was a time when John used to hold her on his lap when she was little. Now he wanted nothing to do with her. The look on his face as he turned to leave hurt Tina more than a trouncing.

Miserable and guilt-ridden, Tina stumbled off to her bedroom. She hated being treated like the foster children, but she also hated the way she fought with her parents all the time. She didn't like yelling, she didn't like always being unhappy and wishing her life could change. Why didn't Joan and John try to understand this?

Tina undressed and crawled under the covers. She looked at her digital clock radio and the figures started racing, just as they did when she set the time. But she wasn't pushing any buttons, she wasn't even touching the clock. In front of her eyes the clock seemed to say it was becoming later and later, closer to the appropriate bedtime of a teenager. Suddenly, music blared; the radio had come on by itself. Tina turned it off, but it came back on. Weird, she thought. She unplugged the clock and the music stopped. Tina was not concerned; she had another clock radio.

Friday morning, March 2, passed without incident. Tina hadn't told anyone about her clock radio, and by the afternoon the incident seemed minor compared to what was to follow.

Joan was in the kitchen preparing dinner when she heard the alarm to baby Anne's heart monitor go off. The six-month-old had been born with a microcephalic brain that could not be trusted to keep her lungs and heart working, so the device was her lifeline. If the alarm sounded, Joan would know that something was wrong. It might be as simple as one of the leads to the chest having fallen off, or the baby's heart might have actually stopped and Joan would need to resuscitate her.

When she heard the alarm, Joan rushed into the dining room where she kept the day crib. She checked the baby. Anne was all right. Relieved, Joan examined the two leads; both were firmly attached to the little chest.

She returned to the kitchen, but the alarm came on again. Again she checked; Anne was still okay and the leads were in place. Joan thought the monitor must be broken and un-plugged it. The alarm continued to sound without power. Be-wildered, Joan would have asked her son Craig to check it out, but he was at work. John was away on an errand; only Tina and the foster children were home.

Joan phoned the supply company for a replacement. A ser-viceman came out right away. He checked but couldn't find anything wrong. To be on the safe side, he installed a new monitor and Joan returned Anne to her crib.

As soon as the serviceman left, the same thing happened with the new device. Joan couldn't believe it. The alarm went off before dinner, during dinner, and afterward, Joan checking Anne each time. Concerned about the baby's safety, Joan took her off the machine. She had never had a problem like this. Worried and confused, Joan had no way to check on Anne short of staying with her all the time.

Joan took Anne upstairs to her crib in the foster children's room, which was close to the master bedroom. When John came home from his errand, he reassured Joan about the monitor, but she was still troubled. Anne's safety and Joan's professional reputation were at stake. As a foster mother working for the Franklin County Children's Services, she was responsible for the well-being of the children in her care. She decided to call FCCS first thing Saturday if the problem did not go away.

Later that night with everyone else in bed, Joan went downstairs to close up the house. She went into the living room to turn off the plant light and caught her breath. A dark shadow hovered. The shape was difficult to make out and there was nothing to explain its presence. Suddenly it disappeared. It was sort of scary, but it was soon gone and Joan had other things on her mind. She went back upstairs without giving the matter further thought.

Saturday morning was cartoon time. In this respect, life in the Resch home was normal. Lisa, David, and Mary trooped into the family room as soon as they had finished breakfast and settled around the television. Tina slouched in afterward and plopped down in the recliner farthest from the set. This was usually Joan's seat. John's matching recliner near the brown-brick fireplace was strictly off-limits, as was his chair at the dinner table.

The younger children were squirming with excitement, but Tina was in a bad mood. Her clock radio was back to normal, but she had woken up with a headache. It hadn't helped when Joan had pestered her about taking a shower and brushing her teeth. What was the point when she wasn't going anywhere? There was always something to be blamed for. When she did finally take a shower, she was blamed for using all the hot water or forgetting to turn off the light. It seemed that the only times her parents paid any attention to her was to blame her for something.

The noise of the cartoons made Tina's head throb even worse than before. She wanted to see a program for teens, but Joan wouldn't let her. "The little children won't understand," she said. Tina made a face and sulked through the kiddie cartoons.

Joan went to the bathroom to set her hair. This was the one time in the morning she could spend by herself, and she treasured the interlude. She used the downstairs bathroom and kept the door open so she could hear the children.

In the meantime, John took Pete to the vet for one of his shots. Craig had already gone off to his job at JAYS, and the house was relatively quiet.

While Tina, Lisa, and the two younger foster children were watching cartoons, the set turned off and would not come back on when Lisa worked the control. Tina watched indifferently as Lisa went to the bathroom and asked Joan to come to fix it; but then the set came on again by itself. Then it turned off, came back on, and so on until the children gave up watching. Tina was amused.

Instead of TV, a different show began. The ceiling light in the family room turned on though no one was touching the switch. Lisa turned it off but it came back on. This went on several times, with Lisa reporting to Joan each time.

"Tina's just playing games with you," Joan told the six-year-old. "Go back and tell her to stop." Joan continued to set her hair. Now what was Tina up to? Joan couldn't be bothered to find out and stayed in the bathroom.

Then Joan was startled by something slamming shut, followed by a whirring noise. She recognized the sound; the clothes dryer had come on. The machine was stacked on top of the washer in a corner of the dining room, and Joan went in and turned it off by opening the door to the unit. When she returned to the bathroom, the door slammed shut again and the engine started up. Again she went in, opened the door, and the machine stopped. This was getting out of hand. She told Tina to stop fooling around.

"I haven't done anything! You're always accusing me of doing things. Now I've got a stomachache and a headache. It just isn't fair."

Joan was disturbed. Tina had never fooled around with things in the house like this and then denied it. This was something new she'd have to contend with. "Okay," she said, "come and sit by me outside the bathroom where I can watch you."

Tina didn't know how to respond. It was the first time in Tina's life Joan had asked her to attend the hair-setting ritual. "I'm not doing it, you know," Tina said.

Then they both heard the dryer door slam shut and start up again. This time Joan knew Tina couldn't be playing games, she was sitting right where Joan could see her, and the foster children were in the family room. A familiar grating noise added to the din. The garbage disposal in the kitchen had come on.

Something was wrong with her appliances, Joan thought; it could be dangerous. Then an entirely new problem started. Water was pouring out of the faucets in the washbowls in the two bathrooms upstairs, and in the tub of the children's bathroom. A few moments later, the faucets to the bathroom sink downstairs went on as well.

Joan didn't know what to make of it. She was scared and gathered the children in the family room, away from the appliances. She hoped John would be back soon.

She checked the time on the wall clock over the love seat. The minute hand was racing like crazy. Another mystery; this time it could not be the house current because the clock used a battery. She asked Tina to go to the kitchen and see what the time was.

The big wall clock as well as the small one on the stove were both racing, each at its own pace. "The same thing happened to my clock radio the other night," Tina told her mother.

Joan looked at her daughter. Could Tina have done it all? If so, Joan sure couldn't figure out how. Tina acted so innocent; usually when she'd misbehaved, it was easy to tell. Tina wasn't good at covering up when she had caused mischief, but this time the girl seemed as puzzled as Joan herself. Something must be wrong with their home; but what?

John returned with Pete at eleven o'clock, and Joan told him about the strange events. He didn't believe her.

"Aw, come on, Jo," he said. "That can't happen. What's really going on?"

Joan insisted she was serious and that the dryer, disposal unit, and water in all three bathrooms had come on without anybody touching a thing. "And you should have seen the clocks!"

John shook his head. "Put your shoes on, Jo!"

"Why?"

"I'm taking you to the hospital to have your head examined."

Tina came to her mother's defense. "It's true!" she said. She gave John a spirited account of the morning's events.

Now John knew what was causing the commotion; Tina was playing tricks on her mother. He was surprised that Joan hadn't caught on. He was just about to lose his temper when suddenly the ceiling light came on, followed by other lights downstairs. The dishwasher and the disposal started up again, just like before. John went and turned them off, but as soon as he stopped one appliance, another turned itself on. The same thing happened with the lights. All he could think was that Tina must be slipping up behind him and turning everything on. His frustration and confusion mounting, he made Tina stay right beside him in full view as he went from room to room and switch to switch.

For the next hour the problem continued. John now made everyone stay together to make certain no one could get their hands on the switches. He was still angry with Tina, but he had to wonder if maybe she wasn't entirely responsible; she was always in sight.

Finally, he understood what was happening: power surges. Bursts of electric power were coming through the wires, triggering the switches. Why hadn't he thought of that before? Relieved, he called the utility company, Columbus and Southern, to come out and fix the problem. A loud screeching sound on the phone almost blocked his call. Probably a surge on the phone lines, too, John thought.

Within the hour, the Columbus and Southern van was at the utility pole outside. Two workers checked the leads to the house, as well as the inside wiring. Everything was in order, they said. There was no problem with the power supply.

Their explanation was interrupted by music blaring from upstairs. Everybody went up to check. The stereo in Craig's room was on full blast, but no one had been upstairs. They turned it off, but it came back on. They repeated this a few times and finally unplugged the machine, but still the music continued—and it wasn't even battery-operated. Then music started playing downstairs. Everyone rushed down to the living

room and found the stereo there competing with the one upstairs. They unplugged this one as well, but it still played without any discernible power supply.

Lisa was watching intently. "It was pugged and it comed
on," said the six-year-old, referring to the unplugged stereo.
This was better than cartoons.

In the kitchen Joan noticed that the small television that sat
on the microwave oven was also on, and it, too, was unplugged. Strangely, only the picture came on, not the sound.
The men from Columbus and Southern were stumped and
suggested the Resches call their electrician. Appliances that
worked without electricity were way beyond anything they
knew.

John thought of phoning his friend Bruce Claggett, the
owner of an electrical repair firm. It was Saturday, but it was
worth a try. He got through to Bruce, but could hardly make
himself understood. The same screeching was on the line as
when he had spoken to Columbus and Southern. Something
was definitely wrong with the power supply to the house. Determined to find a solution, John stayed on the line despite the
noise. He had to—his sanity depended on it.

# 5

# THE FORCE

If it had been anyone other than John calling, Bruce Claggett might never have come to the house. When I interviewed him during the week I stayed with the Resches, he told me he didn't usually work Saturdays. But he was in his office taking care of some bookwork when the phone rang just after lunch.

Bruce could hardly hear who was on the other end of the line. The same squealing and squalling John could hear interfered so much with the call that the two men could hardly complete a sentence without having to stop and wait for the noise to dissipate. Eventually Bruce called John back on another line, but the sound came on anyhow. Between bursts of static, Bruce heard John describe what appeared to be a routine electrical problem, and he agreed to come out to the house and take a look.

Bruce, a tall man in his fifties, had the demeanor of a country doctor—friendly, calm, and confident. If anyone could be trusted to fix the problem, it would be Bruce.

When Bruce got to the house, lights were burning everywhere. He went straight to the basement and inspected the fuse panel. Everything was tight; no loose connections. Perhaps there was a bad switch. He went up to the switch at the head of the stairs and turned it on and off. The lights responded correctly. He then went back down to the basement and inspected the panel again. There were no signs of burning or discoloration of the plastic from heat buildup inside the main breaker. Everything in the panel checked out fine, both when the lights were on and when they were off. Although the lights went off twice while Bruce was checking the panel, there was still nothing wrong with the panel itself, so he snapped it shut and went back upstairs.

In the kitchen, John told Bruce how the lights kept coming on all over the house. Bruce jokingly accused John of hitting the bottle; his inspection didn't bear out anything John was saying. John then told him about the electrical appliances, and Bruce still didn't believe him.

"This can't happen, John. It's just impossible. To turn a light on, you have to complete the circuit, there's just no other way for this to happen."

There was nothing else Bruce could do, and he started to leave. He got as far as the front porch when Tina came running out after him. "The kitchen lights are back on again!"

Bruce thought he must have forgotten to turn them off, and he went back inside and did so. Once again he started to leave, this time with John walking him out, and once again Tina came after them, saying the lights had come on.

Bruce turned to the girl. "Are you sure you're not playing games with me?" Tina swore she was not and that she was telling the truth.

Bruce tried to leave four or five times more, but every time he made it out to the front porch, it was as if he were stepping on a switch. Lights he had just turned off popped back on. It was almost as if something wanted him to stay.

The last time Bruce came back inside, Tina said, "They're moving!" and pointed to the switches in the hallway. Joan backed her up. "Yes, they are," she said. When Bruce took a look, one switch handle was all the way up and the light it controlled was on; the other switch was at the midway point.

At this point Bruce realized something important: he had completely misunderstood the nature of the problem. The lights were not coming on by themselves. The switches in the house were moving up and down, and the lights were responding precisely as they were supposed to.

From here on out, it became a different ball game; who was messing with the switches, and what could he do to prove that somebody was playing games? Scotch tape, he thought. Tape down the switches. If someone tried to change the switch position, they would have to take off the tape and would probably be caught in the act. Bruce had gone from electrician to detective.

Now that Bruce thought he had found an answer, Joan helped him place tape over the downstairs switch plates. That should do it, he thought. But while Bruce was in the kitchen by the hall entrance, facing Joan and Tina, who were standing in front of the kitchen sink, the garbage disposal and the light over the sink came on. There was no way Tina or anybody else could have reached those switches without Bruce seeing.

He was pondering this latest mystery when the two ceiling lights in the kitchen came on. The switch had been taped down, but by Joan, not by Bruce. He didn't want to say he mistrusted her, but he had to be certain no one was playing tricks, not even Joan, so he went and retaped the switch himself. If somebody wanted to get to the switch, it would take some effort to break through the tape. Just as Bruce thought he had it all sewn up, the overhead lights in the kitchen came on. He felt the hair on his neck stand straight up. This was no practical joke.

When the lights came on, Bruce immediately looked to see which set of switches was involved. The tape on the two in the family room that controlled the kitchen lights was gone. It had *disappeared.* No one had been near the switches that turned on the kitchen lights.

The phone interrupted his thoughts. A neighbor had seen Pete. In all the commotion the Resches hadn't noticed their dog was gone; he had probably slipped out when the men from Columbus and Southern left.

John went to get Pete, while Joan helped Bruce tape the switches back in place. But the same thing kept happening: the tape just kept vanishing into thin air, allowing the lights to flip back on. This happened so many times Bruce lost count.

For the life of him, Bruce could not fathom what was going on. It had to be tricks, but by whom? He told Lisa to take the two younger foster children to the family room and to stay by the fireplace. The lights continued to flick on and off; the tape continued to disappear. Tina would cry out excitedly each time a light turned on and its tape went missing, and Bruce would dash in to check. The only time he found some tape was once in the living room where the tape was lightly attached to the wall. This happened two more times. The other pieces of tape were nowhere in sight.

The phone rang again. John had found Pete but couldn't catch him, so Joan went to help. Bruce and Tina were left alone in the house with the foster children. The three older ones were in the family room playing and watching television. The set was working again.

The activity picked up when Joan left, and Bruce became a participant in a game of wits with "the force," as he now called it. This time Bruce kept Tina with him as they went round and round the downstairs, turning off lights and taping down switches. Only the dining room was unaffected. The switches in there remained in the up position. Tina couldn't help but remember that the route she and Bruce followed mimicked the circle she had taken to escape John the other night. Trying to solve the mystery of the vanishing tape with a grown-up who took her seriously was a lot more fun than running from her father.

By the time John and Joan returned with Pete, Bruce had gone through an entire roll and a half of Scotch tape and had run out. Joan found a box of Band-Aids and gave him those. They were stickier than the tape, but they, too, disappeared after they were stuck to the switches. Bruce crinkled one down alongside the switch in the living room. When the switch later moved up, only the piece that was around the handle was still there; the rest of the Band-Aid was gone.

Bruce was determined to catch the force in motion. If he could only see the tape and switches moving, he might begin to understand the phenomenon. At one point he sat in the living room watching a switch for fifteen minutes. Nothing happened. The force was shy.

There was nothing more Bruce could do. He finally left the house at five that evening, telling the family he had no idea what kind of force was operating the switches, but he didn't think it was going to hurt anyone.

Tina was sad to see him go. She liked Bruce; he was nice and had treated her like an adult, listening to what she had to say. With him gone and the problem unsolved, she worried that her parents would just start blaming her again, even when they had seen with their own eyes that she hadn't done anything.

In all his years as an electrician, Bruce told me, he had never had a day like this. This was a once-in-a-lifetime experience. Joan sent him $25 for his trouble. He returned the check, saying he couldn't accept payment for an experience as fascinating as the one he had had in her home. Joan later told me that was the only money she had ever made on "the force."

After Bruce had left, it was clear to John that the trouble was not power surges, at least not the conventional kind. As if to bring the point home, the sound of splashing water came from upstairs. John lumbered up to the children's bathroom, where the faucets to the tub and hand bowl were on full force. The drains were closed and the basin was about to overflow. This was exactly what Joan had said had happened that morning. Fuming, John turned the faucets off tightly, opened the drains, and went downstairs to confront Tina. Damned if he was going to let her get away with this.

Tina was just as angry with John; what was wrong with him? Her head and stomach were hurting, and now she was being accused of something she couldn't possibly have done. Where had John been all day? He'd talked with Bruce; he'd seen the lights and the tape disappear. Tina was always the scapegoat. She hated this house—it was like a prison!

Again John heard the sound of rushing water. He went upstairs a second time and there it all was like some kind of nightmare: the faucets open, the drains closed, and the tub and sink filling. He felt that he was going crazy. Tina was the only one who would do a thing like this, but how she had got past him to go upstairs, he couldn't imagine.

At about five-thirty, the Resches' son Craig came home from his job at JAYS. Craig was blond like his mother and quiet like his father, though more sociable. He wanted to become a clinical psychologist and planned to go to graduate school when he had saved enough money. As soon as he heard about the day's incidents, there was no mystery in his mind. Of course it was Tina.

He and John each had a bottle of beer in the kitchen. They left the two empty bottles on the counter by the sink before going into the family room to watch television. Suddenly a crash came from the kitchen. The bottles had fallen to the floor, one breaking. This was something Tina could not have done because when the bottles broke, Craig saw Tina walking into the family room.

Craig planned to go to a movie with some of the other men from JAYS. He was on his way upstairs to take a shower when he walked past the living room and noticed that something was out of order. As a rule, Joan and John were very orderly, and the living room in particular was kept to perfection. Decorated in shades of green and beige, the spacious, airy room with its white walls and picture window was an oasis of peace for adult use only. Tina and the foster children were not allowed to play on the crushed-velvet couch or to touch the terrarium. But here was a large overstuffed chair sitting several feet away from its usual position by the entrance to the room.

Then Craig saw something move. A picture on the living room wall was swinging back and forth. He jumped when a plant stand in the hallway fell over behind him. Tina walked out of the living room and into the hallway at the same time, but he was certain she had not touched either the picture or the stand. Not sure what to think, Craig went upstairs to take his shower. On his way up, he saw a dark shape moving down the hall. He thought that perhaps someone was using the bath-room, casting a shadow out into the hall. But when he reached the top of the stairs, he realized he was alone. No one else was up there. Somewhat bemused, he carried on and took his shower while the rest of the family sat down for dinner in the kitchen.

Meals were another part of the day for which Joan insisted upon order. She and John liked to eat, and they took it upon themselves to fill the children's plates with good-size portions, John generously salting each plate. The children were expected to eat what was placed before them before they could be excused from the table. Over the years, food had become yet another battleground issue between Tina and her parents. Joan and John were heavy, and Tina didn't want the same thing to happen to her. Joan had also got into the hurtful habit of calling attention to Tina's size whenever they had one of their many arguments. The comments cut Tina to the quick, but when she asked for less food, Joan reversed her attitude and insisted Tina eat a full plate. The huge servings and the taste of salted food had become obnoxious to the girl, and what she couldn't surreptitiously feed to Pete, she often vomited up in private. Resentful for being blamed all day and with her head and stomach hurting, the last thing she wanted was to sit down to another large, salty meal.

Feeding two-year-old David in his high chair, John rested his elbow on the back of a wooden youth chair with an elevated seat. Suddenly, the chair scooted out by nearly a foot. John almost toppled over. His first reaction was that Tina had done it, but she was sitting at the other end of the table, about five feet away. Then it happened again in plain sight of everyone, and twice again after that. Then one of the regular, vinyl-covered kitchen chairs started moving repeatedly, even though no one was sitting in it. The movements were swift and the stops sudden.

Lisa and Mary thought it was a game, a real treat to see the kitchen come to life before their eyes. They jumped off their chairs and squealed with laughter as the chairs scooted around the room. When the chairs stood still, the girls climbed back up, then jumped off to see if the chairs would take off again. They did and the girls laughed harder.

Even Joan was amused. She was also worried. Empty chairs that could move on their own made her feel that her home was occupied by more than her husband and children. Tina thought it was weird, but she was too angry at John to care. During the entire performance he kept telling her to stop pushing the chairs, even when it was obvious to everyone else that she had nothing to do with them.

A sharp crack from the dining room announced that the force had moved and that it was no longer in a playful mood. A wineglass lay shattered on the floor. Joan cried out; it was one of a set of thirty treasured stemware. Scarier yet, the glasses came from the bar behind Anne's crib. Before she could reach the baby, there was another crash and another broken glass. Then more glasses flew against the walls, turning into shards on the floor of the empty room.

Lisa and Mary wanted to see what was going on. "Stay in the kitchen!" Joan warned. "Don't come in here." She got to Anne just in time to find the baby clutching a shot glass that had come into her hands from a shelf on the same bar, well above her reach. Joan was horrified. The combination of small children and broken glass was not something she wanted to think about.

As far as John was concerned, this tipped the scales. It was bad enough to not understand how any of this was happening, but now he had a dangerous mess to clean up.

John and Joan rushed the children through dinner, then herded them into the family room, where the force was less rampant. The foster children went to their toys by the fireplace while Tina sat down on the couch and John and Joan settled in their recliners. Usually they watched the news after dinner, but not tonight.

The Resches had given up power surges as the explanation. Somebody outside the house must be doing the mischief. They were talking about calling the police when a painting on the wall behind Tina began to swing back and forth. John went over and stopped it. When he got back to his chair, it swung again. Irritated, he went back to stop it, only to have it start again as soon as he sat down. After it moved the third time, he took the painting off the wall and stuck it behind the couch. This accomplished, he was on his way out of the room when the painting slid out from the couch as if to follow him.

John could not make the painting stay put. Each time he shoved it back behind the couch and walked away, it slid out as if tied to his leg by a string. John shook his leg, trying to shed the invisible string, Tina erupting in a peal of laughter at the sight. Even Joan had to smile; John looked so comical. Thoroughly fed up, John finally decided to take the painting out of the room. He grabbed it and carried it to the garage, where he boxed it in between a wall and a stack of cartons. The satisfaction he felt from taking control was as if he had caught and caged a wild animal. As for whatever was making the painting move in the first place, John decided it was time to call the police.

Two officers responded to the call. Joan and John realized how crazy their story sounded, but there was no other way to describe the dilemma other than, "Everything moves or comes on by itself."

The officers wanted to see for themselves, and Tina took them upstairs. She went ahead. Slowly, cautiously, one of the officers followed. As Tina turned around to see if he was still there, a metal pan flew out of the children's bathroom behind her. Right away the officer pulled out his gun and aimed to shoot. Tina jumped and asked what he thought he was doing. He was about to answer when plastic lemons started flying from a silk tree downstairs.

"You're throwing them!" the officer said. "You're throwing everything."

"I am not," Tina countered. "This is what we've been trying to tell you about."

The officer didn't believe her. "If another damn thing flies in this house, I'm going to shoot it. Is that all right with you?"

"As long as you make sure it's not me or anybody I love."

The police left a few minutes later. When they returned to the station, they wrote "Mental" on the Resches file and put it away; far away. There was nothing more to investigate.

John and Joan discussed what to do next. It had become clear that whatever was happening in their home was not caused by the kind of power an electrician could turn off nor by the kind of intruder the police could catch. Perhaps they had gone to the wrong experts. Joan decided to call their minister and ask if he would come to the house. They were members of a Lutheran church, though they rarely attended services. Their old pastor had retired and they hadn't become used to the new one. Tina went every Sunday; she was going to be confirmed later in the spring and was taking catechism classes.

Pastor Heinz did not know the Resches well. When Joan told him about flying wineglasses and chairs that moved by themselves on a Saturday night, he suspected the problem was bottled spirits and not the invisible kind. He told her to calm down and call back Sunday if the problem persisted.

The only place in the house that seemed safe to Joan was the family room. She made up her mind that the family would just have to camp out together downstairs for the night. It was a little crowded, but Craig could stay with friends. She and John used the bed that folded out from the love seat, while Tina took the matching couch. The three foster children snuggled into sleeping bags on the floor. For a few hours at least, they were all going to get some rest. Whatever tomorrow would bring, Joan could deal with it better after a good night's sleep.

# 6

# SEEKING DEMONS

Talking to the family, I learned that Tina had to get up Sunday morning in time for catechism class at nine. After that she would attend adult Bible study, then the regular church service, which finished at twelve. John would drop her off in the car and come back after the service.

Tina liked church, especially Bible study. She enjoyed being with adults who listened to her and took her opinions seriously. The teacher liked her, too; Tina was never shy expressing herself, and that stimulated the others in the class. Contrary to Joan's perception of her daughter's behavior at home, Tina was thought of as someone to be counted on to help serve snacks or perform other church duties.

This morning, just a couple of days after the events had started, Tina was apprehensive. What if all the strange things in the house were caused by an evil spirit? Maybe the spirit was attached to her, and that was the reason things seemed to happen only when she was around. If Pastor Heinz came to the house and thought she was possessed, he wouldn't allow her to be confirmed with the other children in April, and everybody would know about it. The friends she had made at church and Girl Scouts would be afraid of her.

Tina was getting ready for church when she heard noises. She looked in the hallway; the force had started up again. Candles that had earlier sat unlit in ornamental wall holders were now flying through the air. Tina noticed that only the white candles flew, not the colored ones, and only white candles were used in church. Candle lighting was an important part of the Lutheran service; was this another sign that something evil was afoot?

It was time to leave. The trip to church was always a silent, uncomfortable journey, but today seemed one of the worst. John didn't have to say a word to let Tina know how much he blamed her for everything that had happened; his heavy mood spoke volumes. Tina couldn't wait to get out of the car.

Back at home, Joan was alone with the foster children. Craig was working all hours to save money for graduate school, and although it was Sunday morning, he had already left for JAYS. Sitting in the family room, which still seemed the safest place, Joan heard rumbling noises from different parts of the house. It could only be one thing: the furniture was moving. After Saturday's events, Joan didn't dare leave the foster children alone so she could go look for herself. Besides, she didn't know what she might encounter; better to wait until John came home. The sounds lasted about five minutes.

As soon as John returned from dropping Tina off at church, she told him to look. He did so and called for her to come to the living room. The furniture was completely rearranged. It was worse upstairs.

In Tina's room the mattresses were off the beds and the chests were pulled out from the walls. Craig's room was no better. His mattress had also come off the bed, his bookshelves had moved, and the wine bottle he used for saving pennies was in the middle of the room with a shoe stuck on top. The bottle, about two feet tall and with a long neck, belonged in the corner by the door. It seemed as if charges of energy had accumulated in the rooms and then gone off by themselves.

John was deeply troubled. Until this time he had stubbornly held to the belief that Tina was causing the commotion; he just didn't know how. Now he was confronted with something she could not possibly have done. Tina wasn't even home; he had taken her to church himself. Craig was at work, and the front door was locked. Impotent anger sat like a lump in the pit of his stomach. What was happening was insane, and it was tearing his home apart. He had never felt so helpless.

Joan worried about what the stress might be doing to John's heart. He wasn't supposed to get upset like this. She told John that the force couldn't go on forever, and there didn't seem to be anything evil about it. In fact, it was even playful, such as when it had scooted the kitchen chairs around for the children, or when it had teased John by making the picture follow him. The way Craig's shoe was stuck on top of his penny bottle was pretty comical, too. Surely it would soon be over and they would all look back and laugh. In the meantime, she would put in another call to Pastor Heinz. John loved his wife and usually agreed with her on just about everything, but he couldn't find anything funny about what was happening, and he doubted that the pastor could help.

Unaware of the latest developments at home, Tina sat in her Bible study class and couldn't believe the morning's topic: devils. That's got to be it, she thought—it had to be the house, something was wrong with it. Maybe it was haunted. The thought that she might be possessed crossed her mind again. Could she have attracted the demon to the house? She knew that she was often bad and couldn't control her temper. And the weird things in the house did seem to be connected to her somehow. Why else would everyone be blaming her? She sat through the rest of the class trying to hide her nervousness.

After the service, Tina stood in line to shake hands with Pastor Heinz. When it was her turn, he asked how things were at home. He had not expected to hear any more about flying glasses and moving chairs, but now Tina was telling him the same things as her mother had the night before. The two of them could hardly be making up the same story, and he knew Tina well enough to see she wasn't lying. Maybe the woman hadn't been drunk after all.

Joan called the church when the service was over. Pastor Heinz said that Tina had already spoken to him and that he would come to the house after lunch. That settled, Joan went to start lunch.

John brought Tina back from church. When she heard Joan tell about the morning's ruckus, she was filled with relief. If rooms could rearrange themselves while she was out of the house, that proved she wasn't possessed. But the short burst of happiness she felt at being demon-free soon left.

Tina had been home just a few minutes when Joan called out for help; the living room was messed up again. Tina went to help her mother. Together, she and Joan pushed chairs and couches back into place; the pieces were heavy and it seemed impossible that they could shift on their own. Their efforts were wasted. As soon as they were out of the room, the furniture returned to its previous state of disarray, but not for long. This was Joan's living room and the force wasn't going to win.

She went back in and moved the furniture to where it was supposed to be.

Craig came home from JAYS and Joan told him what had happened with the furniture. He looked in on the living room. "Everything's okay now," he said. He went on up to his own room to see what Joan had described as the mess upstairs. She had warned him not to change anything, so that Pastor Heinz could see the damage for himself. Craig had some idea of what to expect. Saturday night, before he'd taken his shower, Joan had asked if anything had happened to his room.

"No," he'd replied. "Nothing."

When he'd returned from the bathroom, the lamp on his television was lying on its side and his mattress was partially off the bed. It seemed that his statement had challenged the force. Now it had returned.

Two minutes later, Craig came back downstairs, and there was the living room torn apart again. Craig had to get back to work, but he took a few minutes to help Joan get things back to normal for Pastor Heinz. It was one thing for the minister to see the bedrooms looking as if a tornado had blown through, but Joan was not receiving a guest in anything but a properly furnished living room.

Joan heard more noise; she was almost getting used to this. What now? she wondered. It sounded like more breaking glass. She went to the dining room; the metal drinking cups that formed the centerpiece of the dining table were flying up one at a time and hitting the glass chandelier. At this stage all she could feel was gratitude that the cups were metal and that the chandelier was surviving the attacks fairly well. Only one of the glass balls was broken.

Joan had to get back to the kitchen; the house was filling with visitors. Tina's niece had arrived to help with lunch, as had Pam, one of Joan's married daughters. Pam had brought a friend with her, Joyce Beaumont. Pam was convinced Tina was playing tricks and duping her parents and brother. Joyce was levelheaded and sensible. She worked in the payroll department of Rockwell International, and Pam thought she would be able to reveal Tina's mischief and help get the family back to normal. The plan backfired.

While Tina and her niece began to fry eggs, the eggs flew off the stove and hit the walls and ceiling. These were soon joined by other eggs now escaping from the carton. The eggs flew so fast it was impossible to see how they managed to launch themselves, but one hit the window, others the floor. Raw egg yolk dripped from the kitchen surfaces, pooling with the sticky egg whites. Joan told Tina to put the few remaining eggs into the refrigerator for safekeeping. But as soon as she closed the refrigerator door, the eggs, still in their shells, *started coming out through the closed door!* Each egg emerged slowly, until it was fully outside the door, then it let loose and smashed against the wall. Speechless, Tina could only watch in bewilderment. She turned and then called out, "Mom! Look at the butter!"

Hardly believing her eyes, Joan saw two sticks of butter slide up a cabinet door like two giant slugs. When they reached the top of the door, they stopped. Nobody knew what to say, but Tina was in a turmoil about what would happen when Pastor Heinz came. The demon, if it was a demon, was showing its strength before confronting the minister of God.

For the rest of the afternoon, more visitors and family members arrived to help clean the mess and support the Resches as best they could. Others just wanted to gawk.

The phone rang incessantly as word of the trouble spread. Usually Tina couldn't wait for the phone to ring. Aside from her weekly outings to church and Scouts, the phone was Tina's only link to the outside world. Like any teen, she couldn't spend enough time on the phone talking to her boyfriend and was unhappy when her parents limited her calls. Now she wished she could unplug it; the screeches and chatter were putting her stomach in knots.

Finally, Pastor Heinz arrived. He didn't believe the stories of flying objects, but he saw the mess upstairs and concluded that the family was indeed having problems. Gathering John, Joan, and Tina around him, Pastor Heinz lit a candle and went with the family to bless each of the rooms upstairs. "May there be no evil," he prayed. At the end of the ritual, the minister asked if he could talk to the family. They went into the living room.

As Joan asked Pastor Heinz to sit down on the couch, it shot out toward him, as if inviting him to be seated. Startled, Pastor Heinz looked behind the couch, expecting to see one of the foster children, but no one was there. This was not what he had envisioned. He had come to the home with the conviction that the stories of flying objects and moving furniture reflected family problems he could address. What he saw was beyond his knowledge or capacity to help.

"There are things in this world we just do not understand," he said lamely. There really was nothing else he could do. When Joan and John saw him in church sometime later, he asked how things were, but he didn't offer to come back.

Tina was relieved that Pastor Heinz didn't accuse her of harboring demons. At the same time she felt abandoned because he couldn't rescue her from her plight. The religious intervention even seemed to make things worse. Five minutes after the minister had left, the force turned on Tina with an unexpected malevolence.

Joyce Beaumont had not participated in the ritual and was now sitting on the couch in the family room. Tina came in to join her, but a few moments after she sat down on the love seat, she screamed out in pain. A ten-inch-tall, solid-brass candlestick had flown from the kitchen to hit Tina squarely on the back of her head. Nothing had ever hit Tina before.

Joyce picked up the candlestick and stuck it in the corner behind the love seat so it wouldn't come down again. She hadn't been watching Tina during the incident and now wondered if she had staged it. A crash on her right drew her attention. A candle had hit the wall behind the television. Joyce glanced up at the pair of candleholders on the wall above the love seat. One was empty. This time Joyce knew Tina had not thrown the candle. The candleholders were fastened to the wall on either side of a brass clock about two feet above the love seat. Both the clock and the two holders were embellished with decorative arrows pointing outward. Just as Tina was telling Joyce how much her head and stomach hurt, the clock itself came down and hit Tina with a thud in the back of her head. Tina screamed and threw herself on the floor, curling into a tight ball and holding the back of her head with her hands to protect it. Joyce wanted to help, but a moment later the love seat itself jerked out a few inches from the wall. The strength of the force worried her. The love seat concealed a hideaway bed and sat on wooden legs rather than rollers. With that much power, Joyce thought, the force could be dangerous. She told Tina to stay away from the love seat and to sit on one of the recliners instead.

Tina couldn't stop crying. Everyone was blaming her, she said, hugging her stomach, and she hadn't done anything—none of it. Why was this happening? What was wrong?

Joyce wanted to comfort her, but as she reached out, a telephone jumped across the girl's lap. It had been on a table to her left, and Joyce could see that Tina hadn't touched it. Joyce put the phone back, but it took off again. Tina was feeling worse by the second; now even the phone was after her. How would she call her friends?

A different kind of crying came from the dining room. Something was wrong with Anne, and Joan asked Tina to check. Tina made a face but went in. The baby only needed fresh diapers, and Tina was attending to her when several of the remaining wineglasses in the cupboard over the bar broke, one after the other. Each time, Joyce came in and helped clean up the pieces. After Tina had returned and was back with Joyce in the family room, a couple more glasses broke in the dining room when only the baby was there.

Joyce took a few minutes to step into the downstairs bathroom, then saw the hallway chandelier swinging back and forth. At the same time a wineglass from the dining room, one of the last, crashed by her feet. "Tina?" she called. "Where are you?" She wondered if Tina had thrown the glass.

"I didn't throw it!" Tina exclaimed as she entered the hallway. Her words were hardly out of her mouth when a tape dispenser hit her in the back of the head. Bruce had left it on the microwave the day before. When things hit Tina, Joyce noticed, they usually struck the back of her head.

The dishes from lunch were still on the table, and Joan asked Tina to put them in the dishwasher. Tina was going to do as her mother asked when the cups and glasses, some of them full, took off through the air. Then a crash sounded and pieces of a red coffee cup fell down; it had broken in midair. Tina couldn't stand any more and ran back crying to the family room. Within minutes she was attacked by an end table.

Joyce Beaumont saw that the table had fallen over Tina

and had her pinned to the ground. Tina was screaming hysterically as Joyce tried to pry the girl free, but the table wouldn't budge. As Joyce wrestled with the table, the same telephone that had hit Tina now flew up behind Joyce and struck her in the back. It was almost as if the phone was coming to the aid of the table. Then as suddenly as it started, the table gave up and it was over. Joyce was more angry than afraid.

"Enough of this!" she cried out to the empty room. "Someone is gonna get hurt!" She held Tina tightly, calming and consoling her.

Her lunch break over, Joyce had to leave. "Okay, I'm leaving," she announced to whoever or whatever might be there. She had been in the house for an hour and a half. During that time there were at least thirty incidents. In Joyce's view, the house was possessed. Pam was wrong; Tina was not playing games. There was a force in the house and it wanted to hurt Tina, so much so that it would attack anyone who tried to help her.

Shortly after Joyce left, Tina asked if she could go visit a friend; she had to get out of the house. Joan was at the end of her tether as well, so she said yes. The force departed at the same time. For a few hours the Resches were given a respite, but when Tina returned, so did the force. Chairs, food, candles — it all started up again.

By the end of the day, most of the movables had moved and the breakables had broken. John felt he had reached his own breaking point, but now he was in overdrive. The circus-like atmosphere was more than he could tolerate; close to twenty-five people had come in and out of the house. "Don't be surprised if I'm not around," he told Joan, "because I can't take it anymore."

After a day of constant cleaning, repairing, and unwanted

visitors, John knew that no matter what anyone said, Tina was responsible. Rebellious and headstrong, the girl was nothing but trouble, she had even pulled a knife on him!

"Sit," he ordered. He was going to watch Tina all day and all night if he had to. Tina was furious: Why was he persecuting her like this? But John's mind was made up. Tina was not to leave his sight, not for one instant. Pete came and joined Tina by the couch. But instead of being a comfort, her best friend became a watchdog, barking and warning John every time Tina tried to get up.

The crashing noises continued. Each new sound made Tina wince and cry out; she complained that her head and stomach hurt. John didn't care; she couldn't leave the room. He stared and stared. How was she doing it? She was so clumsy she couldn't walk without bumping into a wall. Craig couldn't be an accomplice, he wasn't around most of the time, and anyhow, he wouldn't do things like this. The same was true for Lisa. This left only Joan and Tina, and it certainly wasn't Joan. It had to be Tina. Why else did things stop when she went to sleep or stepped outside? Then John thought of the mattresses that had come off the beds that morning while Tina was in church; he tried to forget about it.

Joan wanted John to stop hounding the girl. "The more pressure you put on her," she said, "the worse things are going to be. Try and let up."

"I just can't," he replied.

Joan had given up worrying about the breakages. They were small compared to the effect on John's health or the safety of the foster children. With the house in such an uproar, she couldn't possibly look after them in the way they needed. What if they got hit or seriously injured? Any accident would reflect on her ability to protect the children and could harm her reputation. Joan was a professional foster parent, she couldn't afford to lose her position. She called Children's Services to place the three younger children in temporary shelters. Lisa, being older, was better able to take care of herself and could stay at least another day. The decision was painful, but Joan felt there was no other choice.

Craig finished work at nine. The night before he had planned to go to a movie with some of the other men from JAYS. But the events at home seemed far more interesting than anything they could see on the screen. He went back to the store and told his friends what was happening. They thought he was joking. "Come on over," he said, "and see for yourselves!" The invitation was met with laughter, and the men refused to go. Later on he was more convincing and persuaded one of the other men to come to the house along with a girl they knew.

Back at the house, Craig offered his friends some refreshments and had a beer himself. He then went into the family room where Tina was sitting, leaving his two visitors to follow. While he was gone, they saw some plastic cups fly off the kitchen counter, then heard a commotion in the family room. The love seat had slid out from the wall. Alerted that the show had moved to the family room, Craig's friends hurried in to watch. Shortly after they entered the room, an afghan blanket that had been on the arm of the love seat flew up and draped itself over Tina's head. Everybody saw it, and Craig was delighted that the force had shown up for his friends.

Hoping to entertain his friends with more incidents, Craig asked Tina to walk around the house so they could see what else would move. The experiment didn't work, and his visitors prepared to depart.

As the group was on the point of leaving, a wing chair fell

over in the living room near where they were standing. Craig's friends were amazed at what they had seen, and Craig was proud of his success as master of ceremonies.

The force was less playful when there was no one to enter-tain. A while later, as Craig watched Tina come into the family room, something flew toward her from the kitchen. At first Craig thought it was another bottle or glass, but when the thing flew past Tina and hit the fireplace, he knew this wasn't all fun and games. The object was a paring knife that had almost stabbed Tina in the back. The next time it happened, Joan removed all the knives from the kitchen and put them away in drawers elsewhere in the house.

All day long Joan had discussed with her grown children various solutions for ridding the house of the force. Except for her oldest son, Kevin, no one knew what to do other than to just keep cleaning. Kevin, an ardently religious young man with dark brown hair and intense brown eyes, had converted from what he considered his parents' lukewarm Lutheranism to the Mormon faith. When Joan told him what was going on in the house, he offered to ask his congregation to perform an exorcism. "Your faith isn't strong enough," he told his mother. As he went on to explain what the exorcisim would entail, Joan thought she heard him say something about bringing two elders and "someone who's attained the priesthood." Joan was at her wit's end. With all other possibilities exhausted, she agreed to the ritual.

Tina's hopes were raised by Kevin's conviction that his fellow Mormons would know how to deal with the force. She wasn't ready to switch churches as Kevin had done, but Pastor Heinz had been a disappointment.

It was close to midnight when Kevin arrived with Elder Haynes and the two other men from his church. John went to bed. He didn't believe in spirits. He knew who the culprit was; he just hadn't caught her yet.

Elder Haynes chose the family room for the ritual since this was where the spirit had been the most active. He asked Joan for a chair from the kitchen and placed it in the center of the room. Kevin watched from the stoop in front of the fireplace as Tina was instructed to sit down. The three men stood around her and placed their hands on her hair. Following the prescribed prayer for banishing evil, they commanded the spirit to leave.

When they were finished, Elder Haynes guided Tina to the love seat. Immediately it slid out to meet them, just as the living room couch had done for Pastor Heinz. The force treated the two denominations the same, but the Mormons were more persistent.

"Maybe we'd better do it again," Elder Haynes suggested. He was about to start over when Kevin cried out; the kitchen chairs were moving. He was scared to death. Until now his encounters with the force were only what he'd been told. Nothing had prepared him for the reality of seeing it in action.

Elder Haynes remained undaunted and prayed for the evil one to depart even as the chairs continued scampering across the floor. This time the exorcism seemed to stick. He was able to sit down on the love seat without incident.

Holding Tina's hand, Elder Haynes gave her and Joan a lesson about evil spirits and how to get rid of them, when the love seat shot out again, this time carrying both Elder Haynes and Tina. Tina's hopes crashed. The Mormons were as useless as everyone else. She wondered if the force would ever go away.

The priest said they had done what they could, and the group departed, taking Kevin with them. Like Pastor Heinz, Elder Haynes did not offer to return. Neither did Kevin.

Joan wasn't impressed with her son's desertion nor with the ineffective ritual. Nothing had worked. They had called in two electric companies, the law, and two churches, and the force still had the upper hand. Then Joan remembered the one person who might know what to do, the reporter who had interviewed her for the paper last year, Mike Harden. It might be a long shot, but over the years Mike had written on a variety of topics. Maybe he'd heard of trouble like this before or knew of someone who had. We can't be that different from other families, she thought. Or were they?

# 7

# THE PHOTOGRAPH

**P**hotographer Fred Shannon told me he had been with the *Dispatch* for thirty years. Intense at work and impish with his friends, Fred had been described as one of the top news photographers in the country. In his career he had shot everything imaginable from football games to celebrities, but being asked to photograph a poltergeist was a first.

Fred was in his office Monday morning, March 5, when he got the call from Mike Harden. "Mike was at the home of John and Joan Resch," Fred told me when I interviewed him the following week. "He asked me to bring my camera equipment to the house."

Fred didn't mind admitting he was afraid of what he might find; whatever this ghost, spirit, or "force" was, it could be dangerous. But if Mike Harden said things were flying through the air in the home of Joan and John Resch, Fred was going to do his best to capture them on film. He had his reputation to uphold.

When Fred got to the house, Harden met him at the door. "Fred, you won't believe what's happening here."

After introducing him to the family—they were all at home, including Craig—Harden showed him around. First they went to the family room. The Resches had stowed away the holders that had launched the candles the day before as well as the wall clock that had hit Tina.

"I want to get a shot of Tina holding those," Fred said. Wearing a bright red T-shirt, jeans with the obligatory torn knee, and red running shoes, Tina didn't look different from any other teenager as she held the items up for the camera before they were quickly put away again.

They moved to the dining room, where the metal cups had jumped up to hit the chandelier. Fred snapped the damaged glass ball. One wineglass was left in the cupboard, and Fred took a picture of Tina holding it, her arm stretched out as if to put as much distance between herself and the glass as possible. After a few minutes, as they stepped into the kitchen, there was a crash from the dining room.

"Uh-oh, there goes the last wineglass," Joan said.

When Fred went in to look, glass shards in the corner confirmed Joan's statement. No one was in the room when this happened.

Fred stepped out of the dining room and was followed by a clattering sound. Six metal coasters from the bar had hit the wall in the same place as the glass. The room was still empty of people. Fred's fears began to fade; flying coasters were weird, but hardly dangerous. Still, he would have liked to know what was behind it all. Mike had told him that the family suspected Tina, but he couldn't see why. She couldn't have thrown the glass or the coasters since she was with him in the kitchen when they flew. It was the strangest thing he had ever seen. Nevertheless, Fred began to find a pattern to the incidents; the six coasters came from the same place as the wineglass and they followed the same path. That could be important to keep in mind if he wanted to catch the force on film.

Tina was enjoying herself; Fred was easy to talk to, and unlike her father, he was interested in what she had to say. Instead of blaming her, he actually wanted to understand and take photographs. She opened up and, along with Craig, tagged after Fred, pointing out the various locations where the force had shown itself. Fred listened as Craig told him about the lamps and love seat, and how the afghan had flown over Tina's head; Tina described how she and Joyce Beaumont had fought with the table when it tried to pin her to the ground. Then she demonstrated how the phone had flown across her lap.

These are great stories, Fred thought, but unless the force stood still for the camera, he might have to be content with reconstructing the incidents.

While Fred was out of the family room with Harden, Craig looked in on Tina and saw the phone fly across her lap, this time for real. He told her to move to the love seat, and the afghan flew over her.

"What should I do?" Tina asked. Things were happening and Fred wasn't in the room. Craig told her to just keep everything on the floor and he would get Fred.

Craig found Fred, who then rushed back to the family room. The phone was still on the floor by the love seat. Disappointed at being too late, he and Harden sat down opposite Tina, and then the afghan leaped from the floor and draped itself over Tina's head. Craig was watching from the kitchen.

Harden's back had been turned when the afghan went sailing, and he now examined the blanket for strings and other devices. "There's nothing that I can see," he said.

Tina moved to the other end of the love seat. No sooner had she done so than a room divider fell over. It had been standing behind her, by the microwave. It seemed that the force had moved to the kitchen.

While Fred was still in the family room with Tina, a drinking glass in the kitchen flew from the counter by the sink into a corner without breaking. As one of the few remaining glasses, it was put back, but a few moments later it took off again, this time shattering in the middle of the room.

Fred noted that the force had just revealed another of its features, one that was going to be crucial if he was to catch anything on film: an object that moved once would often move again.

He decided he better stay close to Tina since this was where the action was, and he asked her to show him how some of the other incidents had taken place. Tina took him to the living room and pointed to a large lithograph that had been knocked off the wall the day before. Its glass had cracked and some of it was missing. Fred asked her to hold it up so he could get a picture. As he popped the flash, there was a loud crash and he clicked the shutter a second time without the flash. There was enough daylight to get a decent picture.

Fred's first thought was that the lithograph had slipped out of Tina's hands and that the crash had sounded when it hit the floor. But Tina insisted she had not dropped it. "Something knocked it out of my hands," she said, "like it was trying to take it away from me."

Fred considered another possibility; that the glass, already broken, had cracked from its own weight when Tina had held it up, causing both the sound and for it to slip out of her hands. He didn't want to outright accuse her of fraud, but it was hard to tell exactly what had happened.

Worried that Fred might be doubting her, Tina nervously sat down on the living room couch. She was convinced that the force had struck the picture, and she didn't want Fred to think she was lying. "It's okay," Fred said. "There's plenty of other shots we can get. Don't worry about it."

Tina relaxed a little, and as Fred turned to leave, there was a booming sound behind him. He spun around and snapped a picture: the table lamp that had been on an end table next to Tina had crashed to the floor. The lamp had fallen several times before, and Joan had left it standing on the floor to keep it from falling again. She had put it back up at Fred's request.

Had Tina pulled the lamp down? Fred didn't think so, but he couldn't be sure. He decided to keep a better watch.

They headed back to the family room, and Tina seated herself on the arm of the recliner opposite the love seat while Fred watched her from the kitchen. Suddenly the love seat lunged toward her. Fred snapped two pictures, one right after the other. The first caught the end phase of the movement of the love seat. The photo also showed Tina's startled expression, her hands raised to ward off the love seat. The second caught Tina losing her balance and falling backward into the recliner.

Fred put his camera down, and a loud, unnerving sound like a cannon boom came from the same room. He and Mike Harden rushed in and saw a heavy bronze candlestick lying on the floor next to the metal door to the backyard. Two dents in the door attested to the strength of the impact. Next a huge roar, like that of a freight train, filled the room as a second candlestick rolled from beside the love seat into the hallway. Tina thought it was the same one that had hit her in the head the day before. She worried that it might be after her again, but Fred's courage was contagious and she joined him in the hallway. The ceiling lamp was swinging wildly as if in the midst of a hurricane, but at least it was still attached to the ceiling.

Joan felt better with the two newsmen around, but it was obvious they knew no more about the force than anyone else. She decided to call her friend Kathy Goeff at Franklin Country Children's Services.

Kathy, a clerical specialist, did not have any experience with flying objects, but she was composed in the face of a crisis and Joan needed a calming presence. Kathy said she would come over during her lunch break, and that she would bring Lee Arnold, Tina's caseworker.

Joan went back to her guests in the family room and to a series of flights that were unlike any before. The object was the Princess phone. There was nothing new about that, it had flown before. What was different was that the phone flew time and time again for thirty minutes and that it was the only thing that did.

At this point, two phones were in the room. One was the old phone with a base and handset, the other was the new one-piece Princess phone. They were both on the table in the family room between the two recliners.

As Tina sat in Joan's recliner with the table on her left, the phone began making rapid flights over her lap. Fred Shannon watched from the couch opposite her. Each flight lasted about a tenth of a second. Fred did not keep count but thought he must have seen at least seven flights. A couple of times the phone did not get past Tina, but struck her left side, making her cry out.

Finally here was the opportunity to get the kind of shot Fred had wanted all morning. The problem was that he never knew when the phone would move, and when it did, it was over as quickly as it started. He settled down with his eye to the camera, trained it on Tina and the phone, and waited. And waited.

After twenty minutes he gave up and took the camera down. The moment he did, the phone took off. At that point he thought he understood the force; it was "tricky." If he were ever to get it on film, he'd have to be tricky himself.

He brought his camera up to his eye again, focused, then waited with his finger on the trigger for about five minutes. Again nothing happened, but when he brought the camera down, he kept it pointed at Tina. To thoroughly outfox the force, he turned his head to the kitchen while watching Tina through his peripheral vision. Within seconds he saw a blur and hit the trigger. He caught the phone flying in midair about six or seven feet from the table, the retractable cord stretched across the arms of the recliner.

Mike Harden was shaken. He had seen the phone in flight and knew by the flash that Fred had got a picture. The photograph would be crucial to any news report; he needed to leave the room to sort through his thoughts. This was going to be something big, and Fred's picture would make the story.

Mike went into the kitchen to think. A glass mug shattered against the wall and he barely noticed. Suddenly he heard Tina cry out; the footrest to her recliner had shot out and the back had fallen down. Fred, still on sentry duty, was taking more photos, but Mike knew nothing would match that flying phone.

Kathy Goeff and Lee Arnold arrived at around twelve-thirty. Tina was excited to have more visitors and told them what had happened. Kathy was fascinated and wanted to see for herself, but Lee Arnold felt more comfortable in the kitchen. "I'll just watch from here," she said, peering in from the doorway.

Tina sat back down in the recliner, smiling and posing for more phone flights. She braced herself in case she got hit in the side again—that part was definitely not fun, but the look of amazement on people's faces when the phone took off made up for it.

Mike rejoined the group in the family room, and everyone, even Lee Arnold from her post by the kitchen doorway, got ready for the next flight. Nothing happened. It was as if the force had done its duty and left for the day. Tina began to feel uncomfortable. Everyone was staring at her, just as John always did, except now instead of blaming her, they all *wanted* things to happen. She couldn't hold the tears in any longer; why couldn't people leave her alone?

Suddenly the old phone jumped across Tina's lap. The force was back and had changed horses in midstream. Tina's visitors were enthralled. The phone repeated its performance, this time nearly hitting Joan. Lee Arnold gathered her courage and came in to join the others. The nearest empty spot was the love seat. As she started to sit down, Fred warned, "Watch out!" Lee jumped up and the phone soared right to where she was about to sit. Fred took another photo just as Lee was pulling away from the landing site. She wondered if leaving the kitchen had been such a good idea. One thing she was sure of, Tina couldn't have thrown that phone. She'd seen both of Tina's hands when it flew, and the force of the impact when it smacked into the love seat was too great for Tina to have thrown it.

Tina wanted lunch. Her visitors wanted her to stay in the recliner so they could see more flying phones. No way, Tina said; she was hungry. Fred hoped to get more photos and he followed her into the kitchen. The force was quiet. Instead of paranormal flights of eggs and juice, Fred got four shots of something normal, a teenager raiding a refrigerator.

Kathy and Lee had to be back at the Children's Services. On her way out, Kathy saw John down on his knees scrubbing the floor. She stopped to ask how he was, but he didn't seem to hear. During her visit she hadn't worried about the phenomena, they seemed harmless enough, but she was becoming concerned about the Resches. John looked terrible. When she asked him a second time if he was okay, he still didn't reply. Feeling somewhat awkward, she decided to call Joan later that evening after work.

Fred had a full roll of film and wanted to get back to the paper and have it developed. He hoped the force had not ruined the film. He and Mike Harden were about to leave when a large Kleenex box flew from the table with the phones and landed on the side table by the couch. The movement was swift, like the phones, but there was a difference.

In the earlier incidents, the mystery was how the objects started their movements, not how they stopped. When they fell, they landed like any normally thrown objects by sliding or bouncing to a halt. This time, when the box hit the table, it stopped cold, as if it had landed in glue. The box was closer to Fred than any of the other objects had been, about twenty inches away from his right leg. Tina was also on his right, four feet from the box. He was certain she had not touched it.

Fred wondered about the nature of the energy. The force seemed to know when he was looking at the phone, since it only flew when he looked away. At the same time, the recurrent flights, which enabled him to get several photos, showed the force was cooperative. Then, as he was departing, he saw an object—the Kleenex box—whose flight was controlled from beginning to end.

The force, he concluded, was intelligent. It was also fast. In all his years of shooting film, Fred had never seen anything move with such speed. Trying to catch the phenomena on film was the most challenging assignment of his thirty years in the news business. He was later to regard his shot of the flying phone as the most important photo of his career.

# 8

# A MOMENTARY ESCAPE

From my conversations with Tina, it was plain to see she had enjoyed entertaining the visitors. They treated her like a VIP, especially Fred Shannon. She had been glad when it seemed that he got a picture of the phone in the air. But then it was lunchtime and back to the drudgery of the household chores.

The kitchen was in chaos; food and drink splashed against the floor and the walls as Joan tried to put a meal together. John followed her around with his mop and bucket, interrupting his cleaning only to investigate what new mess awaited him in the living room. Whenever he or Joan looked in, it seemed a mindless energy was at work, strewing the chairs here and there, tipping the couch and lamps over, knocking the houseplants down. They had to give up on the terrarium. Weighing forty or fifty pounds, it wandered around like a giant tortoise, sometimes moving up on the couch, at other times preferring the top of the coffer. Being round and large, it was too awkward for the Resches to handle; they decided to leave it alone. The coffer, too, was heavy; like the terrarium it moved about a dozen times that day.

Helping John replace the couch for the umpteenth time, Joan noticed that only the big items seemed to be moving; most of the small things stayed in place. Her two cacti, for instance, behaved quite differently from each other. The big one was always tipped over or set down someplace it didn't belong, while the little one remained undisturbed. She also thought it was odd that when the furniture moved, she no longer heard it moving. The rumbling noises that had scared her so much on Sunday morning had gone away.

Although Craig had spent Sunday night with friends, the force did not forget him. When he retuned home Monday morning, he was again greeted by the penny bottle in the middle of his room with the shoe stuck on top like a sentry at attention.

He had taken the shoe off and returned the bottle to its place by the door when there was a knock. A plastic lemon from the tree downstairs had hit his door; two or three others followed.

When Craig had heard the knock, he halfway expected it was another candle, but Joan had put them away. To give the force something to play with instead, she left the lemons in the pot by the tree. When she later found them around the house where the force had thrown them, she would return them to the pot. She asked Craig and the others to do the same. It was better that the force use the lemons. They were unbreakable and did not scratch the furniture and walls when they hit. The force was playing fetch with the family.

Before going down for breakfast, Craig took the lemons along and locked his door. He dropped the lemons in the pot downstairs, had his meal, and watched some television. When he came back up, he said, the door was still locked, and the penny bottle greeted him from its accustomed place with the same shoe on top.

As the commotion continued, the family unraveled. The three younger children had already gone. Now Lisa was sent away to a temporary home. John was close to all of the foster children, and he was particularly attached to Lisa. The little girl was beginning to think of him as a father. Of course he knew that eventually all the children would leave to be adopted or placed with younger parents, but seeing Lisa go for no good reason increased his distress. John's life was being ruined by something that was impossible.

Joan felt the loss of the children, too; she always valued people over things. But John had extra worries. Although he cared for his family, John's world mainly revolved around the objects they owned. His working life had been to form matter into useful objects—metal at Vorys Brothers, wood and other materials at home. This was a world he was familiar with and thought he understood. If there were problems he could not handle, he knew whom to call. Now this world was breaking apart. The physical losses were not all that serious, and most of the things he could replace or repair. But now, if he were to believe his eyes, he had to disbelieve everything he knew about the world. In some ways it was almost easier to think he had lost his mind, that the problem was all in his head, and not in front of his eyes. He spoke to Joan about leaving, but there was nowhere to go.

Into the midst of the family's confusion, Jack, the Resches' twenty-three-year-old adopted son, turned up in the afternoon for a surprise visit. Jack had been away in the army for two years and was anticipating a warm reception. The family had expected him back, but not before his birthday on Sunday. Instead of open arms, he found flying phones and a family too distracted to pay him much attention. Disheartened, he went to one of his sisters' homes.

The phone rang constantly, Tina jumping each time as friends and family called to inquire if the disturbances were continuing and how the family was holding up. But they could hardly hear through the earsplitting screeches. One of the callers was Kathy Goeff, who phoned after she got home from work. She wanted to know how things were going and if she should come to the house again.

Kathy could barely understand what Joan was saying. "What's that noise?" she asked. It sounded more electrical than human.

"That's been going on all day," Joan replied, "every time I talk to someone."

The sound was more frightening to Kathy than the flying phone had been. It was so intrusive, really hurting her ears. But she did understand Joan to say that she need not come over; they were all leaving. Everyone—John, Tina, Joan herself—their nerves were in tatters and they were suffering from lack of sleep.

"We just can't keep up with it anymore," Joan said. For the sake of their mental and physical health, they had to get out of the house.

Joan phoned a motel for reservations. For a change, the line was clear. Craig was staying with friends, so the family was down to Joan, John, and Tina.

They packed, straightened the living room one last time, and quickly got in the car, John at the wheel. They left all the lights in the house burning, hoping this would discourage the force.

As John steered into the night, he wondered what would happen next. Would the force, all restraints now gone, completely wreck his home? Or would it follow them to the motel? He didn't know which was worse. The house, abandoned but lit, seemed eerily occupied.

The next day, the center of attention shifted from the Resch home to the newsroom of the *Columbus Dispatch*. Mike Harden had no illusions about what was in store for him.

As he had expected, his story was met with ribbing from his colleagues. Hoping for a more receptive ear, he phoned home. His wife, Suzanne, only laughed when he told her about phones and furniture that moved without human assistance. Harden hung up. When he had simmered down, he called back: "I've had enough skeptics on this, I don't need you, too."

The kidding continued with reporters walking by his station whistling the theme from *The Twilight Zone*. One of them suspended a telephone receiver on a fishing line over his desk. The truth of the old adage that a prophet is never believed in his own land was painfully evident.

The editor of the *Dispatch*, Luke Feck, had faith in his two reporters and printed Harden's story and Shannon's photo on the front page on Tuesday, March 6. The force shared the front page with President Reagan, who was addressing a group of Christian evangelicals in town.

In the days that followed, the Resch story and picture appeared in papers around the country, and in the international press as well. Harden, Shannon, and Tina became instant celebrities. Joan's only request was that the family's last name and address not be used. That didn't stop more than 150 requests for interviews from landing on Harden's desk. The photograph of Tina's startled expression as the phone flew over her lap brought calls into Shannon's home from all over the world. It got to the point where his wife, Millie, had to take the phone off the hook so they could eat.

Another concerned party was the Resches' insurance company, Midwestern Indemnity of Cincinnati. Before the family left for the motel Monday night, Joan phoned Dave Miller, their agent, about coverage for glasses, lamps, and paintings that had been destroyed by an intangible force. Miller was amused by the idea. He chuckled, but didn't dismiss her claim. He knew the family; they weren't ones to lie.

Miller brought the matter to the attention of Rein Geller, his boss at Midwestern. Geller's first thought was to deny the claim. He changed his mind when he read the news stories. But he had a problem describing the cause of damage on the insurance form. The Resches had an all-risk policy, which covered things like burglary, fire, and earthquake, but there was nothing about an invisible force that tossed household furnishings around. The category that seemed closest was "malicious mischief and vandalism," except that the perpetrator was invisible.

In the blank where it asked for the cause of damage, Geller wrote the equivalent of "you tell me" and attached all the newspaper clippings. He was sure his explanation would raise a few eyebrows.

Geller told Joan that her losses should be covered since she had an all-risk policy, but it was a difficult call. If Midwestern paid up, he explained, the precedent might make the company vulnerable to bogus claims in the future. Midwestern decided to send their adjuster to the Resch house to figure out what had really happened.

The force was not in evidence at the motel when the Resches checked in. Tina, for a short while, was an only child. She had her mother's undivided attention and no chores. To discourage visitations from the force during the night, she constructed crucifixes from the motel stationery and placed them around her bed. There were no incidents that night or during the next two days.

In total, the family stayed at the motel for three days and two nights. During that time, John made two visits to the house and reported back that things were calm there, too. Everything was peaceful and in its place. But would things stay that way when the family returned? Had the force finally tired and left for good? The questions weighed on Joan and John as they prepared to return.

"If we go back home, and things start to happen again, I don't know what we are going to do," Joan said.

Wednesday, March 7, Tina had an appointment in the morning at Ohio State University for the neurological examination I had suggested. She and Joan returned to the house around twelve-thirty. The minute Tina walked in the kitchen, a candle, a glass, and a bottle of 7UP moved.

She and Joan started back to the front door to get more of the luggage. When they glanced into the living room, Joan felt like crying. The terrarium was on the couch and the rest of the furniture was everywhere but where it should be. Tina went to the family room and the phone leaped toward her like an eager pet. The force had missed her.

Harden had kept his word not to reveal the Resches' last name. To convince his colleagues that Joan and John were upstanding members of the community who would not put over a hoax, he spoke of their work as foster parents and mentioned the column he had written in October. This was the clue the other journalists needed, and they soon tracked the Resches down.

The phone, always busy in the Resch home, became frantic when the family returned from the motel. Reporters, photographers, and TV news crews wanted to come and see what was going on, some to expose a fraud, others to see flying household items and to repeat Shannon's feat of photographing them.

John wanted to take the phone off the hook and keep the reporters out; two of them had already witnessed the incidents, and it would only cause more disruptions to let others in. Joan, always more sociable and forthcoming, did not want to turn anyone away. She pointed out that the publicity might bring in an expert who could make the force go away. They settled on a news conference. In this way they could deal with the reporters all at once and be bothered no more. They chose the following day, Thursday, and told the reporters to be at the house by one o'clock.

The phone continued to ring. Barbara Hughes, a friend of the family's and a foster mother like Joan, called and offered to come by a little later with her husband, Ted, a schoolteacher. She and Ted would also bring their foster son, John Peter, or JP, and their adopted daughter, Connie. JP was fourteen and Connie was sixteen. The Hughes family were born-again Christians and thought they knew how to deal with a demon.

When they saw the state of the house, their worst fears were confirmed. It looked as if a cyclone had struck. The furniture was on end, glass was underfoot; all the cupboards were sticky with juice. It seemed that the force had gained strength during its days off.

Something hit in the dining room. Barbara saw an egg cup on the floor that Tina said belonged on the bar. Next to where the egg cup had been was a stack of metal coasters, the same ones that had flown when Fred Shannon was in the house. "Watch out!" Tina yelled. Barbara ducked; the coasters started flying out from the bar like Frisbees: one, two, three, four.

"Those things have been flying around all day," Tina said.

Barbara saw one remaining coaster on the bar. A stainless-steel jigger sat beside it. When she and Tina turned to leave the room, they heard a loud crash. The jigger had hit the washer-dryer unit in the corner of the room.

JP missed the flying coasters but was treated to a show of his own on the bathroom sink. The soap dish was spinning in circles and "doughnuts," making him think it was some kind of toy. He opened the door and called out to Tina, "Is that soap dish supposed to spin?"

"No!" Tina replied.

Barbara went into the family room while her husband, Ted, talked to Tina in the kitchen. He had brought a crucifix on a chain, which he wanted to give her, thinking it would repel the force. Tina let him put it around her neck.

After Ted gave Tina the cross, a green drinking glass on the sink board caught his attention. Joan had put away her remaining breakables, but had somehow missed this glass. Hoping to save it, Ted took it off the counter and tucked it away at the back of the cupboard, behind the Tupperware.

As he turned away from the cupboard, the glass shattered at his feet. Tina was right in front of him, talking and heading toward the family room. Obviously, she had not thrown the glass. Ted wondered if the demon had smashed it because he had given Tina the cross.

By now it was becoming clear to everyone that if Tina was home, the force would also be in attendance. No one could say why or how, but the combination of Tina and the house on Blue Ash Road was like oil and fertilizer—explosive. As soon as she left the house, the disturbances stopped.

The Hughes invited Tina to stay with them overnight. The force hadn't accompanied Tina to church or the motel, and there was no reason to believe it would follow this time either. Looking after Tina for a while would give Joan and John some peace from the disturbances and a chance to get the house in order before the news conference. They also wanted to help rid Tina of her invisible persecutor with prayer. Joan and John gratefully accepted, and Tina was glad to get away. She and Joan had been arguing again, and she was anxious about the coming news conference.

Mike Harden stopped by for a visit just before Tina left. He found her in the family room by the fireplace, nervously twirling the crucifix Ted Hughes had given her. Her overnight bag was by her side and she was antsy to get out of the house. She seemed upset, and when Mike asked, she admitted she had been fighting with her mother. Tina then said something she hadn't revealed before, that she thought the occurrences were punishment for her anger.

"It usually happens when I'm really mad," she told Harden.

# 9

# NEWS CONFERENCE

A blinding snowstorm swirled through Columbus. People who had been in the house Thursday, March 8, later told me it seemed that nature was matching the force inside the Resch home with a powerful display outside. Barbara Hughes braved both and, along with JP, brought Tina back home in the morning.

Joan told Tina what to expect at the news conference, saying there would be several reporters and that they would ask questions about what had happened. All Tina needed to do was answer their questions. Tina said she didn't want to be there. "You can answer just as well as I can," she said. Joan replied that the journalists had specifically asked for Tina and the conference would only last an hour. After that she could go back with Barbara.

Tina's stomach churned. It was exciting to think a news crew wanted to talk to her and that she would be on television, but what if the reporters thought she was bad? Like the Mormons, the Hughes family seemed to believe an evil spirit had attached itself to her. If the reporters thought so, too, it would be all over town. She could hardly eat when she sat down for breakfast.

It was the worst meal the family had ever experienced. The chairs did their crazy dance while plates loaded with food and glasses with juice flipped through the air, some soaring all the way into the family room. Joan had been up half the night cleaning; now what was she supposed to do? The reporters would be at the house in just a few hours.

Joan's other married daughter, Peggy Covert, arrived with a friend to help clean up. Peggy was a nurse at Riverside Hospital. She had not been to the house during the disturbances and doubted the dozens of stories the family had insisted were true. All she needed was a few minutes in the house to turn into a believer. As she watched lamps fall, juice spill, and the phone fly not only toward Tina but smacking into JP as well, she was convinced the force was a reality.

By twelve-thirty the tension around Tina was almost tangible. Tina had only picked at her breakfast and still wasn't hungry, but Barbara Hughes thought she needed to eat. She had made soup and sandwiches; surely Tina could manage that. As she leaned over the table to serve Tina and JP, two kitchen chairs between her and the table shot out and hit her in the stomach with enough strength to make her double over in pain. Shaken, Barbara finished serving the children and sat down. JP was on her left, at the end of the table, and Tina was facing her, on the other side. The next thing she knew, one of the baby chairs, piled high with visitors' coats, slid over and slammed into her knee. She yelped with pain, and one of the vinyl chairs that had first hit her suddenly turned around and moved away, startling her even further.

From her seat in the family room, Peggy Covert saw the chair strike Barbara's leg. Tina was sitting on the other side of the table a good distance from the chair. Peggy was certain Tina had not kicked or moved the chair in any way.

It was one o'clock. The reporters started to arrive and were setting up their equipment in the living room. Tina waited with Peggy in the family room. She was asking Peggy what she thought the reporters were going to write about when Peggy saw a movement out of the corner of her left eye. As if in response to Tina's worries, the pencil caddy had fallen off the filing cabinet, spilling pens and pencils on the way.

Joan called Tina to the living room; the news conference was about to start. Joan, John, and Tina—the three central figures of the drama—took their places on the couch, Tina in between her parents. The room could barely contain the number of reporters; Paul Alexander, from Associated Press, counted forty. Their presence added a new and disturbing twist to what had already been an eventful week.

Tina was uncomfortable under the television lights. "I didn't want to do this," she told the reporters. "If I say anything, people are going to think I'm crazy."

The reporters assured her it would be okay; just relax and have fun; they'd go easy on her.

"Are you afraid when things move?" someone asked.

Tina began to feel better. "No," she said, objects that moved by themselves didn't frighten her, but "it's a little scary when they're flying. I wish they would stop. I still don't believe things like this can happen." She then mentioned the knives that had almost hit her and told of the time she ducked when she saw the paring knife come at her in the mirror over the fireplace. The reporters hung on every word.

John said, "I see it and I still don't believe it. How a glass can fly at a ninety-degree angle through a doorway and around a corner, or the television can run with no electricity . . . I just try to clean up, to turn my head away when it happens."

Jodi Gossage, a reporter with United Press International, noted that the living room was devoid of decorative touches. Joan explained that the pictures, ashtrays, and mementos that remained intact had been packed away.

"I don't think we have two glasses left in the house," she said. "We've hidden everything that could get broken or hurt someone."

Gossage asked Tina if she had seen the movie *Poltergeist*. When Tina said yes, Gossage asked if the force that had invaded her home and sent glasses flying was like the force in the film. Tina didn't think so. "Nobody has gone sliding across the floor, and no kids have disappeared—yet."

Tina liked the way the news conference was going. Contrary to her fears, the reporters were friendly and nobody thought she was bad or possessed by an evil spirit.

An hour later the news conference was supposed to wind down, but the reporters weren't ready to leave. They wanted to see flying phones for themselves. Even an egg or two would be worth the wait. They knew the incidents followed Tina, so they told her to walk through the various rooms, hoping her presence would get things moving. Like the Pied Piper, Tina led the group from room to room, but everything stayed where it belonged.

"The force," Jodi Gossage noted, "was not with most of the reporters and photographers gathered in the Resch home." Regardless of the force's refusal to show itself, no one was willing to give up and call it quits. The reporters stuck to Tina like burrs; she couldn't take a step without them.

Joan didn't know how to tell the newspeople to leave. It was getting late and they had agreed to stay for only an hour; what were they doing? John glowered with annoyance; he'd tell them where to go, but Joan didn't want to appear inhospitable. They'd have to go sooner or later; she just wished something, anything, would happen to make it sooner.

Tina was center stage in a magic show without knowing how to perform. The force refused to come to her aid. A technician at WTVN, Robert Forest, caught Tina moving the kitchen table with her foot. When he accused her of tricking him, all he got in return was a horse laugh.

The only occurrence that could not be dismissed out of hand was witnessed by Jodi Gossage. At one point, a yelp from Tina and an accompanying thump drew Gossage around the corner to the living room in time to see a chair hit the ground. Tina, who had just come in from the dining room and was still in the doorway, seemed shaken. No one else was in the room.

"It would seem to have happened too fast for her to have touched it," said Gossage, "but the full sequence was not observed."

The day wore on and still the house was full of reporters. Their excitement at being in a house where absolutely nothing was happening reached an absurd fever pitch. Chatting in small groups with Tina or snooping around corners in pursuit of the elusive force, they were turning the house into a carnival. John was nearing meltdown.

Joan took Tina aside. "Something has got to happen," Joan said. Reporters had been in the house for nearly eight hours.

She had tried being nice, and that had only increased their determination to stay. Tina would have to help her out; Joan didn't want them to think she was being pushy or rude. Tina was getting tired of the reporters, too. Several times during the afternoon she had asked if she could go back with Barbara and JP, but nobody had paid any attention. She agreed with her mother that it was time to put a stop to it all.

A few of the reporters had started to leave, Gossage and Alexander among them, but the others still had their video cameras strategically aimed throughout the house in the hope of catching the force on tape. Finally, at nine-thirty, one of them got what he came for, or so it seemed. Drew Hadwal of WTVN-TV in Columbus had his camera focused on a large table lamp when the lamp tumbled to the floor. It was the same lamp that had fallen when Fred Shannon had visited the house. At first Hadwal didn't believe his camera had caught anything, he thought it was shut down. He was delighted when he realized that the camera was still on.

Hadwal rushed back to the station to show his prize catch on the late news. It turned out he had hooked an old boot. The video showed Tina knocking down the lamp with her hand.

On the tape, Tina was seen edging around the sofa, glancing over her shoulder to make sure she was not being watched. She also didn't think the camera was operating. She reached up to test the height of the lamp shade. When she thought no one was looking, she yanked the shade and jumped away as if scared by what had happened. The trick didn't work, so Tina tried again. This time the lamp fell to the floor.

In the mind of the public, the image of the suffering Resch family had been replaced with the suspicion that they had a magician for a daughter. News viewers who saw Tina pull over the lamp concluded that the country had indeed been bamboozled by the teenager. The negative publicity failed to bring anyone who could help the family.

Early Friday morning the doorbell rang. When Joan answered, she found two men and a van from a local radio station. She said the news conference had been the day before and the family was not giving any more interviews. The men replied they weren't reporters and did not want to interview anyone. They were disc jockeys and asked if they could air the morning's music program from the house. This would give the show a special flavor. Hospitable as ever, Joan let them in.

The family escaped to the Hughes home, leaving a friend to look after the house and the deejays to complete their program. When Sue Cross from Associated Press came by to see if the force was still in evidence, the deejays said everything was peaceful except that the phone was ringing all the time, and that they jumped whenever it did.

Tina was walking under a dark cloud, waiting for lightning to strike. No one blamed her outright for having pushed the lamp, but the accusation hung in the air. She stayed at the Hughes home Thursday night and all day Friday. Except for the family's repeated prayers to rid her of the demon, the visit was uneventful.

Sue Cross spoke to the neighbors. Jean Allison, Kevin Resch's mother-in-law, did not bring up demons but said that after seeing the news video, Kevin now thought that the incidents could be due to an electrical force beneath the house. Two other neighbors spoke well of the Resches, saying they did not think they would have made up the incidents. Cross also went to Tina's old school, Parkmoor Elementary, across the street. John H. Jones, the principal, said, "Personally I believe it originally happened, but possibly now [Tina] is doing things."

Later in the day, an FM radio station aired a "Poltergeist Parade" spoof of the incidents. Sue Cross summarized the Resches' current problem: "A family that complained its house was taken over by a strange psychic force is now being beset by a phenomenon of another kind, limelight."

# 10

# OUR INVESTIGATION BEGINS

**M**onday, March 12, was my first full day at the Resch home. I heard a sound just before six and awoke with a start. A white shape was standing by the bed. It turned out that the tall table lamp from the nightstand was now on the floor. Then the children's book about magic fell down. It, too, had been on the nightstand before we went to sleep. I wondered how the two items had come off the table and checked if it was stable. It had a loose leg and was quite wobbly. I thought Kelly or I must have pushed it in our sleep, causing the two things to slide off. That the lamp had landed upright was surprising, but obviously possible.

Someone knocked at eight-fifteen. I opened the door and found three plastic lemons on the floor from the tree downstairs. I wondered if this was a wake-up call by the force or Tina playing games. Ten minutes later two soft knocks came from her room, followed by a louder, impatient thud. I looked in and found her awake in bed. Nothing had moved, she said, she didn't know about the knocks and lemons.

I was finishing getting dressed when there was another thud. Kelly and I agreed that there was nothing strange about any of this and that the incidents were Tina's way of calling for attention.

We arrived downstairs at the same time that Jack came home to celebrate his belated birthday. Joan appeared glad to see her son, but Tina only gave him a tepid greeting. Kelly announced that he was going to take his morning jog and asked Tina if she would like to come along with him. She leaped at the chance to get out of the house. When she left, John went down to the basement to start in on the morning's repair work, and Jack followed. Craig was not up yet, and this gave me another opportunity to talk to Joan. We went into the family room and I sat down on the large couch.

"How often has this moved?" I asked. It never did, said Joan, but things around it had.

"The table beside you, it's moved or been though the air about thirty times." John had removed the picture above the couch because it "just wouldn't stop rocking." Joan added, "The pillows on the couch have moved back and forth probably five times."

She brought out the metal candleholders and the matching clock that used to hang over the love seat. "First the candles wouldn't stay and then the holder would swing on the wall and almost turn over," she said. "After four or five times we put it away. Tina was sitting there, and with those sharp points, we'd be afraid she'd get hurt." The sharp points were decorative arrows, not anything I'd want coming in my direction.

The most active object was the love seat. "The little couch has moved maybe a hundred times either back or out, depending on where it's sitting," Joan said. This was Tina's customary seat, except when Joan was out of the room and Tina used her recliner.

Tina and Kelly returned from jogging. I asked Tina to put the candleholders and clock back on the wall and to sit on the love seat so I could take a picture re-creating how it had looked before the clock had hit her. She put the items up and then quickly took them down after I had taken the photo. Joan stowed them away again.

Tina then went upstairs to her room while Kelly and I stayed to hear the rest of Joan's story. She was saying, "Last weekend that mat—" At that point a sound came from the hallway.

Kelly and I rushed out and saw the ceiling lamp swing back and forth. Jack, who had come up from the basement, was on the phone in the kitchen, and Craig was taking a shower upstairs, so they hadn't done it. I looked at my watch; it was 10:54. Two minutes later, as Kelly and I were going upstairs to check on Tina, we heard a crash from the master bedroom. Kelly got there first and found a picture on the floor. It was the portrait of Tina's nephews Jim and Eric, her sister Pam's boys, which had come down the stairs when we'd first visited.

Tina was sitting quietly on her bed in the foster children's room, but her door was open and so was the door to the master bedroom. She could have tossed the picture in. She might also have set the ceiling lamp in motion, since it could be reached from the top of the stairs.

Kelly and I joined her in her room to chat. I noticed Tina's schoolbooks and asked her if she liked any of her subjects. She enjoyed math and English, she said, especially English.

What did she think of the incidents?

"I think it's stupid, but it's happening," she said.

"What do you think is causing it?" I asked.

Tina was quiet for a moment, then said that at first she thought the incidents were connected to her friend Tina Scott. When Scott was killed, Tina explained, she had had trouble believing her friend was gone. Joan didn't allow her to go to the funeral and she stayed home instead. Tina regarded Scott as her good side, the voice of love and reason.

"When I got in trouble," Tina said, "you know, for something I did, or yelled at Mom, she'd tease me about it."

If Tina did not set things right, like apologize to her mother, Tina Scott would "get real mad about it. She'd get on a strong voice with me." It was a voice Tina could listen to without feeling belittled because she knew Scott loved her.

Scott didn't always have to be present to help. Sometimes it was enough if Tina just thought about her to know what was the right thing to do. "The thought was all I needed a lot of the time. I just seemed to be able to think about her and I seemed to get what I needed to do." Then Tina would be able to take the next step by herself and "I'd go ahead and do it."

Thinking about her friend, Tina would feel happy no matter what was going on around her. "She always promised me when I needed her, she would be there."

Then, all of a sudden, Scott had died. When the truth had finally sunk in, Tina felt lost and then angry that her friend had gotten herself killed. "I was angry when she left, but that didn't last for long."

Over time, Tina came to accept Scott's death. Then something strange happened, Tina said. "She came back."

Tina had just had an argument with Joan. She wanted the name of her birth mother, and Joan, as always, said no. Tina went to her room resentful and depressed. The next thing she knew, there was Tina Scott, right in her room, looking at her with a quizzical smile. Tina was surprised, but not frightened. She needed her friend, and there she was, just as she'd said she would be.

To Tina, Scott looked real. She was sitting on a couch, a pretty handwoven bag next to her that the Resches had given her for Christmas. The only thing Tina didn't understand was that there was no couch in her room; the couch Scott was sitting on belonged in the family room.

Tina told her friend about the argument with Joan and how angry she felt. Scott said not to press Joan too much. Tina would learn about her real mother soon enough.

The visits continued. Tina would need Scott, and she would appear. The two would talk about Tina's problems as they had before, Scott showing Tina the other side of an argument and helping her to calm down.

Sometimes things got out of hand before Scott could intervene. "I do have a lot of feelings of resentment and hate," Tina said, and she would scream at her family or lash out at them.

The disturbances began shortly after Scott's first visit, Tina said. Nothing like this had happened before, and Tina wondered if it was Scott throwing the objects. When the vision appeared, Tina had had the same peculiar feeling in her stomach she had when things moved. But then when she thought more abut it, she realized it couldn't be Scott behind the chaos. Throwing things and upsetting Tina and the Resches was just too out of character, and Tina dismissed the possibility.

I understood that Scott's reappearance was a response to Tina's loneliness and need for companionship, but I didn't think her departed friend had actually returned. More likely the phantom was evoked from Tina's own storehouse of memories. I thought this was indicated by her seeing the apparition on the couch in the Resches' family room rather than in the surroundings Tina occupied at the time.

Kelly and I returned downstairs, and Joan resumed her earlier account. What she was about to describe, when interrupted by the lamp incident, was a series of peculiar movements by a place mat. This mat, which was on the side table next to the large couch, would slip out, she said, while the things on it, a jar of Vicks air cleanser, an ashtray, and a box of tissues, would stay put. This had happened some thirty times, including once yesterday before we'd arrived. It was like the tablecloth trick where the dishes and glasses remain while the cloth is pulled out. Joan used the Vicks to clear her nose.

As Joan finished her description, the doorbell rang. I had arranged to interview the witnesses who had been in the house over the last few days, and Lee Arnold, Tina's caseworker, was the first to arrive. She joined us in the family room and began to tell me of her visit the preceding Monday, when she was almost hit by the telephone while sitting on the love seat. While she was still speaking, Tina came downstairs to announce that Craig's penny bottle had moved to the middle of his room. It was 12:20.

Joan made sandwiches for lunch; afterward Tina said she wanted to write a letter and went to her room. Kelly remarked that something might happen because she was relatively inactive, and he and I went to our room to be ready.

A short while later, at 1:17 P.M., a sound came from Tina's room, followed by another sound a minute later. When we went to investigate, we found Tina sitting calmly on her bed, writing her letter. The first time, she said, a picture of her nieces, Eileen and Cindy, had fallen to the floor, and the next time the picture of Jim and Eric had come down behind the chest of drawers, which was next to her bed. We found it there, the glass further broken. I thought Tina had probably thrown the pictures to get our attention.

Things were peaceful for nearly an hour, and Kelly and I were resting in our room when a series of knocks came from next door. We agreed that Tina wanted attention but we needed to rest, so we ignored the interruption. Ten minutes later there were another couple of knocks.

Annoyed, I reached down from my bed, picked up one of my bedroom slippers, and threw it hard against the wall between the two rooms, hoping this would tell Tina we were onto her game and to stop. There was a yelp from next door and I thought Tina had got the message. But then we heard her go into the hallway and the master bedroom to search for the object she thought had flown. Interesting, I thought; Tina evidently believed things were moving without her assistance.

I went out to the hallway, and Craig came out of his room at the same time. A few minutes before, he said, a candle had hit his door. It had been on the dresser in the master bedroom and was probably what had caused one of the sounds we had heard.

Later that afternoon, new light on the incidents came from an unexpected source. Joan had arranged for Lisa to come to the house and talk to us while Tina went for her weekly tutorial. Usually the teacher came to the house. Because of the commotion, Tina now went to the teacher.

Lisa was six years old, a towheaded, self-confident little girl. Her English was poor, but she seemed bright and observant. Without prodding, Lisa said, "I think Tina is doing a couple of it. You can see her hand going over there and try to put [sic] that lamp over there, you can see that." Lisa was referring to the newscast showing Tina pulling the lamp over. She then moved on to the time Fred Shannon had taken a photograph of Tina holding a picture when it fell to the floor. "It'd be easy to drop that picture, so it must be her."

Next Lisa mentioned a pencil caddy's toppling down behind John's chair when Tina was sitting there. "She was sitting in Daddy's chair. The pencils went down. Right back of Daddy's chair."

Did Tina push them? "No, that happened by itself." Other things had moved without Tina's assistance. "The couch moves by itself. The table moves by itself. All the tables," Lisa added.

"I saw the chairs move and I saw the chair Grandma sits in move and all that kinda stuff. And these move," she said, pointing to the place mat. "It comes off and everything was sitting there." She meant that the things on the mat remained when it flew to the floor.

Tina had not done these things, according to Lisa, but from the first Saturday night, she noticed that they happened when Tina was near. "The night we was eating, the chairs started moving, and when she went in the living room, the couch moved. And the toys were picked up."

I asked, "What do you think is happening?"

"I think really it's a poltergeist happening here," Lisa said. This was obviously an idea she had picked from the adults. When she described the incidents in her own words, what I heard was a child's world of animated objects. The incidents were not due to some extraneous force, but to the intentions of the objects themselves. They were alive and wanted to catch or hurt Tina. When the phone and the lamp moved toward Tina, it was because they wanted to "trech" her, Lisa's version of "trap."

Lisa pointed to Joan's chair. "In the morning the next day the phone tried to trech her when she sat down right here.

"And when she was sitting with the baby, [the lamp] tried to catch her baby and her. The candles tried to catch her, too. And knives came out of the drawer and tried to cut her." In Lisa's mind, there was no mysterious force in the house, so there was nothing for her to be afraid of. The things were out to get Tina, not her.

We went into the living room and Lisa pointed to the stereo. "This was pugged and it comed on." She meant it came on after it was unplugged. "And the TV was off and it comes on by itself."

Had Tina done any of this? "No," Lisa replied.

Then to indicate that the interview was over, Lisa pointed to my tape recorder and said, "You can turn it off 'cause that's it."

Tina returned from her tutorial around seven, and she and Kelly went upstairs for a counseling session in our room. In the meantime, Kathy Goeff arrived to tell me about her brief visit the previous Monday. Three times, she said, she was looking at Tina when the phone came up and flew past the girl. The last time Fred Shannon snapped a picture of it as it landed near Lee Arnold. The description matched what Lee had told me. Unlike the few occurrences that had happened after Kelly and I had arrived, it was hard to believe that Tina could have staged this incident.

Tina's counseling session with Kelly was not going well. She did not want to discuss her relationship with her family when her mind was filled with a more immediate one—her infatuation with Kelly himself. He cut the session short, and Tina tried to catch his interest in another way. She went out to the hallway. There was a noise, followed by an exchange with Craig.

"What are you doing?" Craig asked.

"Oh, nothing. I just dropped something."

"You're throwing something? Why are you throwing this?"

Kelly did not say anything to Tina about what he had over-heard. He suspected she sometimes threw things to get our attention, but he also thought some of the incidents were real. Instead, he asked her if she thought she could bring on the movements at will. As if in reply, there was an occurrence. One of Tina's barrettes apparently zinged off a table and hit a wall. Kelly wasn't sure of the barrette's exact starting location, but he was certain that Tina had not had it in her hand and that she had not thrown it. Kelly decided to keep a closer watch on her.

They went downstairs and Kelly waited for Tina while she was in the bathroom. When Tina came out of the bathroom, Kelly heard something fall into the toilet bowl. It was a small, blue plastic cup. Recounting the events for me, Kelly said he was certain she had not thrown the cup because she was standing outside the bathroom when he heard the splash inside.

First trickery and now phenomena that Kelly vouched for as genuine. I wondered if Tina had him fooled. After all, he was new to this sort of thing.

"I really enjoyed being home," John told me. There had been a lull in the activity and I asked John if we could talk. "I like to tinker around the house and take care of the kids, so I was really having a good time." Looking around the living room, he added, "Of course, this seemed to shatter most of that."

John pointed to the dented furniture, the crooked table lamps, and to the places where pictures were missing. "The things that have happened, all of them together is just a little much. Just like the planter is all twisted there where things have either fallen off or bumped against it."

He had repaired it once. "It hasn't been too long ago I had that thing out in the garage and squared it up. I see it's all tipped over again."

Before the force had struck, John and Joan had bought another picture and a wall clock that he planned to put up. "I never did hang them," he said. "We've just put it back behind that folding table there and stuck the chair up against it in hopes to save it. I don't know whether it's still any good or not, I haven't looked."

John's mood was lighter than on the day before. "Right now, things are quiet and we haven't broke anything for the last couple of days." He added, "I piddled around with some stuff I've been working on in the basement, and that kind of relieves you, do something to take your mind off of that. It's been real nice today."

I thought to myself that he could thank Kelly and me for that. But the events of the last ten days lay heavy on John. "I couldn't understand any of it," he said. "And the more things happened, of course the less I understood, and the more frustrated I get just trying to clean up everything."

He did and he didn't blame Tina. "Like I say, I blame a lot of it on her. I keep trying to tell myself that she really doesn't have that much control over it. But when you see what things are happening, you've got to believe that some of the turmoil she is going through is probably what's causing our problems now."

As John was talking, the events were beginning to make sense. "In essence, what's happening is a reflection of the whole setting here. She's just revolting against everything. It seems to be the things that she feels are things she doesn't want. It's a way of getting rid of them."

The conversation turned to the foster children. "I've gotten so that I enjoy seeing them grow and improve," John said. "I get rather attached to them, having thought that I put an eight-to-five job behind me for a while."

I said, "It must be hard to bring children up and then—" I was going to say "see them go," but John cut me short.

"The parents are younger, they want children, and they can probably give them a lot better life than we can. A lot longer."

John paused, then speaking of his family said, "It's a fairly close circle. We don't have too many friends." He caught himself. "Jo has a lot more friends than I do really, and I'm satisfied with that. She's a different type of person. She needs more people. I don't."

John thought of all the strangers who had been in the house the past week. As difficult as it had been to watch his prized possessions destroyed one by one, the reporters and curiosity seekers were nearly as disruptive. "That's what bothers me the most," he said, "that people are either questioning or just generally inquisitive about it. And I'm a very—I don't know, what shall we call it—introverted person. I don't feel good about it."

Of the four members of the Resch family still at home, John was the most troubled. I had hoped the force would resume its activity so that I could learn what was going on, but now I was worried about what it would do to John.

John was finishing his account and Kelly was winding down a counseling session with Tina when an incident occurred. She had complained that Craig had taken the radio from the foster children's room so that she was now deprived of music. Kelly said she could borrow his transistor radio and went to fetch it from his duffel bag. Searching around in the bag, he found a teacup partially hidden among his clothes. It was the same cup I had left on Tina's dresser earlier in the day.

Kelly had noticed it there a few minutes before going down-stairs to get some water. The event reminded him of a similar incident that morning. After he and Tina had come back from jogging, he had placed his gloves on the same dresser. A little while later he found them half-tucked into his suitcase. He didn't give it much thought, he told me, "because it seemed kind of silly," but the teacup brought it to mind.

I thought Tina was trying to engage Kelly in a way she knew would catch his attention by mysterious movements of objects, and that she had placed the two things in his bags while he was out of the room. Kelly thought this might be true for the gloves, but not the teacup. Just before he found it in his bag, Tina had talked about the traumatic events in her life and seemed depressed and drained. She had also overheard John tell Joan that he was thinking of leaving, and she was upset at the thought of being blamed for any trouble between her parents.

"There was not the usual chaotic activity around her," Kelly said. "She was sitting very quietly and kind of staring into space. It's possible she could have done it, she had enough time, but just the feeling of it doesn't fit. She's gotten the most attention from banging and rapping and obvious, bla-tant noises that you could hear a mile away, and this is so sub-tle that you wouldn't notice it except by accident."

I was doubtful. I had no problem supposing Tina had tucked the cup into Kelly's bag. She would know that a subtle incident would be more appealing than bangs or throws. I found the incidents involving Kelly's bag and suitcase interest-ing, not as examples of psychokinesis, but because they showed that Tina was using the movement of objects to en-gage people.

# 11

# UNWELCOME VISITOR

Tuesday morning, March 13, started on a jarring note. While Kelly and I were still in our room, we heard muffled shouts from next door. Hoping Tina was all right, I looked in and found her asleep, apparently having a nightmare. I woke her up and she said she was dreaming that John was in the basement burning the rug and intending to burn down the house. Her distress was real and I asked Kelly to speak with her while I went downstairs.

Joan was in the kitchen cheerfully preparing breakfast. The eggs and toast were behaving themselves, and the juice stayed right where it was supposed to be, albeit still in Styrofoam cups. Even John seemed less somber. I wondered if the disturbances, genuine or concocted, had come to an end. Perhaps Kelly had succeeded in relieving the tensions in Tina that seemed to feed the incidents. In that case, it was time to leave.

There was also another possibility. Kelly and I had satisfied

Tina's need for attention and made the incidents unnecessary. Maybe the peace would only last as long as we were in the house. If it all started up again while we were on the plane going back to North Carolina, our mission would have been a failure.

I suggested to Kelly that we leave the house at some point during the day and see if things still remained quiet. In another case where objects were moving in a warehouse of novelty items in Miami, Florida, the phenomena stopped when I arrived, but resumed when I left for a short period. After that the phenomena continued when I was present. We didn't discuss our plans with Tina, as I was afraid this would make her self-conscious and inhibit the force.

The morning had been quiet. I used the time to speak with three of the Resches' grown children, Peggy, Craig, and Jack. Peggy and Craig gave full accounts of the incidents they had witnessed, but Jack had seen nothing. By one o'clock John had to leave for a doctor's appointment, and Jack also was on his way out the door. Peggy was still visiting with her mother and Tina, and it seemed like a good time for Kelly and me to leave the house. I told Joan that I wanted to buy some film for my camera. There was a shopping mall a twenty-minute walk from the house; Kelly and I would be back in an hour. What we didn't tell Joan, mistakenly I realized later, was to be prepared in case the force started up again during our absence.

When we returned from the mall, Joan was sobbing and Tina's eyes were filling with tears. The force had returned with a vengeance.

After Kelly and I had left the house, Joan had walked Peggy to the front door to say good-bye. Hopeful that the force was gone for good, she looked forward to getting her life back in order. "I think it's over," she told her daughter. The words were hardly out of her mouth when there was a loud thump upstairs. Joan braced herself.

"It's probably nothing," she said.

Peggy wasn't so sure. "Why don't you check before I leave?"

Craig was home, and Joan told Peggy she would be all right. Tina ran upstairs to see if anything had happened. She called down from the top of the stairs, "His wine thing has moved and the mattress is off the bed." She was talking about Craig's penny bottle.

Despair replaced Joan's optimism. She had clung to the hope that the counseling session with Kelly had relieved Tina's stress and that things would now be quiet. Joan's back started to hurt, the same pain that always flared up when she was tense. All those years of carrying little children were taking their toll.

Peggy took off her coat, went back with Tina and her mother to the kitchen, and tried to calm Joan. The phone rang and Joan took the call, leaning against a chair to relieve her back. Suddenly it was pushed against the refrigerator, hard. Then the chair fell over. Tina was nowhere near.

Peggy had to go. Just after she left, a glass that had been put away for safekeeping days before suddenly broke on the kitchen floor. Joan had no idea where it had come from, but she knew where Tina was, right in front of her, helping in the kitchen.

Listening to Joan's depiction of events, I felt sorry for the family. At the same time I was relieved. The phenomena were apparently genuine and still strong. We did not have to cut the investigation short, and we might still succeed in witnessing the incidents ourselves.

I was uncertain about what had happened in the kitchen. It seemed possible that the chair had slid away from Joan when she was leaning against it, and that Tina had found and thrown the glass. But she could not have pulled Craig's mattress off his bed since Joan had heard the thud when Tina was downstairs with her. I thought it unlikely that Craig had sneaked in and staged the two incidents; this seemed too much out of character.

Kelly and I consoled Joan as best we could. Kelly pointed out that there had at least been a reduction in the occurrences since we'd come and he'd begun working with Tina. "It's like a temper tantrum that she'll get under control more and more," he said. "If you'll hang in there another day or so, we'll keep working at it."

The question was whether Joan could hang on for those extra days. John was ready to move out, and Joan, who had weathered the storm until now, seemed close to a breakdown.

I thought I might have a solution that would appeal to everyone. I would bring Tina to North Carolina and continue the investigation and counseling there. In addition to the Psychical Research Foundation, two parapsychological centers, the Institute for Parapsychology in Durham and Spring Creek Institute in Chapel Hill, were nearby. I felt certain my colleagues would rise to the challenge of exploring the occurrences around Tina. But I needed to find a psychologist who was willing to do volunteer work with the girl. Kelly was due to go to New York by the end of the week.

I thought of Rebecca Zinn, a psychotherapist in Chapel Hill. I had met Becca in the same way I had met Kelly, at the Patricia Hayes School, where she was taking a course in psychic development. Becca had a doctorate in clinical psychology, and she was highly intuitive, a skill that is important for a psychotherapist. But Becca might not be able to fit Tina into her schedule. In addition to her practice, she owned a plant nursery and was busy.

Then the vexing issue of money came up. Assuming Becca could see Tina, would she be willing to donate her time? I had no funds for counselling and neither did the Resches. I decided to phone Becca and find out. Kelly was also on the line and gave Becca his impressions of Tina.

Becca was sympathetic and said she would work with Tina, assuming she and her parents wanted this. During our conversation, Becca got an earful of the force's strength. The screeching noises others had described to me as "terrible" and "painful" kept interrupting and threatening to drown out our talk altogether. Three times we had to wait until it died down long enough for us to resume speaking.

Fifteen minutes after we finished the call, Tina complained of hearing a "siren" in her right ear. Another fifteen minutes later, she heard the noise again. Each time, she said, it lasted for about ten minutes. Tina had not been in the room when Kelly and I had spoken with Becca, and we hadn't told her about the noise. I wondered if there was a connection between the din on the phone and the ringing in Tina's ear.

It didn't take long for Joan and John to agree to have Tina go to North Carolina. The prospect of an interlude without the force visibly elevated their mood. But there was yet another hurdle to cross. Would my wife agree to have Tina as a houseguest?

Muriel was not enthusiastic when I phoned. We had a collection of Danish porcelain and other breakables on open shelves in a long hallway. Muriel had a mental picture of Tina walking down the hallway with our treasures breaking in her wake. I reminded her of two other psychokinetic youngsters we had hosted, Ernest, a twelve-year-old African-American, and Julio, an eighteen-year-old Cuban who had been the center of the disturbances in the Miami warehouse.

In neither case was there any damage while the boys stayed in our house.

Thinking back to these peaceful visits, Muriel said I could bring Tina and that she could use our daughter's room. Lise had married and was living in Sweden, so we had a spare room.

Kelly and I did not mention the possibility of the trip to Tina. I still hoped to witness the occurrences myself and did not want to do anything to change Tina's state of mind.

In the meantime the incidents were coming closer to my vicinity. At 4:20 P.M. I was walking into the kitchen from the family room when there was a loud crash ahead of me in the dining room. I dashed in and found the crib turned over. The crib was unused and empty now that Anne had been sent away with the other foster children.

I looked for Tina. She was sitting quietly by a card table in the living room, filling in a psychological questionnaire. The table was just the other side of the door to the dining room. Her back was to the door and it was closed. Could she have pushed the crib? She would have had to be fast and quiet. I did not hear the door between the two rooms open and close. Joan was on the phone in the kitchen, and John was behind me in the family room watching TV. Craig was upstairs. None of them could have tipped the crib over.

Two hours later Kelly and I were on our way to dinner when we were caught up in a commotion outside the house. Earlier in our visit I had asked the reporters who called not to phone or come to the house during our investigation. Instead I said I would hold a news conference at the end of our stay to present my conclusions. Doing so would help both parties, the reporters, who could turn to other matters without fear that the competition would scoop the story, and Kelly and me, who could conduct our study free from distraction. In spite of my request, here was a group of journalists and television cameras circling the driveway. At the center of the group stood a short figure in a black cape. With his full white beard and penetrating eyes behind horn-rimmed glasses, I recognized him at once: James "the Amazing" Randi. Randi was a stage magician, but he was best known as a psychic sleuth who exposed fraudulent psychics and preachers.

"I don't believe in things that go bump in the night," Randi had said in a telephone interview with Steve Berry, a reporter with the *Columbus Dispatch*, the day before. "It's the same reason I don't believe in Santa Claus and the Tooth Fairy."

Berry had reached Randi in Dallas, where he was performing in a magic show. Randi now continued his performance outside the Resch home. "I've never seen a bona fide paranormal event, but that doesn't mean I won't," Randi said. "When you've sat by the chimney on Christmas Eve for thirty-five years and have never seen Santa Claus, you don't say he doesn't exist. I'm always ready for a soot-covered fat man in a red suit to bounce down the chimney."

Randi was accompanied by astronomer-physicist Steve Shore and astronomer Nick Seduleak from Case Western Reserve University in Cleveland. The three had been sent by Paul Kurtz, the founder of the Committee for the Scientific Investigation of Claims of the Paranormal (CSICOP), to conduct their own investigation of the Resch case. CSICOP specialized in debunking reports of psychic phenomena, and the TV segment showing Tina pull down the lamp was wind in their sails. Kurtz had originally been contacted by Paul Alexander, one of the Associated Press reporters at the house during the now infamous press conference. Alexander had wanted a second opinion on the incidents to go with the accounts he had heard from the Resches themselves. Kurtz, a philosophy professor at the University of New York in Buffalo, told Alexander, "We want to be open-minded and we think the public deserves an explanation. Offhand, it seems to me there's a hoax being perpetrated and the whole country is being bamboozled."

Displaying his flair for the dramatic, Randi pulled out a check for $10,000 from his cape. Posing for the cameras, he said he would give the Resches the money if they could show him an object that flew without human aid. More than six hundred people had tried to collect the prize over the past twenty years, he said, and none had succeeded. He added that he had exposed many tricky teens whose fraud was perpetuated by indulgent parents and journalists hungry for headlines.

Hospitable as always, Joan said that Shore and Seduleak could come to the house after Kelly and I had left, but Randi would not be welcome.

"I don't want him in the house," she told Shore. "It's been rough on us. We've had a circus. Now we have a magic show. No, not here." She added that she did not like the offer of money.

Mike Harden was standing outside along with the group of reporters. He thought Joan should have let Randi into the house. "In a case like this," he said, "I think you're almost obliged to have a second opinion. A magician possesses the skills to come in and show how these might be staged. If he can come in and by sleight of hand replicate them, that's something the public needs to know."

But Randi had offended Joan with his showmanship, jokes, and offer of money. He had predicted that the Resches would not let him in, and he was right. Shore and Seduleak turned down Joan's offer to investigate the occurrences on their own. I was surprised that the two scientists did not trust themselves enough to reveal the supposed tricks of a fourteen-year-old girl. But Shore laid the blame on Joan. "She refuses to cooperate in the spirit of scientific inquiry," he told the press.

Randi's quips and the refusal of the two others to go in on their own made me wonder how serious CSICOP was about investigating the phenomena.

The next day came in like the proverbial lamb. Except for Mike Harden's story about Joan's encounter with James Randi—"Visiting Magician Told to Disappear"—the morning was uneventful.

# 12

# FLYING TEACUP

After lunch on Wednesday, March 14, Kelly took Tina for a second neurological exam, and I took advantage of the quiet to draw a floor plan of the house. This would let me trace the incidents for later study.

While Kelly and Tina were gone, Barbara Hughes and JP came by to tell me about their own encounters with the force. The subject of James Randi and CSICOP came up, and Barbara mentioned that she had been approached by the group but had chosen not to speak with them. When I asked why, she said, "I don't feel this group is coming with an open mind. I'm not about to help them make more ridicule of a situation that's already bad enough. If I thought I could help them by explaining to them like I have to you, I would, but I think it would get twisted and turned."

Barbara was one of the few people other than Tina who had been physically attacked by the force. Having experienced its strength and speed for herself, she knew the amount of danger it held. We went into the kitchen and Barbara began to describe the morning she had brought Tina back from the overnight stay at her home after the press conference. Joan and a neighbor were there.

"I became frightened for Tina's safety," Barbara said. Tina had sat down in her usual seat at the kitchen table, her back against the wall, when the chair next to her slammed back against the wall and then hit her chair. Barbara was on the other side of the table. The next thing she knew, the table scooted away from under her. She and Joan put it back, and it slid out again. JP saw it spin itself around.

"Things happened in twos," Barbara said. "Twice the table—like faster than a speeding bullet, faster by three times. This is a heavy table. It just went right out from under me."

Tina had decided to make instant coffee. She had heated the water in a kettle on the stove and taken out four Correll cups from the cupboard as Barbara anxiously looked on. Barbara tried to stop her: "I said, 'Don't use it, Tina.' "

Tina replied, "Mom says it doesn't break," but Barbara told her not to take any chances, and Tina returned the cups to the cupboard. It was too late. One of the cups flew back out and smashed to the floor. Tina began to cry, worried that Joan would be angry. Joan kept her feelings in check, but Tina was punished in another way. As she walked by the stove, the kettle came off and splashed hot water over her.

JP saw it. "It burned her," he said. "She was over here crying." He pointed to where Tina had stood.

Barbara said that the phone then rang and Joan took the call on the kitchen extension. She needed to write a note and put the handset down so she could fetch a pad and pencil from the counter. As she returned, one of the kitchen chairs turned around behind her and followed her back to the phone.

In the meantime Tina had made coffee and served it in Styrofoam cups to Joan and her two visitors, pouring herself a cup as well. Remembering the chair that had hit her before, she sat down at the opposite side of the table.

Barbara noticed something was bothering Tina. She was holding her hand over her cup instead of drinking from it. She said, "I feel sick. My stomach!" By now everyone knew this was a sign that something scary was about to happen.

Tina seemed increasingly agitated. "Would you just do me a favor and hold on to your cups everybody," she said.

Joan told Tina to move her chair away from the table. Barbara watched Tina push her chair back, while at the same time leaning forward to keep her hand on her cup. Suddenly Tina's chair tipped backward, flinging her legs into the air and throwing her to the floor.

Barbara's voice was a mixture of shock and amazement as she told me what she had seen. "That chair raised up off the floor, just like that. Her feet flew up into the air and it dumped her, chair and all, onto the floor, onto her right side. And she just laid there and cried, 'Oh, my hip!'"

Moments later, Tina pulled herself together and got back up on the chair. Then she was thrown again. "Now that happened twice," Barbara said. "The second time her glasses went off."

JP found the incident no stranger than a horse throwing a rider. "The chair just—poof—flipped her right off."

After Tina had recovered from the second fall, Joan urged her to stay on the floor. Tina pushed herself over to the refrigerator and leaned back against the door. The refrigerator had two vertical units, a cooler and a freezer. As Tina was hugging her knees and leaning against the cooler, Barbara noted, "It wasn't three seconds and that freezer door flew open and smashed back against the corner of the pantry."

Others less courageous than Barbara might have fled after these displays of power. Barbara not only remained in the room, she tested the strength of the force. Going up to the freezer, she pulled at the door to see how much effort it took to open. "And that's suction," she said. "You have to really pull." She persuaded the Resches' other visitor to test the door as well.

"We pulled on the door and felt it to see how hard it was to open." When the women had finished testing the door, the force repeated the feat, slamming the door open again. They told Tina to sit in the middle of the room, and the door stayed closed.

Massive manifestations of power alternated with minor incidents. JP and Tina were in the downstairs bathroom when two hairspray cans started "going crazy."

"I saw them," said JP. While Tina was hunting in a drawer for bobby pins, "They just went 'Whew!'" One can landed in the trash bin and the other in the corner on Tina's right.

JP also reported the only incident known to have taken place outside the house. One day he visited, Tina came out on the porch to greet him and get the mail, when a log of firewood took off from the woodpile and flew toward her.

"The log was setting [sic] about right here," JP said, pointing to a place about two feet to the right of the door. Tina was reaching up to the mailbox when the log "just picked up and flew at her and flew right between her legs. And then she looks out, and it's still sliding." The log slid to the other end of the porch, about fifteen feet from the pile, before it stopped.

Neither JP nor his foster mother showed much fear of the events. "I came here believing as a born-again Christian there were demons," Barbara said, "and the devil is alive and well on planet Earth." But she did not sense any sinister presence. "I don't feel anything demonic here. I feel very much at peace in this home."

If not a demon, then what was causing the phenomena? Barbara had read an interview with Paul Kurtz, the leader of CSICOP, where he suggested it was all a hoax.

"There's no doubt about it," Barbara said, "it is not. I've been here. I've seen it. I've been hit. All we're interested in is getting it stopped. I just feel the Resches' helplessness in this. They didn't turn it on and now they can't seem to get it stopped."

After the interview with Barbara and JP, I took a cup of tea upstairs to my room. Ever since living in England, I had adopted the custom of afternoon tea, and I now looked forward to a few moments of relaxation. No sooner had I stretched out on the bed than I was interrupted by noises downstairs.

I went back down to find Joan and Tina standing by the front door, staring at a roll of Scotch tape by the bottom of the stairs. It had flown there from its position atop the microwave in the kitchen. Joan said that this was the third flight this afternoon. Earlier, when Tina and Kelly had returned from the neurologist at four-thirty, Joan was seeing a visitor to the front door when the tape fell from the microwave to the floor. Tina replaced it, and while the visitor watched, the tape flew again, landing in the soap dish by the kitchen sink. Now here it was by the stairs.

I knew Scotch tape held a special significance for Tina be-cause the tape had convinced Bruce Claggett, the first witness outside the family, that the force was more than a tricky teen. Tina hugged herself and said, "I've got shivers."

"Do these things make you shiver?" I asked. "Or is it just—"

"I'm not cold." Tina turned to Joan and said in her adult voice, "I wouldn't tell Dad if I were you."

Joan seemed troubled by the incidents and what would most likely be John's reaction, so I thought it would be a good idea to take Tina back upstairs for a while. When we got there, a call came through from Mike Harden, which I took on Tina's extension. Tina went out in the hallway. At 5:17, as I was speaking with Mike, I heard a metallic sound. Tina came in to inform me that a metal pot on the edge of the bathtub had fallen in and the top of a bottle of lotion had broken off and was now on the floor. I finished my call, and as I went out into the hallway, something hit the floor behind us. It was a bottle of Pert shampoo that belonged to Jack. Tina said he had been packing in their parents' room, so it must have come from there. I was slightly ahead of her when the bottle hit and could not be sure if she hadn't thrown it.

The incidents were getting closer to me. I told myself that if anything happened again, I must keep a better watch.

Because the activity was starting up again, I wanted to remain where we were. For the same reason, Tina was anxious to go downstairs. I persuaded her to stay, and she decided if she was going to be stuck upstairs, she might as well keep busy. We went into her room, which I now shared with Kelly, and Tina began to rearrange her bookcase. I finished my tea and placed the cup on the nightstand between the two beds. Just then Tina upset a Styrofoam cup of water Kelly had left on the bookcase. As I watched her mop up the water, a sound came from behind me.

"Now we have an incident," I said into my tape recorder. "When I was looking at Tina, something fell."

I turned. Tina's closet door was open and the cup was resting on a pile of clothes. I continued recording: "A cup moved from the little table behind her. This was a cup I'd just finished tea. It's now 5:29. The cup moved from behind her to inside the closet. It's not broken. Tina was nowhere near [the cup] when this was taking place."

When the cup moved, Tina was in full view, both hands occupied, standing by the bookcase with a bed between her and the nightstand. The cup had moved twelve feet. There was no way she could have thrown it without my seeing it.

A weight fell from my shoulders. After four days of uncertainty, I had finally witnessed a genuine occurrence of recurrent spontaneous psychokinesis, or RSPK, in the home. Whatever Tina might have thrown in the past, she did not throw the cup.

Tina wanted to continue straightening up her belongings, and we went into the foster children's room. But as soon as we entered the room, she seemed uneasy and said she wanted to get out. As we stepped back into the hallway, there was a sound behind us and Tina jumped. I supposed something had fallen in the room we had just left. I turned on the tape recorder and went in to check, telling Tina to follow me. She appeared tense and I kept up a chatter as much to calm her as to record what was happening.

"She was walking, we were walking out, she was with me stepping out, when we heard a sound from her room and now we're going to look. It's 5:34."

We returned to the foster children's room. "So let's see," I dictated, "what happened in here? There was the sound of something falling—I don't see anything out of place so far.

There's got to be something lying around, isn't there?" At this point my soliloquy was interrupted by a sharp crack behind us that the Sony picked up.

"There was an explosive sound behind us, sounded real strange." I surveyed the scene and saw a bottle on the floor. "Here's a little bottle lying here."

"No, that's been there," Tina said.

I picked it up; it was a bottle of perfume. " 'Cotillion,' " I read. "Let's put that back." I placed it on the dresser and noticed that one of the beds was askew.

"This bed is a little out of whack," I said, when there was another explosive sound. "Something else: a cracking sound. We don't find anything, but there are these cracking sounds. She's with me all the time." The Sony picked up the sound.

The three sounds seemed to originate somewhere behind Tina and were separated by about a minute's interval. Each time Tina jumped like a jack-in-the-box.

We returned to Tina's room and I asked her to go back to tidying her bookcase as this was what she had been doing when my teacup flew. I replaced the cup on the nightstand, hoping it would move again.

Tina went to work on the bookcase, and as I was watching her, the window curtain on my right fluttered. I looked down and saw a box of Tic Tac candy on the floor, which had evidently hit the curtain before falling down. I didn't know where it had come from, but I knew it wasn't from Tina.

Tina was getting hungry. "Bill, let's go have dinner. I haven't had anything to eat all day except two cookies."

I felt as if I, too, had had two cookies—the cup and the candy—and I was hungry for more. "Let's wait a little longer," I said. We could eat at six, in about fifteen minutes. I noticed something sticking out from under Kelly's bed and asked Tina to see if anything was there that didn't belong. I needed to know where items in the room were located in case they moved to another place.

While the recorder was running, Tina crouched down between the two beds. As she reached under Kelly's bed with both hands, the table lamp suddenly crashed to the floor, accompanied by the sound of shattering glass. My cup slid off the table at the same time and Tina screamed.

I picked up the lamp; nothing was broken. The wall-to-wall carpeting had prevented any damage and I wondered what had caused that explosive sound. Tina had been on her knees with both hands under the bed when it fell. I considered another possibility: the nightstand was unsteady, and Tina might have pushed something against it as she was reaching under the bed, but this did not explain the noise.

I started to describe the incident on the Sony, saying, "She had both hands underneath—" when another crash came from the opposite side of the bed. "And now something was falling over on the bookcase." I went to check and found a volume from *The Funk and Wagnall's New Encyclopedia* on the floor.

"Where does this book belong?" I asked.

"Downstairs." Tina's bookcase was on the other side of the bed, two to three feet from it. The book could not have fallen from Tina's pushing the bed and the bed bumping the bookcase.

Flat on her stomach and using both hands, Tina continued to search under Kelly's bed. I was still watching her when there was yet another crash on the floor behind me. This time it was a bottle of deodorant.

"Okay," I began recording, "we were just looking underneath the bed to see if we had some other messes lying around, and as Tina was lying on her tummy on the floor, right behind her and me a little bottle called Secret came crashing in, apparently from her room, where she had just been arranging things. Both hands were occupied, This happened just a minute ago at 5:47." Tina had obviously not thrown the bottle. She said the deodorant had been among the things she had been organizing on the dresser in the foster children's room ten minutes earlier.

By this time Tina had had enough of flying objects and crashing sounds. She went over to the other side of the room and sat down on a chair, her chin resting on its back. "I'm not feeling good," she said.

"How are you not feeling good?" I asked. I expected she had a headache or the stomach cramps she often complained of after the incidents.

"I'm not sick or anything," she countered. "My head's wandering and thinking about everything."

"Tell me some of the things you're thinking about."

"Jonathan and Kelly and Mrs. T. and Laura, the other Girl Scout leader." Jonathan was Tina's boyfriend from church, who had just broken up with her, or she with him, it wasn't clear. Mrs. T. was her Girl Scout leader, Chris Tinnerillo.

"How are the thoughts coming in?" I asked. "Are they strong thoughts or weak little thoughts that are wandering around?"

"Strong thoughts."

"What are you thinking about right this minute?"

"This stuff that's falling on me," she replied in a low voice as if not to tempt whatever was causing the havoc. She started chewing the back of her chair.

"Well, at least you have your chair to eat," I said.

Tina looked at the bite marks covering the wood. "I always bit on that since I was a baby. It was always my protection chair. It protected me from spankings. I'd sit down in it like this and they'd go, 'Ahhh.' "

A magical chair, I thought, that could protect her from the magical force.

Tina got up and fetched the rag she had used to wipe the water from the bookcase. "I need to take this to my parents' bathroom," she said. I followed with the tape recorder. As we came out of the bathroom into the master bedroom, something hit the floor behind us. I turned the Sony on: "As I was watching Tina, a piece of soap from the shower fell down." I supposed it had been on the soap dish in the shower stall. "Where did it come from? Up here?" I pointed to the dish.

"I would guess," Tina replied.

Then a loud bang came from behind us. Tina screamed, the Sony picking up both sounds. A painting had come off the wall, and I duly noted the occurrence on my recorder. Tina appeared dazed and I had trouble getting her to respond.

"Where did this come down from, Tina?"

She ignored the question. "My head hurts." Her voice was barely audible.

"Your head hurts?"

"Yes."

"Which side?"

"Right here." She held the back of her head.

"When did that start hurting, right now or before?"

Her voice became stronger. "Right now. Sometimes I can get warnings of what's going to happen, but usually, as in this case, the warning waits until it's happened."

"What kind of warning is that?" I wondered aloud.

"I keep thinking, it's some kind of warning, but it's after," she replied, her explanation as confused as before.

I asked her how she felt now.

"I either get headaches or I get the shakes." Lightly she added, "We're going to have to tune my brain in to make it come before it happens."

"Now you keep working on that," I said, doing my best to keep my voice playful. We had come to a watershed, and I didn't want to lose this newfound ground. Tina had just worked out for herself that the pain at the back of her head was a sign that she, or her "brain," was causing the occurrences. Until now, she shared the prevalent idea of the Hughes family and others that she or the house was possessed by evil spirits.

Kelly and I had undoubtedly helped to shape this new realization, for we had never brought up the demon or spirit theory, focusing only on Tina and her feelings. More than anything it was probably my constant questioning about how she felt before, during, and after the occurrences together with Kelly's more general inquiries about her home life that made Tina understand that she, and not some external agency, was involved.

But this new understanding carried a heavy price. If Tina was causing the turmoil, she could be blamed for it, as John thought from the beginning. There was enough ill feeling between Tina and her parents already; the thought of further blame and punishment was more than she could bear.

I turned to the fallen painting. It was leaning against a wall of the master bedroom. Tina cried out, "That's my mom's best picture — she's going to be so mad at me!"

"No, she's not going to get mad at you," I said. "Let me take a look at it." The picture wasn't broken and I scanned the wall for the nail so that I could put it back up. The nail was on the floor and Tina bent down to retrieve it. She jumped at a crash from the other end of the room.

"Okay, all right," I said, trying to calm her. Into the Sony I said, "We heard a big crack from the closet doors. Tina was about three inches from me then."

The new incident cleared Tina's mind of her anxiety about the painting. "That door is like all the way across the room," she said, impressed at her newly discovered talent.

"So, let's go and look," I suggested. We went to the closet and found a bottle of Keri lotion and a jar of Diaperene by the closet doors. I asked Tina where they had come from.

"The lotion is supposed to be in my mom's bathroom," she said. The Diaperene belonged on John's dresser.

I could not be certain that the two containers hitting the closet had made the sound we'd heard. I had not examined the room for stray objects, and these would have been out of sight, on the other side of the bed.

In any case they had ought to be returned to where they belonged. I knew that objects never moved from where they'd landed. If they were to move again, they had to be put back in their original locations.

Tina told me where to replace the toiletries, and we took the lotion into her parents' bathroom. Tina caught sight of herself in the mirror above the bathroom sink. She began combing her hair.

"I'm now beginning to comb my hair," she said for the benefit of the tape recorder. "Can you turn the light on please? See how I like the way my hair curls, like that, it's so cute."

I turned the light on. "Aren't you lucky being so cute?"

"My hair's cute but my face is so ugly."

"Let's see." I looked at her. "Yeah, it's true."

She laughed, then stopped. "Something's moving," she said in a low voice.

My attention was on a piece of soap she was playing with

and I didn't hear her. Only the recorder caught what she was saying.

"Put that soap back, Tina," I said, thinking she might drop or throw it. She replaced it and I felt I had been overly harsh. I made a clumsy attempt to change the subject. "What's your full name?"

"Christina Elaine Resch." The words were hardly out of her mouth when there was a sharp retort and she jumped back. A lipstick was rolling on the floor in front of the toilet.

"There, I saw it move on the floor," I dictated to the recorder.

"I told you something was going to move."

Because I hadn't heard her the first time, I said, "You didn't tell me something was going to move. How do you feel now?"

"Shaky."

I returned the lipstick to the drawer where Tina said it belonged. Had she been thinking of using her mother's lipstick when it came out? When Joan reproached Tina about some minor infraction, she would use her full name, Christina Elaine Resch. Because the incidents sometimes seemed to reflect what was going on in Tina's mind at the moment they occurred, perhaps I had triggered the negative association.

We went into the bedroom to put the painting back up. A pair of pliers on the dresser near the door to the bathroom would serve as a hammer. With the recorder still running, I placed it on the dresser where the pliers had been and hung the picture, Tina watching by my side. Suddenly there was a thud behind us. My Sony was lying on the floor near the door to the hallway, about eight feet from the dresser.

Of all the things in the room that could have moved, I expected this the least. The dresser stood against the wall to the left of Tina and was about eighteen inches behind her. When the recorder moved, Tina was to my left, her left hand flat against the wall close to where I was hammering in the nail. Her right hand was by her side. She clearly did not throw the Sony with her left hand. Her right hand was outside my line of vision, but she could not have reached back for the Sony, let alone thrown it without turning, and she was standing quietly.

Looking for a reason for this incident, I wondered if I had offended Tina when I'd contradicted her a moment before, claiming she hadn't spoken when in fact she had. Feeling un-heard by her parents was a major cause of Tina's sense of isola-tion and frustration, and now I had stepped into their shoes. Perhaps the Sony's flight was her way of complaining about my inattentiveness. The tape machine was a natural target; it was mine and it held the record of my negligence.

I replaced the pliers on the dresser and went to collect the tape recorder, keeping Tina slightly ahead where I could see her. As I was sitting on my haunches in front of Tina, testing the Sony by narrating its flight, I was startled by a violent crash from Joan and John's bed. The pliers had flown from the dresser and hit the bed's headboard six feet away.

When the pliers flew, Tina was standing serenely in front of me, her hands at her sides and about eight feet from where the pliers had been. She could neither have picked them up nor thrown them without my seeing her do so.

I called out to Kelly, who was still downstairs, to come up and bring our Polaroid. I wanted pictures of Tina and me as a reminder of our positions before and after these last two occur-rences.

Kelly took the photos and returned downstairs. Tina and I went back to her room. I was placing a new tape in the recorder while Tina sat on the floor in front of the nightstand, leaning against the bed, about a foot from me. Suddenly the nightstand collapsed, bringing the lamp down again and Tina to her feet. This was one incident, I thought, with a simple explanation: Tina must have inadvertently jostled the bed and thereby the table, which was right next to it. The loose leg had come off, and as I put it back, Tina made a startled sound.

"What's up?" I asked.

"The bed moved."

"Okay, well, just sit down on it." Even I had had enough moving objects for the day.

"I'd rather sit on the floor if you don't mind." Tina resumed her seat on the floor and I put the lamp back. She began breathing heavily, sounding upset. "You ready to go?"

"Okay, I think we're ready to eat," I said.

It was nine minutes past six. There had been at least fifteen movements of objects and five unexplained sounds in fifty-two minutes, about one occurrence every three minutes. Six of the objects—the cup, candy, book, Secret, Sony, and pliers—moved when I had Tina under observation and she could not have interfered with them in any visible way. I didn't include the painting because the nail might have been loose and could have come out on its own. In no instance was there evidence of strings or other devices that might have brought on the occurrence.

I had handled three of the objects immediately before they moved. This precluded the further possibility that they were attached to trick devices before the event. The teacup had the additional distinction of being in my line of vision when it flew. I hadn't seen it in the air, I supposed because I was watching Tina, who was six feet to its left, and because the cup went too fast. Other witnesses had commented on the speed with which things moved.

Tina was delighted to finally be on her way to dinner. She

went on ahead of me and I watched her walk out the room and down the hall, bumping into the walls as she went.

"I like the way you weave in and out between the walls as you walk," I said.

Tina laughed. She was happy and so was I. Now I knew it wasn't all chicanery; things were actually flying by themselves. The day that had started like a lamb was going out like a lion.

# 13

# TESTING TINA

When Tina and I came downstairs, we were greeted by a new arrival and a new project. Bill Cacciolfi, a sergeant at Wright Air Force Base, had read about Tina in the paper and thought she would make a good subject for a "thoughtography" test. I knew about the tests, in which a person attempts to project mental images on photographic film or paper without light or other known forms of energy, although I had never seen any conclusive evidence of the phenomenon. But I was open to whatever Cacciolfi had in mind. When he called earlier in the day to ask if he could work with Tina, I told him to come over that evening; we would conduct the tests if Tina agreed.

Tina had no objection if she could eat first. With only two cookies to sustain her all day, she was starving. The four of us, Bill, Kelly, Tina, and I went out to dinner, Tina as bubbly and excited to be out of the house as ever. She ordered her favorite foods, cheeseburger with relish and onions, with a side of fries and sour cream. After our meal and our return home, Bill went upstairs to prepare the children's bathroom for his tests. It was the room that could most easily be made lightproof, and Bill required total darkness to be certain that any results were not simply due to light seeping into the room.

While Bill worked on making the room lightproof, Kelly and I chatted with Tina in the hallway. Suddenly it sounded as if something had hit wood in the foster children's room. I turned on the Sony recorder: "We were upstairs, Tina and I, at 8:23, talking to Kelly, when there was a bang, and now we're going into the little room and looking around, wondering if anything is out of place."

The noise had been loud, yet nothing was amiss in the room that we could tell. We went into Kelly's and my room, all the time watching Tina hunt for whatever had caused the sound. She looked behind my suitcase and found a bottle of Secret deodorant, presumably the same one that had flown earlier in the evening. I thought I had replaced it on the dresser in the foster children's room, but couldn't be sure. If it was the same bottle, it had probably hit the window frame before falling down behind my suitcase.

Tina was perplexed. "How does it go around corners like that? If it came out of my room, it would have to come out like this, then like this." She described the supposed path of the bottle with her hands. "That's weird. I'm going to get changed before anything else happens, because my head doesn't feel too good."

I wondered how changing clothes would make her head feel better, but asked her where the pain was. "Which side? Is this another premonition after it happened?"

Tina placed her fingers at the back of her head.

"Right here?" I asked, touching her head. "In the middle? Just under that little bump we all have?"

"Yes!" Tina replied.

"Is it feeling better now?" Her head evidently still hurt because she didn't reply. "How long does it take for it to get better?"

"About ten minutes." A similar headache had come on, Tina said, when we had been leaving the house for dinner. "I got a headache when we stepped onto the driveway." She had asked Kelly if anything had fallen, but there was nothing that he knew of.

Tina went to change her clothes and I put the bottle of Secret back on her dresser. Since so many things had happened upstairs, I decided to check Craig's room to see if anything was out of place. If it was, I knew Tina could not have moved it as she had been with me for the past five hours.

Craig's door was locked, but Tina said she could open it with a bobby pin. I wondered if that was a trick she used to get into the room before announcing astonishing flights of the wine bottle or the mattress. I encouraged her to try picking the lock.

"You have to get it in a certain hole in order to unlock it," Tina said. The lock resisted her efforts and I suggested she try a nail.

"A nail won't work," she said. "See, they used to lock me in my room, so the only way I could get out was with that certain key. And I forget what I did with that key."

Tina was not an efficient burglar. We went back to her room for a nail file, but that also didn't work. "I can't use anything up here," Tina said, "because, one, it belongs to my dad, and if he catches me using it, I won't be here, and two, anything that will work will be downstairs."

Tina went downstairs and found a key and we entered the room. Instead of Craig's penny bottle with his shoe stuck on top, we found a dirty dinner plate, two empty beer cans, and a pair of pants on the floor; nothing paranormal about that arrangement.

We left the room, and when Tina was out of sight, rather than lock the door, I stuck a broken toothpick between the door and the frame. If the penny bottle should move and I found the toothpick on the floor, this would tell me that she or someone else had been in the room.

It was almost nine, but Bill Cacciolfi wasn't ready yet. Tina and I went into her room, where she sat down and began to draw a flower. She asked how long Kelly and I would be staying. I replied we would probably leave Friday.

"What happens if this stuff doesn't stop and you have to leave on Friday?" she asked.

"What do you suggest?"

"I don't know, but I'm just wondering who we can call then. There's nobody left to call. I know my mom is going to freak as soon as you leave."

I asked how she thought John was feeling right now.

"He's not feeling good at all," she said. "I think he wants out but he knows there's no place for him to go. I'm not very close to him, so we don't speak that much."

"Were you ever close to him?"

"When I was a little girl. He was very nice to me then. He just said I grew up and I learned too much." She finished her drawing. "So when are these tests going to happen?"

I explained that we were still waiting for Bill Cacciolfi to get the room ready. Tina didn't say anything for a while, then: "You know what makes me very, very sad?"

When I didn't say anything, she continued, "That I like you

and Kelly very much, and when you guys leave, I mean, I might come to New York or something like that if I'm lucky, but I will not see you again probably ever."

I thought this might be a good time to broach the possibility of her traveling back home with me. "How would you like to come for a little visit to North Carolina?"

"Really? Oh, God, I'd love to!"

"Well, now you sound happy." I added tongue in cheek, "But do you think you could leave your mommy and daddy for a little while?"

Tina didn't hesitate. "I've been away a month before and haven't missed them. Oh, that would be great! Hey, I wouldn't mind going to North Carolina or anyplace else, that's fine with me. You could take me a couple of miles down the road here and that would be fine with me. Just so I can get out." She was beaming.

It was five minutes past ten and Cacciolfi was ready to conduct the thoughtography tests. The only equipment he had along were several sheets of photographic paper, still in their packing envelopes from a box which had been opened that morning on the air force base.

For the next hour, Bill, Tina, and I sat in the darkened bathroom while Bill led Tina through his series of experiments. For some of the sheets, Cacciolfi asked Tina to trace her name with her finger on the outside of the envelope; the others he asked her to place against her head and body. Although the hour was late, Tina performed the tasks with reasonably good humor. We finished up the session and Bill said he would develop the sheets the next day. If the experiments had worked, we would see fogging or other unusual effects. I didn't hold out much hope anything would show up, but it was worth a try. After Bill left, we called it a night and turned in.

＊        ＊        ＊

"Peter's a little strange this morning," I said. There had been two incidents in the family room, and the Siberian husky was looking at Tina strangely alert, head high and ears up.

"What is it, Pete?" I said, reaching down to pet the dog.

"Does he detect something in me?" Tina asked.

"I don't think so. Has he been like this before?"

"No, never." Until now, Pete had taken the incidents in stride. It was the confusion afterward that he reacted to, preferring to be outside rather than in the midst of all the yelling and crying. Cats and dogs often react in odd ways in homes where the occupants tell of seeing apparitions, sensing presences, and hearing footsteps. But pets usually behave normally around psychokinetic people, and Pete was no exception.

"Okay, Pete," I said, and to Tina, "Let him go up to you and sniff you."

It was Thursday, March 15, a week after the news conference and the embarrassing clip of Tina fooling with the lamp, causing many to doubt the events. This morning I was scheduled to hold a conference of my own at the Park Hotel in Columbus, and I looked forward to setting the record straight.

The conference went well and gave me the opportunity to outline Kelly's and my activities over the past four days. I gave a detailed description of the incidents with my tape recorder and the pliers. I told the reporters, "I was impressed by these occurrences. I cannot explain them away easily. In my opinion it was not possible for Tina to have thrown these and other objects."

After I came back from the press conference, I thought of what we would do when we left Columbus. In addition to research in North Carolina, there was a woman in Florida, Mary Rossi, I wanted Tina to meet. Mary was a medium at Camp

Cassadega, a residential center for psychics near Orlando. I had met her during a research trip and heard stories of moving objects during her sessions. She was a warm, motherly woman, and I thought she might help Tina bring her psychokinesis on at will.

I was on the phone at ten to twelve, asking a friend in Florida to put us up, when two incidents occurred: Joan and Tina were in the family room when Joan's Vicks bottle on the table by the large couch hit the wall behind the table, followed by the mail caddy scooting to the floor. The mail caddy was also hers.

Pete was still acting funny and Tina asked me why.

"I don't know," I said. "Maybe you seem tense; how do you feel?"

"Fine, I guess."

I had forgotten to ask her before, so I added, "How did you feel, by the way, after those last two incidents?"

"Fine."

I persisted, "Any different? I mean, did you have that feeling afterward?" I was thinking of the headaches or stomach butterflies that usually went with the occurrences.

But Tina said, "No." This time she felt okay; it was her dog that was acting peculiar. Pete was still watching Tina in an alert, inquisitive way that was new to her. Although the dog was not behaving aggressively, Tina held him off, half-scared.

"Let him do what he wants," I said. "He's curious." I wondered what was making Pete so wary. Perhaps Tina was emitting some sort of energy that only the dog could sense.

I told Tina not to worry about Pete, and we went upstairs, Tina to pack and I to call home so Muriel would know when to pick us up at the airport. The phone worked fine.

I was still on the phone making arrangements for the trip

when Tina went downstairs on her own to look at family pho-tos. Glad as she was to get away from John's silences and her mother's reproaches, she couldn't help but think how it would be without her parents and familiar faces. A few minutes after she sat down on Joan's recliner with the family photo album, the mail caddy shot off from the table again. Joan called me down. Whenever there was an occurrence in the house, she made a mental note of Tina's location. She told me, "I was keeping an eye on her. I do that all the time anymore, after this long. It will be two weeks tomorrow and I just keep look-ing—and she wasn't touching it."

The spilled pens and pencils may have matched Tina's thoughts. She liked writing and receiving letters and may have been thinking that she could stay in touch this way.

I reminded Tina that we hadn't had lunch yet. "It's one o three—have you eaten today?"

"No, I haven't."

"Aren't you hungry? How come you never eat?" I added jokingly.

Tina didn't get it. "Because I never have time. But I eat a lot more than you think I do, believe me, I do."

Joan interrupted to ask Tina to run the electric carpet sweeper. Tina resisted until Kelly gently persuaded her, but not without a scowl and a complaint. "I'm getting annoyed," she said.

I thought there might be an occurrence because of her irri-tation. Remembering the incidents in Craig's room while Tina had been downstairs, I went up to his room, closed the door, and wedged a toothpick in the opening as I had done the night before. Throughout the evening I went up to his room to see if the toothpick had moved or if the room had changed in any way. Each time I checked, everything was just as I had left it, even with Tina having had ample opportunity to enter the room had she chosen to do so.

This time when I returned downstairs, Tina's scowl had changed to sadness. "I think Kelly's mad at me."

Kelly was making flight reservations in our room, and I said I would speak to him. I asked Tina to wait in the children's room. Kelly's call dragged out and I joined Tina. "He just seems very mad," she said softly.

"Okay, I'll find out," I reassured her.

Tina hung her head.

"What's up?" I asked. "How does your head feel?"

"Fine." Her hand went to her stomach.

"Your stomach doesn't feel so good, huh?" I thought she was lovesick and anxious that Kelly might be rejecting her.

"I think it's just that I'm a little excited to go to Girl Scouts tonight," she said. "I haven't been for a while and I miss my friends."

"You have butterflies in your tummy?"

"Yeah." She headed for the bathroom. I noted this on the tape recorder and her mood changed abruptly. "Got you!" she snapped. "Why does everyone follow me?"

"Oh, I don't know, you're just a very nice, attractive girl, people are just attracted to you."

"Or is that people don't believe me?" Tina shot back.

"Well, it's that people believe you, but when I'm together with you, things don't happen quite as much."

"But they do sometimes."

"Sometimes they do," I agreed, "and then we should be in a position to know what happened, where it moved, and also it helps you to be not quite so nervous when I'm around."

"But everybody acts like they don't believe me."

"I sure believe you because, first of all, of all the people I spoke to, and then mainly because of the things I've seen myself."

Tina began to calm down. "At least somebody believes me and doesn't call me a liar."

"If they call you a liar, they have to call me a liar, don't they?"

"Yup, I guess so."

I asked Tina if I could come along to her Girl Scout meeting that evening. I hoped to speak to her troop leader, Chris Tinnerillo. Tina said I could.

Before we left for the meeting, Bill Cacciolfi returned with the results of his thoughtography tests. Bill showed me the photographic sheets. At best they could be labeled inconclusive. On some of the sheets the glossiness of the paper had gone in places. I supposed it was due to the development process. The rest were unaffected. I could tell that Bill was disappointed and so was I.

Tina and I then went to her Girl Scout meeting. Scouting was an important part of Tina's life. She had earned more badges than her uniform sash could hold, ranging from reading and writing, which she loved, to volunteer service work, canoeing, and building a campfire. In the same way that Tina was valued at her church, her Girl Scout leaders regarded her as helpful and always ready to take on responsibility. Despite Joan's account of Tina's disastrous attempts at crafts in school, the girl had become more confident in her abilities. She had learned to sew by hand and had even made herself a kimono when the girls had studied the Philippines. But in the last few months, the Scout leaders had noticed a slight change in Tina.

During a break I spoke to Chris Tinnerillo, one of the leaders, who said that Tina had been withdrawn after the last few meetings. Other than that, she seemed fine. "I've known Tina for so many years," she said. "I've watched her grow up, and she's suffered so many traumas and had so many problems over the years, and this little withdrawal was no big deal to me because I know big deals."

"Big deals were mainly with peers in school?" I asked.

"Yeah. When we do things with children or elderly people, Tina just blossoms and is beautiful."

I thought back to Joan's wistful remark the other night when she acknowledged the difference between her relationship with Tina and that between Tina and Chris. I had seen Tina's anger when Joan had insisted she run the carpet sweeper. Maybe the trip to North Carolina would give mother and daughter some breathing space. They both needed it.

Fourteen-year-old Tina Resch having a snack in the kitchen of her home in Columbus, Ohio. FRED SHANNON

Tina and her foster parents, John and Joan Resch, posing for photographer Fred Shannon in the family room in March of 1984. FRED SHANNON

"Tina was sitting on the arm of the chair by the telephone," recalls photographer Fred Shannon. "I was in the kitchen area looking at her when I saw the loveseat move about eighteen inches towards her. I saw this with my own eyes." FRED SHANNON

"I sat on the long couch with [reporter] Mike Harden when the afghan jumped off the floor and draped itself over Tina's head," said Fred Shannon who took this photo immediately after the event. Tina's brother, Craig watched the event from the kitchen. Harden examined the afghan but found no strings or other devices to explain the occurrence. FRED SHANNON

By the time Fred Shannon came to the Resch home, all but one wine glass had shattered inexplicably. Shannon had Tina hold the last remaining glass for this picture.
FRED SHANNON

s Tina's caseworker, Lee Arnold, watched, the telephone hit the loveseat. "Tina was facing me and I saw her hands," said Arnold. "It really shook me up because I couldn't explain what was going on."
FRED SHANNON

Fred Shannon considers this shot of the telephone in flight and crossing the room "the photograph of a lifetime." Recalls reporter Mike Harden: "I was seated across the room, facing Tina . . . I saw [the phone] in motion without it being aided in any way on her part." FRED SHANNON

Photo sequence reconstructs the
unexplained movement of several objects:

(1) Tina stands next to parapsychologist William Roll, who is using a pair of pliers to hammer in a nail for a painting that has come off the wall in the master bedroom.

(2) Roll had placed his tape recorder on John Resch's dresser. When Roll hears a sound, he discovers the tape recorder on the floor, about eight feet from the dresser. Roll places the pliers where the tape recorder had been.

(3) Roll checks the tape recorder while Tina watches.

4) After hearing a
ud bang, Roll
nds the pliers by
e wall next to the
esches' bed, about
ven feet from the
resser. SEQUENCE
IOTOS BY WILLIAM
OLL

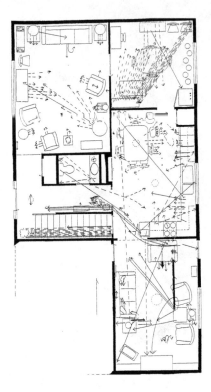

This ground-floor plan of the Resch home shows the unexplained movements of objects. The solid lines indicate movements of objects witnessed by visitors, the broken lines show other events, and the heavy lines several incidents with the same object. The living room is located at the top left; the dining room is top right. The kitchen lies between the dining room and the family room. Below the living room is the foyer, with the main entrance and the steps leading to the second floor.

This second-floor plan of the Resch home also shows the unexplained movements of objects. The solid lines indicate movements of objects witnessed by visitors; the broken lines show other events. The master bedroom is located top left; Tina's room is top right. The foster children's room is below Tina's room, and brother Craig's room is bottom right (the door in Craig's closet opens to the attic above the garage). The star figures in the foster children's room indicate unexplained explosive sounds.

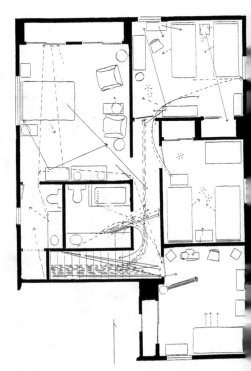

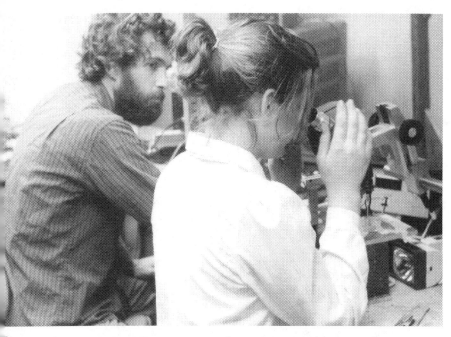

Neurobiologist Stephen Baumann watches as Tina attempts to affect a nerve cell from a sea snail in an exploratory test for micro-PK (psychokinesis) at the Spring Creek Institute in April 1984. WILLIAM ROLL

In October of 1984, Tina attempted to affect a piezoelectric crystal in a test of micro-PK in Stephen Baumann's lab. WILLIAM ROLL

Could the psychokinetic events occurring in Tina's presence be due to an anomaly in her brainstem, where instructions pass from the brain to the rest of the body? Stephen Baumann tested Tina's brainstem at the University of North Carolina, Chapel Hill, in October 1984.
WILLIAM ROLL

Tina seen during visiting hours at the jail in Carrollton, Georgia, in October 1992.
WILLIAM ROLL

# 14

# CAMERA SHY

After the Girl Scout meeting, my son, Tertius, arrived at the house to join me for the final segment of the investigation. Kelly was leaving in the morning and Tertius had agreed to help me make a video recording of Tina and any occurrences that we might be lucky enough to catch on tape.

Tertius was on spring break from Denison University, a short distance from Columbus, and was on his way home to North Carolina. He had asked to meet Tina, and I thought this was a good idea. When Tina came back with us, she would have someone close to her own age to talk to. Tertius was actually named William George, like my father and me. To not confuse him with Bill Sr. and Bill Jr., we followed a British custom and called him Tertius, Latin for "third." Joan, always happy to receive visitors, welcomed him straight into the household. Tertius had brought a sleeping bag, but Joan insisted on making him a proper bed on the hideaway in the family room.

Tomorrow would be my last day in the house and my last chance to get a videotape of any incidents. Because the force had never followed Tina outside of the home to either the motel, the church, the Girl Scouts, or the Hughes home, I did not expect the occurrences to resume in North Carolina. It was even more unlikely that the incidents would continue at places that were completely foreign to her, such as the parapsychology laboratories where I planned to bring her for further research.

I thought if I could succeed where the TV news crews had failed and catch an actual incident on tape, it would do two things: give added credence to the reports of flying objects and throw light on the energy that propelled them.

I asked Tina to help Tertius install the camcorder in my room, as this was where my teacup and other items had flown. I hoped Tina's participation would make the equipment less intrusive and make her less anxious about being filmed.

To approximate the earlier events, I had Tertius aim the camera at the table with the teacup and the bed where I wanted Tina to sit. There was a problem though. When the camera was focused on the bed and the bedside table, the two dressers were out of view. With Tina on the bed, I wondered if the things on the table would move, or those that were out of the camera frame? In fact, would anything move at all? Tina's mind was filled with the trip ahead, perhaps to the point that there was no energy left for psychokinesis.

Shortly after eleven the next morning, we were ready to begin taping. Joan had given me three glasses from the cupboard as a sacrifice on the altar of science. I placed one with a cup on the night table. Hoping to duplicate the flying-teacup incident, I was again having a cup of tea. I put another glass and a plastic cup on the brown dresser to the right of the bed, and the third glass and a white plastic cup on the white dresser next to the door and facing the bed.

The Resches had agreed to stay downstairs during the taping, and Tertius stationed himself on the stairs to make sure no one went up. If things should move in the other rooms upstairs during this period, I would know that neither Tina nor anyone else in the family was involved.

Aside from keeping Tina in camera view as much as possible, I did not restrict her movements. The more natural the situation, I thought, the more likely things might move. My only rule was to ensure a continuous recording. If something moved beyond the camera range and the recording had been interrupted, critics could argue that the object had been taken from its place during the interruption to simulate an occurrence.

As I was making some final adjustments to the camera and while Tina was sitting on her bed, some clothing she had tossed on top of her bookcase fell down, partially covering her. I didn't see how this had happened and asked her to come over to where I was working with the camcorder so I could keep better watch. As she came and stood with me for a moment, the glass on the white dresser shattered against the floor.

"Too bad it wasn't on," Tina said, referring to the camcorder.

I agreed, but it was also a good omen. Tina's back had been to the glass, so she couldn't have thrown it. I replaced it with the one from the night table and turned the video on.

In spite of the camera, Tina did not seem at all self-conscious and she entertained herself by humming and cracking her knuckles. I sat down on the other bed and picked up my teacup. "Well, I think I'll have my cup of tea, actually."

"Aaa-ctually," Tina repeated, imitating my mix of British and Danish accents.

I finished my tea and went back to check if Tina was still in camera range. She slid off the bed, then crawled to the door and hid behind the white dresser. After some more horsing around, she got into a housekeeping mode and took the sheets off what had been Kelly's bed and went out for fresh linen. A moment later there was a sound from the hallway while Tina was still out there.

She called into the room, "Bill, one thing. Something just fell."

"Where did it fall?"

"In Craig's room."

"Don't go in there."

Tina came back and was standing in the doorway when there was a louder crack from the hallway. She jumped. "Ah, shit!"

This was no good. Two incidents before I began taping and now two more beyond camera range. "Okay," I said, "let's close the door. Tina, go back and sit on the bed." She returned, and I said, "Put a pillow behind you so you can be comfortable. How are you now?"

"I've got a headache."

"Is that something you just got or did you have it before?"

"Yeah," she said, she'd got it now.

I went out to the hallway to see what had fallen, then came back to report the incident on the tape. "Okay," I said to the recorder, "it's 11:28. There's a brush that was in the bathroom that hit the right-hand side of the wall in the hallway. It came from the drawer adjacent to the door." It was Craig's brush, Tina said, which she often used. I put it back and Tina turned on her favorite tape, Cindi Lauper's "Time After Time."

Halfway through the song, Tina's boyfriend, Jonathan, called. Tina had trouble speaking and began to stutter in a slow, labored way. "I can't pronounce my *w* too well," she said, though the *w* of *well* came out fine. She made another attempt at a sentence, which seemed to be intended as, "So what's new?" but again got jammed on the *w*.

Finally she said, "So, anything new? You still coming?" Tina was not eager for a visit. To me she said, "Bill, can I talk to him for just a second?"

I agreed, "You stay where you are, okay?" I left, keeping the video running and hoping that my absence would trigger an incident.

Tina was lying flat on her stomach speaking to Jonathan and listening to her tape. "I'm going to be in North Carolina for seven to ten days, and then I'm going to go to Florida—

"What?"

Jonathan was blaming her for their not getting together, and Tina was alternately defensive and irritated. She twirled Jonathan's ring and played with the phone cord. Finally she hung up, saying she'd call him back in ten minutes.

"I hope he can't come," she told me when I returned. "I have too much stuff to do without him being here."

She called Jonathan back in less than two minutes. She didn't reach him and called her friend Elizabeth, hoping she could visit.

I was getting impatient. "Tina, let's wait with that. Let's see if we can clean things up in here." Housework seemed to have encouraged the force before.

Tina headed for the door to get fresh linen, but I didn't want more incidents out in the hallway. "Let's stay in here, Tina. Let's close the door."

Before she did, she caught a glimpse of Tertius on the stairs. "Hello, whoever's on the steps? Stop playing games. Who's on the steps?"

"Come, close the door," I said. "How was your talk with Jonathan?"

"Awful. I really don't want him to come up today and he's thinking of every reason why he has to. I'll send his ring back to him through the mail."

Tina took my empty cup and smelled the tea bag. "That stuff stinks.

"Want to see a flying saucer?" She pretended to throw the saucer. She went up to my tape recorder on the white dresser and saw it had been on during her talk with Jonathan.

"I'm going to kill you! You left the tape recorder on the whole time!"

I thought she knew. "This has been on, too," I said, pointing to the camcorder. Tina picked up the tape recorder. "Don't press any buttons," I implored. "You can say some sweet things to it."

"All right, what's your name? *B-iiill*," she filled in with a Southern drawl. She tapped her fingers on the recorder and made scratching sounds, then returned to the bed.

"Can you see my right hand?"

She rolled around, fell off the bed, hid under the other bed, pushed it up, stuck her tongue out, hid again, covered the camera lens, and laughed. "Having fun, Bill? Let me film you for a while." She again went out for bed linen. This time I didn't object and went along. On the way she pretended to throw the plastic cup from the white dresser. Nothing happened outside. When we returned, I sat down on the bed and she started operating the camera.

"Say something, Bill."

"The weather is a little warmer than it was yesterday. The snow has about gone and we are preparing now for another shoot of this famous movie, *Tina and Pete*. It's a story about Tina and her pet dog, Pete."

Tina laughed, and between the two of us we spent the next few minutes concocting a silly story that worked its way from *Tina and Pete* to *Tina and Kelly the Gorilla.*

The phone rang and Tina grabbed it, hung it up when it wasn't for her, then flung herself on the bed with such vigor that the mattress slid into the nightstand and Tina and the lamp fell to the floor. I groaned.

"Let's get everything straightened up, Tina."

But she wanted to talk about Kelly. "Okay, we've talked about Kelly the ape. Now let's talk about Kelly Powers—I'll start out. Kelly Powers is a twenty-seven-year-old [*sic*] man that is very tall and very cute, and gets along great with other people and is very nice. And I hope you get to see this soon," she added for Kelly's benefit.

After more storytelling about Kelly, there was a curious incident, which I only noticed after I played back the tape. Tina was pulling the little finger of her left hand when the finger next to it cracked with the sound of an electrical discharge. Tina laughed and said in a teasing voice, "Whoops, what's that, Bill? I didn't quite catch that!" imitating my voice. I stowed the occurrence away in my mind. Probably nothing of interest, but then again perhaps a piece that fit somewhere in the puzzle.

"What's green and goes one hundred miles an hour?" Tina asked. I couldn't think of a reply. "Kermit the Frog in a blender!" She fell over laughing. She reached back in her nightstand and picked up a small paperback, *Come Laugh With Me.* Tina settled down a bit and began to read some more of the jokes to me.

After five minutes, Tina tired of the book and flung it away. She started to play with the camera, first showing Kelly's bed. "This here at one time was where Kelly slept." She panned to the other bed. "This is where Bill slept. This is the room that they slept in. This is the mess that Bill always kept. You see the mess. This is where Kelly always kept his stuff very nice and neat." She swung the camera back and forth. "Kelly, Bill, Kelly, Bill."

My impatience was back. "Why don't we see if we can get the feeling back we had before so we can get something moving."

Tina accidentally pressed the off button, so I asked her to again film the target placings. "Let's set up the TV and forget about it," I said.

Tina returned to the bed.

"When do they happen?" I asked, speaking of the incidents.

"When I don't have my mind on anything."

"When your mind is a blank?"

"But right now my mind is on Kelly."

"How about if you keep your mind a blank screen? Can you keep your mind blank?"

Tina's reply was to call Jonathan. "Is Jonathan home?" He couldn't be reached.

I tried to get her attention. "See if you can keep your mind blank and see if we can make things happen."

Tina pretended to make her lamp fly. The phone rang; it was Jonathan asking to visit later. Tina didn't want that. "We are leaving at seven, we are going to eat first and get all our luggage." Jonathan was disappointed and they talked about keeping in touch by phone.

That problem settled, Tina wanted to eat. I left the camcorder running and we went to the hallway. I hoped things might happen in the room once we were outside. Immediately there was an explosive sound.

"At 12:44 we heard a noise the moment we got out of the

room." I continued, "Tina and I are standing outside and her brother's brush moved out. Again it was in this drawer here in the bathroom. So how do you feel, do you feel anything different now?"

"I feel fine."

"So it's not always when there is an event that you're feeling different?"

"No, not always." She added, "So, you want to turn the camera off so we can go eat?"

I remembered Wednesday, when there was a striking sequence of incidents after Tina said she wanted to eat. I said, "It's interesting that something happened out here. It seems to be outside the room rather than inside the room right now. Did you notice that?"

"Is it because that camera's in there?" Tina asked.

"You think that's why?"

"I don't know. It always shies away from the cameras."

I said, "It happened when we were away from the camera or before we set the camera up."

"Then the stuff will happen," Tina concluded.

As if to verify this observation, a moment later a plastic lemon hit in the hallway while Tina and I were still outside her room. It was 12:46. She went in, then as she came back out, there was a loud cracking sound. "Whoops," I said, "something came out of her room behind her." It was the white plastic cup I had set on the dresser by the door.

"So how do you feel now?" I asked.

"Fine, just jumpy." Two sharp bangs followed. Another lemon had apparently hit the open bathroom door, and a shampoo bottle had landed on the first step of the stairs. The bottle belonged in the bathroom closet by the door.

As I asked Tina to put it back, a metallic sound seemed to

come from her room. But Tina thought it was her toothbrush, which she had just put down in the bathroom. Before we could solve this inconsistency, a piece of soap from the bathroom landed in the hallway, followed by a loud falling and bumping noise clearly coming from Tina's present room. A bottle of shampoo had fallen from my travel bag, which I had placed on the white dresser.

"Things are quite active now," I noted unnecessarily.

Something hit near Craig's door. "We now have the top of a bottle of some sort, an orange top. Where does this come from?"

"The bathroom," Tina said. "Here, I'll put it back." It was 12:50. "And everything's going strong."

A rattling sound made me say, "Right behind us an object came from . . . ?"

"That's not mine," Tina said. A bottle of Tylenol was lying on the hallway floor. Tina picked it up and put it in the bathroom drawer.

I thought, if only I could get some of this on film. I asked Tina to hold the tape recorder while I went in to fetch the camcorder.

In the voice of a news reporter, Tina said, "Things are really flying in the Resch home today—" There was a bang and she screamed.

I came back out. "Things move behind us, forward. Here we have a bottle of some candy, Sugarettes, outside the bathroom."

I saw that the white plastic cup had flown from Tina's dresser to the left of the bookcase. "The cup is missing, the plastic cup that we just had. It's down here, the plastic cup is to the left of the bookcase." I returned it to the dresser.

"I think one of my perfume bottles is destroyed," Tina said when she didn't find it on the dresser.

In the meantime the video had run out of tape and I tried to get the camera back in operation while Tina held the tape recorder.

"Okay," I said, "the TV is off now." I told Tina to just keep still and hold on to the tape recorder. Something from the bathroom moved outside of Craig's door.

As I went to get a videotape from my briefcase to put in the camcorder, telling Tina to follow me, there was a clattering sound and a shout from Tina: "The tape!" A roll of Scotch tape, probably from the bathroom, had hit the wall in the hallway.

"All right. Just stay there," I told her. Another sound followed.

"Something else just hit," Tina said. She jumped and cried at each sound, spasmodically clicking the tape recorder off and on.

"Don't leave me in this," she cried. "I don't want nothing to do with it. Shit, I'm sick of this. Now I've got a headache—"

Tertius heard the commotion from the stairs and ran up. "What happened?"

"Every time we turn around, stuff happens," Tina said.

I began picking things up off the floor.

"Hey, that's my perfume bottle," Tina said, relieved, her mood swinging 180 degrees.

"Did you get anything on film?" Tertius asked.

"No," I replied sadly.

I brought the camera into the master bedroom. From there the cord could also reach the hallway. As I was about to plug it in, there was a bang from Tina's room. Her face puckered up and she held her neck as if it hurt.

I touched her neck and she cringed.

"It's itchy," she replied when I asked how her neck felt. "I'm allergic to jewelry. So I've broken out back there."

Tina went into her parents' bathroom, caught sight of herself in the mirror, and brushed her hair. "Isn't that cute?" she asked, "I may as well get my hair looking good while we're going to be on camera." Her fear and tension had vanished.

We left the bathroom and I was ready to film again when there was another loud bang, this time from behind us. Tina began to shake and I reached for her hand. It was limp so I took her by the wrist, and as we went back to the bathroom, a large phone book fell to the floor in the bedroom. Into the recorder I said, "We go in very cautiously to the bathroom and there's a little thing on the floor which looks like your mother's—"

Tina interrupted, "That hurts, Bill."

"Sorry."

"I've got a sore wrist. Try the other one."

I did, and she said, "That one's sore, too."

"Okay, you hold me. Hold my finger." I went back to recording our movements. "Now we walk out and there's no one else up here. Tertius is on the stairs. I know that nobody was in the bedroom when the phone book fell. Its position apparently was on the dresser, but I don't know exactly where it was. But anyhow, I was holding Tina firmly, too firmly, when the phone book fell."

As we sat down, there was another loud sound. "Whoops. And here she was sitting right next to me and something hit somewhere here in the bedroom and let's see what it is."

Tina seemed dazed. She stood up to see what had fallen, but I did not want her to go on her own.

"Stay here. Just leave it," I said. She didn't seem to hear. "Leave it!" I repeated. I went to check, keeping her next to me.

"A small bottle of spray," I said, only to be startled as a tremendous bang came from the clothes closet across the room.

"Shit!" Tina screamed.

One of John's shoes had kicked the closet—if *kick* is the right word when there is no foot in the shoe. Into the tape recorder I said, "Again she was nowhere near there. She was right next to me."

We waited for a few more minutes. Silence. The kick marked the end of the events.

It was a little past one. I thought about Tina's bodily sensations. In the past when her neck and the back of her head had felt sore, she had been hit by objects in those places. Now her wrists were sore as well. I wondered if this had had anything to do with these last occurrences.

Keeping Tina in her room for two hours—the time it took to run one videotape—had been like keeping a wild bird in a cage. She was continuously on the move. As soon as she was out of the room and standing quietly, things around her were moving. It was the most active run of psychokinesis I had ever experienced.

After lunch Tertius went back to Denison to pick up something he had forgotten. At two, Tina and I went to her room so she could pack. Sometime later, in the kitchen, when she was taking Pete's bowl to the sink for water, a high chair fell across the door to the dining room as Tina walked by.

This was the last incident in the home while I was there. Interesting, I thought, that the two weeks' turmoil was framed by occurrences involving the foster children, first the heart monitor and now the high chair. Fred Shannon then came by and took Tina, Tertius, and me to the airport for the flight to North Carolina.

How did the evidence for recurrent spontaneous psychokinesis stack up at the end of my visit? I realized that striking feats of sleight of hand could be accomplished by a magician, but Tina showed no evidence of magical skills. On the contrary, she was uncoordinated and her faulty depth perception made it difficult for her to estimate distance. From her failure with crafts in first grade to her debacle with the lamp in front of reporters, she had demonstrated a marked inability to match sight with movement. Tina just didn't have the agility or sophistication to successfully fake the occurrences, at least not from what I had observed of her in her own home.

As far as I was concerned, the occurrences I had witnessed around Tina were genuine. What I couldn't be so sure of was what would happen in the lab.

# 15

# ON THE ROAD

y wife, Muriel, picked us up at the airport. Tina had never
been on a flight before, and earlier in the afternoon Tertius had done his best to set her worries to rest. He'd also tried
to describe our house in Durham. "You've never seen a house
like it before, I'm sure," he told her. "Kind of like a motel.
About ninety feet long." The house jutted out from a small
hill, and Tertius's room overlooked the woods in the back of
the house.

"Seriously, just one long hallway and the rooms are off it?
That's weird!" Tina said.

When I'd offered to take Tina to North Carolina, it was like
a prison door having sprung open; she was euphoric. Though
happy to be away from her parents, Tina felt betrayed by Joan's
lack of hesitation in letting her go. She knew that Joan trusted
me to take care of her during the trip, but how did Joan really

know who I was and where I would be taking Tina? The thought that Joan was so ready to get rid of her deepened Tina's feeling of being abandoned. She made up for the feeling by continuously calling Joan on the phone. In spite of their constant round of arguments and punishments, it was obvious Tina missed her mother. I was surprised that her bond to Joan was that strong.

I had asked Tina before we arrived to please not make our porcelain move and break. I didn't believe that she had voluntary control of the incidents, but I thought there must be some part of her mind where she controlled the levers that produced the phenomena.

Tina was still big news, and her arrival in North Carolina produced stories in both the Ohio and North Carolina newspapers. The articles said that Tina was on vacation and having fun, and that she was also receiving counseling. Neither item was enough to bring reporters to the house. This was a relief. The last thing I wanted was the media circus in Columbus to be repeated in Durham. Our porcelain remained intact during the six days Tina stayed with us.

Freed from her parents' constant scrutiny, Tina became even more playful than she had been back home. Table-tilting during meals became a favorite game to the extent that we couldn't eat and had to ask her to desist. I was reminded of the playfulness the psychokinetic occurrences had sometimes shown, especially those in her brother Craig's room, where his penny bottle periodically showed up in the middle of the floor with one of his shoes stuck on top. The force was playful and so was Tina.

As part of my research with Tina, I had planned to take her to Florida to work with the medium Mary Rossi. Mary evidently had PK abilities herself, and she believed she could bring Tina's powers under conscious control. Together with Tertius we traveled to Orlando and spent five days working with Mary to make objects move. Kelly had taken time off from his work and assisted Mary. Mary didn't succeed, but felt Tina could become a psychic healer if she was trained.

Our trip then took a recreational turn. Before my visit to Columbus, I had promised Tertius to take him snow skiing at Beech Mountain in North Carolina. Instead, it became waterskiing in Key West, Florida. Emmy Chetkin, whom I had met at one of Patricia Hayes's workshops, put us up in her home. Florida was a series of firsts for Tina: her first view of the ocean, her first lobster dinner—a real change from burgers and fries—and her first boat ride. Emmy took us out on the water, and Tertius tried to teach Tina water skiing. She never managed to get up on the skis, but she shone from the attention.

While she was taking a moment to catch her breath, Tina said she saw Tina Scott in the boat. Oddly though, Tina saw her friend sitting on the couch in the Resches' family room, yet she was in the boat, and she was wearing beach attire like the rest of us.

I knew that the appearance of Tina Scott usually was a response to stress, and I wondered why the vision had come to Tina at this moment. The outing was supposed to be a fun and relaxing excursion. I realized later that being in a small boat on the ocean and trying to get up on skis must have more stressful than Tina showed. At the time, seeing Tina laugh and enjoy herself, I interpreted the vision as a sign of things to come, since Tina had seen Scott at her home shortly before the incidents began.

When we returned to Durham, I arranged for a seriously

sunburned Tina to visit Richard Broughton, the director of the Institute for Parapsychology. Richard had dark hair and a full beard. His eyes are intense, but he has a relaxed manner that I thought would help to make Tina comfortable at the institute.

On the morning of March 29, Tina went to the institute and tried to marshal her abilities for a game that Richard was running testing psychokinesis. The results were flat chance; there was no evidence of PK.

When I answered the doorbell that afternoon, Tina and Becca Zinn were at the door. Becca was the psychotherapist I had called from Columbus who had offered to spend time with Tina. She had chauffeured Tina to and from the institute, stopping at her own house on the way back. Now standing on my doorstep, Becca looked drained. On their way over, she said, the hood to her car had popped open and the car itself had slipped out of third gear into neutral. If once wasn't bad enough, it happened two more times. In the four years she had owned the car, Becca said, "It's never done this before."

Tina and Becca came inside. Apparently the car troubles were just the last in a string of incidents that Becca found downright frightening. The first incidents, she said, were innocuous enough and had started while she was in her office using the telephone. She had just brought Tina back from the institute. When she went to make a call, she said, "I heard that loud, shrill sound on the phone that I have heard only twice before in my life—and those were both times that I was talking to Kelly while he was at Tina's house. The noise was so bad that I had to hang up the phone."

Tina had been outside Becca's office. When Becca asked her what was occupying her mind at the time, Tina said she had been thinking about Joan and her natural mother. She also complained of the familiar feeling of an upset stomach, as she often did following the incidents. Becca tried to make another call, but the interference on the line continued.

Tina then joined Becca inside her office. While she was standing by her desk, Becca said, two pens dropped off a table in the room, one after the other.

"Tina deliberately placed a pencil on the bookcase," Becca said, "and we laughingly told it to stay put. We hugged each other, and then, out of the corner of my eye, I saw the same pencil land on the floor across the room. We looked at the bookshelf, and the pencil was no longer there.

"I began to be a bit alarmed and started moving Tina toward getting ready to leave. We were standing in the middle of my office when a twist-off top to a Coke bottle flew off of my desk and landed on the floor." Becca hadn't seen it take off, but she saw it land. She took Tina by her left hand and began to lead her out of the office, walking about half a step ahead of her.

"The next thing I saw—again out of the corner of my eye," Becca said, "was the telephone hitting Tina in the back. There is no way that anyone could have touched it since we were the only ones in the office and since it flew at Tina from behind both of us." Tina screamed in pain, fell to the floor, and began to sob. Becca tried to console her, holding her and telling her it would be all right. Tina said that she had again been thinking about Joan and her real mother when the phone hit. Becca managed to calm Tina down enough for them to go out to the car.

"When we got in the car," Becca said, "the horn began blowing by itself." They drove to Becca's house. As Tina got out of the car, Becca said, "A tube of toothpaste—Crest, for scientific accuracy—flew out of my car and hit Tina in the chest. Again I saw only the end phase of the movement."

Tina wanted to call Joan, but Becca's home phone only emitted a dial tone. She tried again with the same result. Becca then tried, also unsuccessfully, but on her second attempt she got through. After Tina had spoken to Joan, Tina asked Becca to talk to Joan.

"As I talked to Joan, Tina began hugging me. She had both arms wrapped around me when at the exact same moment the phone disconnected and the lamp fell over. The lamp was to Tina's right."

Becca thought that Tina might be safer outdoors, so they went downstairs and outside. Tina again asked Becca to call Joan. Becca told her to stay on the porch while she used the kitchen phone. While Becca was on the phone, Tina came back inside and was asking Becca to tell Joan about the lamp that had fallen, when a closet door opened by itself. Becca sent Tina back outside and continued speaking with Joan.

Tina was by the front door, waiting for Becca to finish talking to Joan, when suddenly the door slammed into her, knocking her onto her back on the front porch. Becca didn't see the door at the start of its movement toward Tina, but she saw it hit her—hard. Becca was convinced there was no physical way for Tina to be in front of the door and then slam it from behind with that kind of force. The fall left Tina dazed, further intensifying Becca's fears.

"I heard, felt, and saw the force of her impact when she fell," Becca said. "It was a powerful fall." There was no wind or other ordinary explanation for the door to swing shut like that.

I was stuck by several aspects of the occurrences as Becca explained them to me. They followed Tina's frustrating attempts to deliberately use PK on Richard Broughton's machine. I thought that Tina's efforts in the lab had built up energy that had now come to the surface. I noticed that the movements took place only when she interacted with Becca, and that nothing happened when Tina was by herself in an outer office. Several of the incidents revolved around phone calls to her mother. Added together, the incidents could have been Tina's way of telling Becca about her love-hate relationship with Joan and her guilt and need for self-punishment.

What alarmed Becca more than anything was how the hood of her car flipped open during their drive and how the car went into neutral. Becca sensed real danger and was terrified. But at the point when she felt most frightened, Tina said that a voice was telling her that everything was all right and that things would not happen anymore. Glad for any hopeful straw, Becca encouraged Tina to listen to the words and to feel what they were saying. This seemed to relax Tina, and the rest of the drive to my house had been uneventful.

After Becca left, Tina phoned Kelly to tell him about the day's events, but the phone cut off. This could have been normal interference, and nothing further occurred that day. The next morning there was another phone malfunction and then eight movements of objects, three when I was watching Tina. Fortunately, our porcelain and fragile belongings were spared. Only unbreakable or inexpensive items such as candles or things made of metal or wood moved. The message was clear: Tina's psychokinesis was still present and responsive to our needs.

The time for Tina's return to Columbus was approaching. Then, on March 31, Tina visited Jim Carpenter to play ESP and PK games with his daughter, Ferrell. Ferrell had a motorized three-wheel trail bike and Tina asked to try it out. Almost immediately she hit a tree and broke her left leg in two places.

Tina had a history of being accident prone, something Joan found both exasperating and a source for countless anecdotes. Tina's accidents, some of which were probably due to her problems with depth perception and balance, also had an element of self-hurt that seemed to be reflected by the psychokinesis, as when objects flew out and hit her. Tina's escapades had become part of the family mythology. One time as she was mowing the lawn, she stepped on her shoelace, tripped, and went over the handle of the lawn mower to land on the hot engine, smashing her nose. As painful and embarrassing as the accident was to Tina, Joan never ceased to find humor in the story, taking it as one more example of "What do you do with a kid like this?"

Tina's latest mishap with the three-wheeler resulted in two stays at the hospital and eight days of difficult mending in my home. During the twelve days Tina was in bed, there were no psychokinetic incidents. I went from being a parapsychologist to a paramedic. The damage to her leg was severe, and the best the hospital could do was stabilize it in an open cast until Tina could return home. Even using crutches was an exercise in pain, forcing Tina to stay bedridden with her leg elevated to reduce the swelling.

While Tina was trying to recuperate, reporter Joel Achenbach visited my home. His story on Tina came out in *Tropic*, the Sunday supplement of the *Miami Herald*, on May 20, 1984, and also in supplements to papers elsewhere in the country. Achenbach may have been hoping to witness the same kind of phenomena Mike Harden and Fred Shannon had seen, but all he got was a fidgety teenager snapping her hospital wristband and juggling a bottle of nail polish. Both items "flew," one of them landing at Achenbach's feet. Tina quickly apologized and said they were accidents because she was nervous at being interviewed. "Sorry," she said, smiling.

A few days later her parents and Craig drove down from Columbus to take her back home. With Tina's leg on a pillow, Joan asked every few minutes how she could have done such a thing. It was the longest drive of Tina's life.

# 16

# THE AMAZING RANDI

**B**efore James Randi left Columbus, he sent an arrow my way. He was giving a press conference about his theory of the Resch case and said, "Parapsychologists don't need to jog. They get enough exercise jumping to conclusions." To show what he meant, Randi set up some hoops to have me jump through.

The annual convention of the Parapsychological Association (PA) was scheduled for August 1984 at Southern Methodist University in Dallas, Texas. This scientific association was founded by J. B. Rhine at Duke University in 1957, the same year I came over to the United States from England, and he invited me to join the council as a European representative. Over the years I had presented most of my poltergeist investigations at the PA's annual conventions and in the written proceedings of these conferences, the *Research in Parapsychology* series.

In many ways Tina's case stood out from the previous ones because so many individuals had witnessed the phenomena. In addition to telling about my own observations, I wanted my colleagues to hear from the other witnesses, in particular Bruce Claggett, Mike Harden, Fred Shannon, and Becca Zinn.

The chairman of the program committee was my friend and fellow explorer of the poltergeist, Jerry Solfin, and the idea of a panel discussion appealed to him. But he had a suggestion: why not also invite James Randi? Randi was an entertaining and effective speaker with his mixture of fun, facts, and fiction. Including him would certainly make a lively addition to the panel. Jerry was aware that Randi had not investigated the Resch phenomena but that he thought he knew how they were produced—by fraud. Jerry thought that a magician of Randi's expertise might also provide some good tips about how such phenomena could be produced by magical tricks.

Fred Shannon was the only witness who managed to attend the PA convention in Dallas. The others sent written reports of their experiences. I sent copies to Randi, including my own. Randi ignored them all.

Fred and I gave our presentations before it was Randi's turn. He did not discuss Fred's written report, but directed his remarks almost exclusively to Shannon's photos, showing slides that he had copied from a selection of the thirty-six pictures Fred had taken during his visit to the Resch home on March 5. Without citing Fred's statements about what he had actually seen in the house, Randi told the audience how Tina could have produced the incidents by simple trickery.

I was amazed and distressed at what was in effect an attack on Fred's intelligence and ability to observe what was happening right in front of him. Randi did not propose that Tina was performing magical tricks but simply that she was throwing, pushing, or pulling the objects that moved when Fred and the others present were not looking. Photographic evidence is often considered especially reliable, and Randi used his slides to particularly good advantage because the pictures he used to build his case against Shannon were Shannon's own.

There was not enough time during the discussion to adequately reply to Randi, and he clearly won the day. I felt sorry that Fred had been the victim of Randi's attack. He had come to the meeting expecting to be among friends and to have his photographic work in the Resch home appreciated. Instead he was treated like a fool.

But Randi didn't reserve his sarcasm for Fred. In the paper Randi wrote for *Skeptical Inquirer* magazine the following spring, he turned the incidents of March 14 into farce: "Immediately prior to the rush of phenomena, Tina had spent some thirty minutes upstairs, alone (only the two of them so far as [Roll] knew, were in the house). Then she appeared at the top of the stairs screaming for him to rush up there and see miracles. A bar of soap, he reported, fell into the bathtub. Next, while they both were standing four feet from it, facing away, a picture fell from the wall. The nail had been pulled out of the wall. Roll and Tina rushed to it."

Randi is a master of sleight of hand. I have seen him place a small ball in one hand and have it turn up in the other. He is also good at sleight of word. You say one thing and he turns it into another. What I had actually said was that Tina and I had spent thirty minutes upstairs together before the events occurred. I did not say we were alone in the house, we weren't, but that we were alone upstairs. By placing Tina there by herself, Randi had her prepare the soap and painting incidents.

The scene where Tina screamed for me to rush upstairs to

"see miracles," Randi created out of thin air. It never happened. I was already upstairs and she did not scream for me; we were in the same room.

Randi then conjured a shower stall into a bathtub and made the soap, which had come out of the shower, appear in the tub. There is no tub in the Resches' bathroom. These are minor errors but they demonstrate a careless reading of my report.

In the next scene I became the straight man for Randi's jokes. "Roll described his own observing abilities in such a way that we must place his performance in the paranormal category . . . he saw the tape machine fly away from a position directly behind him."

I never wrote that I "saw" the tape recorder fly, only that it moved while I was hammering in the nail with Tina standing right next to me. If she had reached back, taken the recorder from the dresser, and tossed it, I am certain I would have seen it.

Having invented my description of the event and then disposed of it, Randi went on, "I postulate that, since [Roll] could not see the tape recorder, Tina had ample opportunity to throw it along the dresser, from which position it fell to the floor. Then she picked up the pliers as the two of them went to recover the tape recorder and threw them against the far wall as Roll examined the recorder." To back this up, Randi made a drawing of the path of the recorder and the layout of the room from a news video he had seen.

This took another magical feat. On his drawing, a solid piece of furniture in the Resches' bedroom has disappeared. Joan's toilet table, which was standing next to John's dresser, is gone. If the toilet table were conjured back, and if Tina had shoved my recorder along John's dresser, as Randi would have her do, the recorder would have landed on the toilet table, not on the floor. But the recorder moved about eight feet, not just off the dresser.

I didn't think it was possible for Tina to have picked up and thrown the pliers without my seeing it. With Tina on my left, away from the dresser, I placed the pliers on the dresser and then went to retrieve the recorder. There was no opportunity for her to pick up the pliers.

Having reduced my account to inanities, Randi dispatched me with a coup de grâce: "Roll is myopic and wears thick glasses; he is a poor observer." What could I say to this? One thing I can say is that I am not myopic but farsighted. Randi should have been able to make out what kind of glasses I was wearing. The photo that accompanied Mike Harden's story in the *Columbus Dispatch* about Randi's visit to the home showed us facing each other in the driveway, no more than three feet apart. The two types of lenses are distinctly different, and it's easy to tell them apart. Farsighted lenses magnify the eyes, nearsighted lenses make them smaller.

Randi judged me a poor observer and at the same time demonstrated that he couldn't see what was right in front of his eyes. I wonder what he would have seen, or not seen, had Joan let him in the house.

What Randi did have at his disposal were contact prints of Fred Shannon's photos. The *Columbus Dispatch* supplied him with all thirty-six pictures as well as some enlargements, probably the same enlargements the paper gave me. In addition I sent Randi the reports by Bruce Claggett, Mike Harden, and Fred Shannon, together with my own.

Steven Shore, the astronomer-physicist and fellow CSICOP member who had accompanied Randi to the Resches, had told reporters that the direction in which the phone was pointed in

Shannon's famous photograph (the twenty-fifth on his roll of film) violated the laws of physics because it did not show a "straight-line trajectory." Shore implied that Tina had picked up the phone and thrown it. Randi ignored the idea proposed by his scientific colleague, but came up with another technical term, *transverse blurring*. The cord, he said, displayed transverse blurring, which showed that Tina had picked up the phone and thrown it.

My enlargement of the same photo shows blurring of the phone cord, but it seemed no more transverse than lengthwise. Still the photo by itself does not prove that Tina hadn't thrown the phone. This issue could only be settled by the people who were present and saw what took place: Shannon and Harden. Fred Shannon only saw the event in his peripheral vision when he put the camera down and deliberately turned his face away from Tina and the phone. But Mike Harden, who was seated on the couch next to Fred, was facing Tina when the phone took off. In his report, Mike said he saw the phone in motion without its being aided in any way by Tina. Randi simply ignored Mike's report.

Randi did try to speak with someone he considered an important witness, Lee Arnold, Tina's caseworker, who had been in the house at the same time as Fred and Mike. Lee is seen in one of Fred's pictures, which Randi reproduced over the caption "The major witness watches as the phone 'flies' at her." Randi phoned Lee Arnold, he said, but she would not discuss the incident. Children's Services had asked her not to get involved with the magician.

Craig Resch appeared in three of the pictures. In one photo, Craig is looking in from the kitchen at Tina after the afghan blanket shot up from the floor and covered her head. In the same way Randi ignored Fred and Mike, he made no attempt to reach Craig for further information before writing his version of the events.

Randi was intrigued by "Miss 'X.'" Referring to the twenty-fourth photo on Fred's roll, Randi wrote, ". . . and there is a little girl—Miss 'X'—standing and watching on the right. She was an eyewitness to this event and shows up in five other frames as well." In the photo Fred shot after the phone incident, "Miss 'X' is looking at the camera as if wondering whether that throw was convincing." Randi also found "the ubiquitous and mysterious Miss 'X'" in three more photos. The Miss "X" seen by Randi in one of the shots is invisible to anyone else. To the normal eye, the picture shows only the legs of a large Raggedy Ann doll on the floor.

"Miss 'X,'" Randi suggested, "could reveal a great deal about Tina's actions during the time those photographs were being taken. But try as we may, no one will inform us how we may contact her. That is most unfortunate since her testimony might reveal very interesting data."

Miss "X" was probably also the only witness who might have believed in Santa Claus and the Tooth Fairy, beliefs that predispose one to see flying objects, according to Randi. Miss "X" was six-year-old Lisa. I did not ask Lisa about magical beings, but I found her down-to-earth about flying objects.

Randi saved his best shot at the flying phones for last. "It is the last of the flying telephones on Fred Shannon's film that really asks a great deal of our patience," he wrote, referring, with characteristic confusion, to the next-to-last photo in the sequence. Randi continues, "It shows Tina Resch seated in the chair, her pointing left hand extended to her right across her body. The telephone cord is horizontally stretched out and the telephone handset is so far away as to be out of the frame altogether. Tina is in a stance suggestive of a major-league baseball player completing a throw to first base. Now, with the simple principle of parsimony in mind, we must ask ourselves if we will choose to believe that this is a photograph of a girl being affected by poltergeist activities or a photograph of a girl simply pitching a telephone across the room."

He reproduced the photo with the caption "Tina appears to have been *holding* the phone base, and has *thrown* the handset out of the frame."

There is a problem with this explanation. Randi made Tina out to be a left-handed pitcher when in fact she was right-handed. If Tina were throwing the phone, as Randi would have us believe, why use her left hand? When she pulled down the lamp three days later, she used her right. With Fred Shannon and Mike Harden sitting directly opposite, Tina would need to be fast and adroit. If she had decided to throw the phone, it would have made much better sense to hold the base with her left hand and throw the handset with her right.

Except for one photo where Randi supposed Tina threw the phone with her right hand, in all other cases Randi had her use her left hand. He supported this unlikely scenario with the claim that the phone cords showed "longitudinal blurring." It's uncertain what this proves, but it has a nice scientific ring.

Randi next turned his ridicule toward Fred Shannon. Fred had discovered that the only way to catch the telephone in flight was to take his camera down and look away; he would then snap a picture whenever he caught a glimpse of movement. Sometimes he would get a shot of the phone as it flew past Tina, sometimes he would be too late, the phone having already fallen to the floor, and sometimes he would only get a picture of Tina squirming in the recliner. One such time Tina is shown holding the armrests of the recliner, a startled expression on her face as she leans back. As she does so, she must have accidentally released the footrest, causing it to pop out. In Fred's report there is no indication that he regarded this as anything unusual. This did not faze Randi, and he played the picture as further proof that Fred had been fooled. "While he snapped frame number 26, photographer Shannon, as he looked elsewhere awaiting a miracle, must have believed that something 'psychic' was happening."

Randi added a jab at Tina: "Her startled expression would indicate to me only what she has proven in the past—as in the videotapes—that she is an excellent actress."

In most instances the problem with Randi was his insistence that people had not seen what they said they saw. The most startling occurrence Fred claimed to have seen was the movement of the love seat. He was in the kitchen looking at Tina, who was perched on the arm of Joan's recliner, when he saw the love seat move some eighteen inches toward her. "I saw this with my own eyes. Tina registered shock. I snapped a picture but of course the couch had stopped moving by then and there's really not much to see in the photo."

The magician saw a great deal. "[In one of the photos] . . . we see a roll-away couch 'jumping out' from the wall at Tina, who is again startled at another wonder of poltergeistery.

"But examination of a small lower section of a previous frame . . . reveals an interesting fact: Tina clearly has her right foot hooked under the end of the couch! A sudden pull backwards and the couch would jump out at her easily."

An examination of the two photos shows fast footwork, not by Tina but by Randi. The first photo Shannon took in the house (the second on his roll) shows Tina holding up the wall clock, which had come down and hit her. She is standing near the place over the love seat where the clock had been hanging. The front of her right foot is indeed under the love seat, but flat on the floor, not "hooked." Later in the day, when Shannon said he saw the couch move out from the wall and snapped a picture, it showed Tina on the arm of the recliner opposite the love seat. In the next shot, she is toppling into the recliner.

To complete his tale, Randi transmuted the couch. With its hideaway bed, the couch was heavy, and it was planted on wooden pegs, not rollers. Randi made it into a "roll-away" that Tina could "easily" pull out with her foot. If Tina had in fact performed "a sudden pull backwards" with her foot, the likely outcome would have been a serious strain, not a movement of eighteen inches by the couch.

What of Fred Shannon's eyewitness description of this occurrence? Not a word from Randi about it nor any of the other incidents Shannon said he had witnessed. Yet Randi regarded the photographer as "the most important witness of the phenomena exhibited in the presence of Tina Resch." As for Bruce Claggett, who witnessed the lights turn on and the tape disappear when no one was near, Randi said only that Bruce "gave strange and contradictory accounts of the wonders in the Resch household."

Randi's only revealing observation was not about the incidents that Shannon and the others could not account for, but an incident no one had any problem explaining, Tina pulling over the lamp the day of the press conference. I did not see the video, which was taped by WTVN-TV (ABC), but Randi said he saw the part used for the broadcast plus a longer unedited version. The latter, as described by Randi, is important because it is the one instance Tina can be seen both setting up and performing an attempt at illusion.

The lengthy preparation and clumsy execution of this simple trick is in sharp contrast to the way the witnesses described the occurrences. The movements, they said, were fast, sudden, and often happened when they were watching the girl. The witnesses seemed to be sane and serious people. I didn't think that they invented what they told me. The incidents that took place when I was present convinced me personally that genuine psychokinesis was involved.

But the occurrences took place under informal circumstances in a private home, not in a laboratory. In my report to the media, I emphasized that my opinion was personal and I said, "This is not a scientific laboratory. It is somebody's home." I added that we hoped to do controlled testing with Tina in North Carolina.

Most of the witnesses were unwilling to be the butt of Randi's jokes. But he spoke to Bill Wolfson, a reporter from Cleveland who attended the press conference in the home. Wolfson said he saw a Styrofoam cup hurl itself off a table, but was apparently less certain after talking to Randi. "NBC-TV news reporter Bill Wolfson, at first fascinated by Tina's performances, changed his mind after prolonged exposure to events, contradictory reports, and reconsideration of what he actually saw — or didn't see."

Randi said that the occurrences around Tina, if genuine, would amount to "a repeal of the basic laws of physics." Physics does not say that objects cannot be affected without tangible contact. The moon revolves around the earth and magnets attract pieces of iron without visible contact. Recurrent spontaneous psychokinesis requires an extension of the laws of physics, not their repeal as Randi imagines.

# 17

## HYPNOSIS

It was October 1984, and there had been no further incidents in Tina's home since her return from North Carolina in April. Her stay had told me that the recurrent spontaneous psychokinesis, or RSPK, was not confined to the house in Columbus. But the main purpose of the visit, to demonstrate PK in a scientific laboratory, fell by the wayside when she broke her leg.

I phoned the Resches to ask if Tina could come back to Durham, and they agreed to a second visit. Tertius was back at Denison University, so Tina could use his room. I asked Becca Zinn if she would assist in another round of experiments, but Becca wasn't ready for more car trouble or flying objects. As a possible replacement for Becca, I contacted Jeannie Lagle, a psychotherapist I had met during a visit to West Georgia College (later renamed State University of West Georgia), where Jeannie had received her master's degree. We had discussed parapsychology and I knew she was interested in the topic. She was a skilled hypnotist and used it in her practice, an ability that was going to be important for our work with Tina.

Jeannie was a spirited brunette with shoulder-length hair, and high cheekbones inherited from an Indian ancestor. When I reached her in Kentucky where she was living with her husband and explained that I needed someone to act as companion, counselor, and trained observer of Tina during the five days of experimentation, she jumped at the chance. "Are you kidding?" she asked. The idea of working with Tina seemed "like a gift from the gods, an opportunity of a lifetime."

Back in March, I had taken Tina to the Spring Creek Institute in Chapel Hill to meet Stephen Baumann, a neurobiologist at the Chapel Hill campus of the University of North Carolina. In his spare time, Steve conducted PK tests at the institute, and he was building a machine to test people's ability to directly affect the nerve cells of a sea snail. Tina's results were promising and Steve had asked us to come back when his equipment was fully operational. Steve had curly, brown hair and a full beard. His serious expression would easily turn into a wide grin.

The evening before Tina's arrival, Steve, Jeannie, and I met in Tertius's room to review the tests we had planned. Steve's equipment was ready; the main problem now was whether there would be any PK to detect. If Tina's PK had vanished for good, her trip to North Carolina would be a waste of time. We then tackled the question of whether to use hypnosis to reactivate Tina's PK. Jeannie regarded the occurrences, including the sensations that went with them, as a form of behavior. She thought that the memory of this behavior might be brought back by hypnosis, and that this could result in renewed RSPK.

Hypnosis might also help to reduce Tina's fear and guilt about the RSPK and produce a supportive frame of mind for the intentional PK on Steve's equipment.

Tina arrived on October 18 with a short haircut and a purse with silverware. Back in Columbus, she said, she had been experimenting with bending metal as a way to test her PK. She said she had got the idea when the bowl of a spoon suddenly flopped down while she was eating. She knew about people who claimed that silverware could be bent or twirled just by rubbing the metal; sometimes the metal would even bend without being touched. After I had phoned the Resches to invite Tina back to Durham, Tina wanted to see if she still "had it" before coming, and she had intentionally bent a fork and three spoons, which she now carried with her. She also had a packet of cigarettes.

Both Joan and John had smoked when Tina was little, and one of Tina's favorite games back then was to sit on John's lap and pretend to smoke pretzel sticks. She would puff on the pretzels and tap them into an ashtray, saying she, too, would smoke for real when she got big. When John's doctor told him to stop smoking because of his bad heart, he and Joan gave up their cigarettes. Tina was not allowed to smoke at home, and smoking had become a way to both imitate her parents and rebel at the same time. Jeannie and I told her we didn't object as long as she smoked outside.

Later that evening Tina met with Jeannie, who then explained the plans for the upcoming experiments. She asked Tina if she wanted to try hypnosis. Tina said that she did; she wanted to understand what was going on. Jeannie then told her to select eight items from her purse to be used as RSPK targets. Personal articles, Jeannie thought, would have an emotional charge and be better than impersonal objects. Tina chose her toothbrush, hairbrush, lipstick, deodorant stick, the fork, and the three spoons.

The next morning, October 19, was sunny, and by noon the weather had turned hot. I had to leave the house for a few hours, and Jeannie worked with Tina outside the house away from our porcelain.

Tina brought her eight objects, and the two sat down across from each other at a metal table surrounded by a cement patio next to the swimming pool.

Tina said, "Something's going to happen." She said that she had the same weird feelings she often did just before something moved. Jeannie began with suggestions for relaxation and asked Tina to name the eight objects she had brought. Jeannie also asked her to recall a psychokinetic episode that wasn't threatening and to watch it in her mind as if she were watching a movie.

Tina replied that this was difficult to do. She said that all the events had been frightening and that many of the objects had struck her or someone else. Jeannie asked her to just stay connected to her body as she remembered the event she was concentrating on. When Tina acknowledged this image and feeling, Jeannie asked her to continue to pay attention to her body and to describe any area where she felt a heightened sensation. Tina's right hand moved to her stomach and she grimaced in pain.

"Are you feeling something there?"

"Yes," Tina said, "it hurts."

Jeannie instructed her in another minute of relaxation to decrease the pain. She asked Tina to concentrate on her stomach and suggested this would turn into a sensation of warmth, an easy task as they were sitting under a hot, noonday sun. Tina said she felt her stomach getting warm. Jeannie then asked her to mentally select one of the objects on the table. When she had done so, she was to name them all again.

Tina said she felt her chair was about to flip the way it did at home. Jeannie looked at the chair and assured her that what she felt was due to her own rocking. She asked Tina to visualize the movement of a target object while continuing to feel the warmth in her stomach. Tina fell into deep concentration, and Jeannie thought she saw an expression of fear cross her face. "Are you scared?" she asked. Tina said yes, she was scared.

For the next few minutes Jeannie and Tina talked about how frightening the past events had been to live with, and Jeannie suggested Tina try imagining them in a new light. She told her to think of how something soft and harmless like a pillow might move on its own and not hurt anyone.

Tina cocked her head to one side, as though listening to a voice other than Jeannie's. "I'm talking to my friend Tina," she said, referring to Tina Scott. "She's telling me not to do this. She's telling me that I am being used."

Without missing a beat, Jeannie suggested Tina take a few moments to talk with her friend and reassure her that she was safe. Tina closed her eyes, waited, and then said, "I told her I wanted to learn how to do PK so maybe other people could learn and we could help people who had the same trouble I did. When she heard that, she said it was okay."

Jeannie thought this was a good time for a break. As she and Tina were walking to the door to get a drink in the house, they heard a noise behind them. One of the spoons was on the ground about two feet from the table. Jeannie hadn't been watching Tina and thought maybe she'd picked up and thrown the spoon. They replaced it on the table and proceeded back to the house. As Tina approached the doorway, a sound again made Jeannie turn. This time she found the deodorant stick under a chair about six feet from the table. Jeannie was certain that all eight objects had been on the table before they left, and she had Tina walk in front so she could see her hands. Before they headed for the door a third time, Jeannie again checked that all eight objects were on the table, and again she kept Tina in front of her.

They had got as far as the kitchen when a clattering sound from the patio announced another spoon had fallen. Jeannie found it on the cement three feet from the table. When it fell, Jeannie was watching Tina in the kitchen, a wall separating them from the patio.

At about this time I arrived home from an errand to take Jeannie and Tina to Spring Creek. Jeannie told me what she had seen and asked me to watch while she and Tina walked from the patio table to the house, hoping for a repeat performance. Nothing happened, and I went to the car while Tina went back to the table. Jeannie remained in the hallway waiting for her to return.

As Tina approached the doorway, Jeannie saw something hit the back of her head. Tina cried out and covered her head with her arm. They found the fork on the ground outside the doorway.

"Stop hurting me!" Tina screamed. She flung the fork into the pool.

Tina had been in full view of Jeannie both before and at the time the fork hit her. Jeannie was convinced the incident could not have been faked. I wondered if Tina's failure to perform in front of me had made the fork strike her in self-punishment. In any case, it was time to leave.

❋            ❋            ❋

Spring Creek Institute occupied a suite in an office park on the main road between Durham and Chapel Hill. The modern, one-story red brick buildings made a nice contrast against the greens of the lawns and the pine trees that surrounded the complex. Besides Steve Baumann, two other people were working that day, Ed Kelly, the director of the lab, and Robert, a technical assistant. Ed's office was next to the room where Steve would conduct the experiments with Tina. Robert had a large workroom next to the computer room. The computer room was next to the experiment room.

Steve showed Tina the PK detection devices and explained the experimental procedure. He had arranged two tests, the first being with his sea snails. The snail, *Aplysia californica,* is about six inches long and is found along the coast of California. Steve kept his snails in a saltwater aquarium and extracted the neurons as needed for his experiments. The neurons Steve used were pacemaker cells that regulate the biological functions of the animals. He liked to work with these neurons because they were large and fairly easy to handle; they also continued to fire for hours after they had been removed. When I had gotten over the fact that the snails would die after their neurons were removed, the tests appealed to me. If Tina could affect animal neurons without tangible contact, perhaps she could do the same with humans. PK might supplement conventional medical procedures that treat the nervous system.

Tina's task was to slow down or speed up the firing of the neuron according to Steve's instructions. The neuron was placed in a saltwater solution on a slide under a microscope in front of Tina. It was monitored by a probe leading into a recorder that registered changes in the firing. A computer in the adjacent room would assess the results.

In Steve's second test for Tina, she would attempt to put pressure on a piezoelectric crystal. The word *piezo* comes from the Greek verb "to press," and piezoelectric crystals produce electric current when they are subjected to even slight pressure. This, too, was relevant to the question whether Tina's PK could contribute to healing. Piezoelectric crystals are found in the teeth, bones, and connective tissues of the body and also in rock formations. When the body is infected or injured, piezoelectric currents from the pressure bring on pain and alert the person to seek treatment.

Steve used two crystals. One was the experimental crystal on which Tina was to concentrate. This was suspended from the top of a bell jar. The control crystal was concealed on the bottom of the jar. Both crystals were monitored by probes leading to a recorder that would detect even the slightest pressure. The experiment would succeed if the experimental crystal showed a response while the control crystal remained inactive. If pressure was recorded from both crystals, this could be due to an extraneous source, such as vibrations of the test equipment. To reduce this possibility, Steve had mounted the piezoelectric crystals and the neuron detector on a heavy metal slab.

I waited in the conference room while Steve conducted the first experiment. Jeannie assisted by helping Tina focus on the two devices while envisioning success. After thirty minutes Steve announced a break. Tina was free to walk around while he stayed in the experiment room to prepare his equipment for the next round of tests. Jeannie and Tina had gone into the computer room and were just about to step into the hallway when Jeannie heard something hit the floor behind them. A six-inch screwdriver had fallen from the desk by the window onto the floor. It was 3:10. Jeannie watched as Tina picked up the screwdriver and defiantly replaced it on the desk. She was here to work with neurons and crystals, her action seemed to say, not pesky screwdrivers.

They turned to leave again, and passing the doorway, Jeannie heard the same sound; the screwdriver was back on the floor. This time Jeannie walked behind Tina and paid close attention to her movements. For the screwdriver to land where it had, Tina would first have had to pick it up and then throw it back over Jeannie's head. Jeannie was convinced Tina had done neither.

Two minutes later, Tina was placing the screwdriver in the desk drawer in the computer room when they heard something land on the carpet in Steve's office across the hall. Steve was still in the experiment room and his office was empty. Jeannie went into the office and found that five coins she had seen earlier on Steve's desk were now on the floor. Again, she thought, Tina could not be responsible. When the coins fell— a distance of approximately eighteen feet and on the other side of a wall—she had been watching Tina put the screwdriver away.

The occurrences seemed to upset Tina, and Jeannie suggested they continue their break outside where there was a concrete walk. Rising from the walk was a series of eight steps. They sat down on the fourth step, Tina on Jeannie's right. Tina placed her purse between Jeannie and herself and lit a cigarette. For the next few moments they talked and Tina smoked. Then Jeannie heard something hit the concrete at their backs. They got up to look and found Tina's hairbrush on the walkway at the top of the steps. Tina said it had been in her purse, and Jeannie recognized it as the brush they had used as a target in the hypnosis session earlier that day. When she heard the brush hit the ground, Jeannie was looking at

Tina and saw her left hand hold the cigarette while her right hand was on her right knee. It was 3:20.

At 3:30 they were back in the computer room standing in the doorway to the adjoining workroom and talking to Robert, the lab assistant. Jeannie caught a sudden movement out of the corner of her left eye and turned just in time to see a pen fall to the floor. Robert said it was his; it had been on a cart beside him in the workroom. The pen must have traveled about fifteen feet, flying over their heads to end up in the other room. Jeannie saw the pen land while Tina was standing next to her. She didn't think Tina could have thrown it.

Before they began the second set of experiments, Jeannie and Tina went into the rest room. This was situated along a hallway outside the suite of offices. Tina entered first and went straight to the mirror over the sink while Jeannie checked the room for loose objects. Tina then went into one of the stalls and Jeannie took the one beside it. To make sure Tina stayed in her stall, Jeannie had her put her foot in the open space below the partition and locked her own foot around Tina's. It was awkward, but Jeannie wasn't taking any chances. After a short while, a loud crash was followed by a strong fruity odor. Jeannie came out of her stall to find the floor covered in shattered glass and red deodorizer liquid. She looked up and saw that the lid to the deodorizer's plastic container, which was attached to the wall above the mirror, was raised. When they had entered the rest room, she had noticed the container and saw that it was closed. Jeannie climbed up on the counter; the box was empty. Since Jeannie had been with Tina outside the stall and held her foot while inside, it was impossible for Tina to have faked the incident.

When Jeannie gave me her account of these events, she

noted that the bottle fell at 3:35 and was the last of the occurrences. I couldn't figure out why the bottle should move except that Tina was "hot" and the bottle was the only movable object in the room.

Tina and Jeannie returned to the lab, Tina completing the second and last part of the PK tests for the day. When they were finished, Steve came to join me in the conference room. There were promising signs that Tina was able to affect the snail neurons, but problems with Steve's test protocol made the results difficult to evaluate. Jeannie and Tina were still in the hallway when they heard a noise, followed by a loud bang from the now empty experiment room. At the sound of the noise, Steve and I rushed in. The test devices were intact, but in the wall on the other side of the room was a half-inch gash. This and the bang were apparently caused by a square, one-volt battery weighing about a pound that had been on the table with the PK detectors. Steve said he had seen it there a few minutes earlier. It must have sailed twelve to thirteen feet across the room, hit the wall, and landed under a table. Steve was certain the gash was fresh.

Robert was alerted by the activity and came in from the workroom to see what was going on. Tina was still in the hallway, and as Robert went over to talk to her, he was startled by a noise. A nine-inch crescent wrench he had seen only moments before on his work cart in the workroom was now on the floor behind him. The wrench had moved at least eight feet. The time was 4:42, one minute after the battery incident.

It was getting late and we had had enough flying objects for the day. The North Carolina State Fair was in Raleigh for its annual visit, and we had promised Tina an evening at the fair. As we were leaving the building and Tina was at the front door, Jeannie heard a rattling sound on her right. A black rubber bag attached to an anesthesia machine was swinging back and forth as if waving good bye. The machine was four feet away from Tina, well out of her reach. We then went to the fair and watched the carousels and rides, all moving objects, but none that went by themselves.

No tests were planned with Steve for the following day, so we stayed out late, giving Tina free rein to enjoy herself. The next morning Jim Carpenter took Tina to his office to play a computer PK game called Psychic with his daughter, Ferrell. Tina was also scheduled to take the Rorschach inkblot test as well as the thematic apperception test (TAT). I had asked Jim to give her the tests in the hope that they would uncover the emotional tensions I thought must be behind the occurrences. Jim expected that the Rorschach would tell him about Tina's emotions and intelligence by the way she interpreted the colored inkblot designs. In the TAT, he would show her black-and-white pictures of people in ambiguous situations and ask her for an interpretation.

Tina spent most of the day with the Carpenters. Besides administering the psychological tests, Jim had set up a few targets for her RSPK. Before picking Tina up at my house, he had placed two objects on the desk in his office, a pencil sharpener and a metal figure of a unicorn. Hoping, but hardly believing, the items would move, Jim left Tina and Farrell together to play their game.

While the girls played on the computer, a loud noise came from an office across the hall. Ferrell went to investigate and found a light fixture on a bookshelf. Ferrell had seen it on a shelf above the computer before the game. The computer was on a desk in a narrow space between two offices, and Tina was sitting farthest from the office where the fixture landed. Tina could have picked up the fixture, but she could not have taken it into the office without interrupting the game and passing Ferrell. If she had thrown the fixture from her position by the computer, it would have hit a wall.

Ferrell returned to the computer, Tina working the keyboard and looking at the monitor. Suddenly, the two objects Jim had placed on his desk appeared in the computer area. Again, a wall was between the starting position of the objects and where they ended up.

Like some of the objects at Spring Creek, the light fixture, sharpener, and unicorn must have turned corners to land where they did. The pencil sharpener and unicorn also revealed a new and unexpected feature—they had been on Jim's mind rather than Tina's. Tina had no idea that Jim had chosen the two items as PK targets and may not even have seen them. Instead of objects that were significant to her, she had apparently activated items that were important only to someone else.

Jim and Ferrell brought Tina back home, telling me there had been several other incidents, some involving telephones, but I'd have to wait for the details; they needed to get home. After they left, Tina was too excited to go to bed, and Jeannie said she could take a swim. In the meantime we had a beer. Tina wanted one, too, but Jeannie reminded her she was underage. She could tolerate Tina smoking, but she drew the line at serving alcohol to a fourteen-year-old. Tina pleaded, saying she was allowed to have beer at home, but in vain. Instead, Jeannie told her to get ready for bed.

I was on the phone to Jim, who had called to ask if there had been any more activity, when Tina went into the kitchen, followed by a crash. Jeannie's empty bottle, which she had placed on a counter, lay shattered on the floor.

"A bottle just fell and broke," I told Jim, explaining that Tina couldn't have done it because I was looking right at her and she was only about five feet away. Jeannie was also there and we could both see Tina's hands. It was 10:30.

Anticipating more incidents, we decided it was better that Tina stay in the pool area than in the house. Tina was still full of energy and excitement from her day with the Carpenters, and she let off steam for the next three-quarters of an hour by performing a series of highly energetic dives. Finally Jeannie announced it was bedtime. As the three of us went into the house, there was a crash behind us. We turned and found the pieces of a second bottle on the hallway floor. It was evidently my bottle, which I had left on the patio table. Five minutes later, as we were sweeping up the glass, a third bottle crashed on the patio. Tina and Jeannie went to their rooms a short while later and the incidents stopped.

Afterward, when Jeannie and I had a chance to discuss things, we agreed that the broken bottles reflected Tina's irritation at being denied a beer. At the same time they followed our admonition that only objects of no value be affected.

Soon after Tina woke up the next morning, October 21, Jeannie went to Tina's room. The room was below the living room and overlooked the woods behind the house, where the trees were showing their fall finery. As Jeannie and Tina stood talking, they were interrupted by something landing on the floor in front of the bookcase. It was Tertius's silver-colored plaster-of-paris candlestick, which had been on the corner of a chest of drawers close to where Jeannie was standing. She returned the candlestick to its place. One minute later she saw the same candlestick in the air above the head of the bed and saw it drop to the pillow. She and

Tina were standing in almost exactly the same positions as before.

The first time the candlestick had moved six feet; this second flight went four feet farther. Tina was standing quietly, her hands by her sides. Jeannie took the incidents in stride; by this stage she was getting used to objects that could fly on their own.

# 18

# HARNESSING THE FORCE

Tina had a degree of control over the events, insofar as only inexpensive objects were affected rather than Steve's delicate test equipment or the porcelain in my house. She also seemed capable of focusing on specific objects that we had selected without her knowledge. We decided to test this ability formally by setting up an experiment in the conference room. Steve chose about a dozen tools and lab supplies as PK targets and placed them on the conference table. Most were small and fairly light, including a plastic level, a box of drill bits, a hose clamp, an L bracket, and an AA battery. An exception was a twelve-inch socket wrench that must have weighed a pound or more.

With the targets in place, I thought this could be my chance to film an object in motion. My experience in the Resch home had told me that nothing would happen within camera range if Tina knew that she or the objects were being filmed. To prevent detection, I concealed my video camera in an unused testing console and focused it on the table. Unfortunately I had not consulted Steve about my plan, and he felt it was unethical to film without Tina's permission. I showed Tina the camera. "What do you think?" I asked. Tina was clearly upset, and after some hesitation she said the camera would be okay; but I could tell she wasn't happy.

Besides Tina, only Steve, Jeannie, and I were in the lab that day. For the next two hours we waited for an object to move, Tina's mood steadily going downhill. Finally Tina announced there would be no incidents because "it" did not happen in front of cameras. I turned the camera off, but Tina's sulky mood remained the same.

Jeannie tried to help by taking Tina into another room for a hypnosis session. We knew that the first four incidents Jeannie had witnessed followed hypnotic suggestion, leaving little doubt that this had led to the movements. As before, the suggestions Jeannie gave Tina included three components: a request to Tina for movements of objects; attempts to trigger the movements by evoking the bodily sensations that had accompanied earlier incidents; and assurances that Tina would be safe if the movements started up again.

When they were finished, there were three events involving nontarget objects while Tina wasn't supervised. Then at 5:10, while Steve was in the experiment room and Tina and Jeannie were outside Steve's office, Jeannie heard a noise. She looked in the empty office and found the hose clamp on the floor. Even if Tina had gotten away from Jeannie, she couldn't have stolen the clamp from the target table since I was sitting by the table guarding the objects. To land where it did, the clamp must have taken a left turn down the hallway and then another left turn into Steve's office, a distance of about thirty-three feet.

After the clamp, a roll of wire also landed on the floor in Steve's room and in almost the same spot. The wire wasn't a target but came from a table at the far end of the room, about eight feet away. When it fell, Tina was with Steve and Jeannie, her back to Steve's office and her hands on the doorframe.

I left for home at 5:24, and Jeannie and Steve went into the conference room to pack the camcorder, careful to keep Tina away from the table. At 5:35 a loud noise behind Tina sent Steve and Jeannie to the storeroom down the hall, where they found the socket wrench. In a powerful show of force, the wrench had careened nineteen feet, apparently flying right past the three of them, then curving right, hitting the door, and falling down inside the room. A deep dent in the door explained the noise. At no time did Tina have the opportunity to pick up the wrench without either Steve or Jeannie seeing her do so. When they later reported the incident to me, I wondered if it was connected to Tina's irritation about the camcorder, which Steve and Jeannie were packing at the time. Although we had eventually turned the camcorder off, just seeing it again may have brought back Tina's earlier feelings of not wanting to be taped; emotions strong enough to send the wrench flying. It was a dramatic conclusion to the day.

On October 22, the last day of testing, a small object moved a great distance. After the first experimental session with Steve, at 1:31, Jeannie and Tina were standing by the desk in the computer room, Tina searching for her plane ticket in her purse, when Jeannie heard a sound at her back. She turned and saw movement in the paper that was hanging from the computer's printer. At the same time she discovered the plastic level on the floor below the printer. Evidently the level had first hit the paper. When Jeannie had heard the sound, she had seen that both of Tina's hands were in her purse. I was certain that Tina had not been near the conference table. The level must have moved some forty feet, first taking a left turn and then a right. At 1:50 and 1:51, a hose clamp and a pen moved when Tina was not observed, so it was possible that she had picked them up. Neither object was a target.

Jeannie and Tina went into Steve's office so Jeannie could use his phone. They were sitting on his desk next to each other, Jeannie talking on the phone and Tina holding Jeannie's free hand with both of hers when there was a loud noise across the room. Steve, who had also heard the sound, came in and found his pocketknife on the floor. It had been on his desk, he said, behind Jeannie and Tina, about twelve feet from where it landed. Tina might have picked up the knife but could not have thrown it since she was holding Jeannie's hand. The time was 2:01.

A minute afterward, while Jeannie was still on the phone and Tina was still holding her free hand, there was a noise from the hallway. Steve checked and found a metal bracket from his computer that had been in a drawer in the computer room. Tina could have picked up the bracket sometime during the day, but she could not possibly have thrown it. At 2:14 Jeannie's attention had momentarily strayed from Tina when a pair of scissors moved.

Then Steve's wallet hit Tina. The wallet had been behind her on the desk, next to the knife. Jeannie actually saw the wallet slap Tina on the side of her head. It was 2:16 and Tina was becoming distraught; Jeannie felt a relaxation exercise might help calm Tina down and also reduce the number of occurrences.

I was still sitting in the conference room guarding the target table when Jeannie brought a very upset Tina in to join me. Keeping her a safe distance from the table, we had Tina sit down in front of us by the window. Within minutes, two of the targets, an AA battery and an L bracket, hit the window above her head. Neither Jeannie nor I saw Tina make any suspicious movements.

I had conflicting feelings about the recent spate of occurrences. I was glad there were incidents that we could vouch for, but I was worried that the disturbances would continue after Tina had returned home. If the disturbances resumed in the home, they could be attributed to our work with Tina. Far from helping the Resches, we would have further disrupted their lives.

Tina's mood was mixed. She was clearly unhappy about going home, and she was agitated by the upswing of occurrences. I thought her depression about returning had brought on the increase. I speculated that many of the occurrences were Tina's way of communicating with us. Whatever she was uncomfortable or incapable of saying with words, her psychokinesis could express. I wondered if that's what was going on now. Was Tina asking to stay by showing that she could still produce PK?

She got up from her chair by the window and went to the door to the hallway, Jeannie and I following and still making sure she kept her distance from the table. Tina stopped, and as we sat down by the table watching her, there was a sound behind us. A drill bit from the box on the table had landed by the window where the battery and the L bracket had fallen, some ten feet from its box, which had remained on the table.

One more incident occurred at the institute when Tina was

unobserved, and also one at my house when she said she was hit by a stone. The next day, October 23, Jeannie and I took her to the airport. It was Tina's fifteenth birthday.

When Tina came to North Carolina, she was mostly with people who appreciated the occurrences and had become fond of Tina herself. I thought that, for this reason, we were favored with incidents. The occurrences at Spring Creek Institute usually took place when we were looking at her, talking with her, holding her hands, or for the incidents in Jim Carpenter's office, playing a computer game with her. Even when Robert, who was not a member of the research team, interacted with Tina, his pen and crescent wrench moved into the area where they were talking.

Two factors suppressed the activity: sleep and deliberate attempts at psychokinesis. During the four nights Tina stayed in Tertius's room, the things on his dresser and bookcase remained in place when she was asleep. But just being awake did not ensure PK. When Tina was concentrating on the crystals and neurons at Spring Creek, there were no incidents. They occurred only during breaks in the tests when she was no longer focused on the PK tasks. It seemed that release of effort to produce PK on demand opened the door for its spontaneous expression. Tina's psychokinesis was active as soon as she stopped concentrating and was able to relax.

I had asked Jim Carpenter to give Tina TAT and Rorschach tests so I could learn more about her. When I received Jim's report, I sent a copy to the Resches.

"Tina was a fourteen-year-old girl at the time of testing," Jim's report began. "She was at the center of a storm of apparent RSPK activity, and of controversy about that, during the time testing was carried out. She was several hundred miles from home, under parapsychological observation and receiving psychotherapy, while staying at the Roll home."

Jim continued, "Tina was cooperative during the testing. Her rather large vocabulary showed good mental ability, but the quality of her percepts on the tests showed emotional immaturity, and a particularly immature understanding of other people and interpersonal needs."

Tina's world, Jim said, is "unpredictable, chaotic, periodically very distressing. Nothing hangs together in a normal, organized, reliable way. It seems quite an apt reaction to a world in which static objects might fly around, fall down on one, hit one in the back of the head, etc. At the same time, these themes in Tina's testing are so pervasive, and are so often tinged with human content, that I don't think they're just responses to a few months of RSPK activity, no matter how disturbing. These themes are congruent with such activity, but they represent much deeper and older currents of neglect, danger, neediness, and insecurity. It would appear that for a long time Tina has experienced life as frustrating, neglectful, and possibly abusive; and if the RSPK phenomena are genuine, they may in part be an extremely odd but emotionally consonant expression of these same deep and troubled themes.

"On the TAT," Jim said, "several themes emerged that seem to color her perceptions of others and of herself in the world of people. There is a general tone of unhappiness. Parents are seen as having high expectations and of being critical and disappointed in a child whatever the latter tried to do. The disappointment is mutual, as longed-for approval doesn't transpire. Mother, in particular, is seen as potentially nurturant and more or less reliable, but she too is more often disappointed than not."

Jim turned to the Rorschach. "Tina's perceptual style shows a tendency to overgeneralize in her thinking, and to miss complexities and discrepancies. She tends to jump to conclusions about things, and to oversimplify them, and the emotional coloring of events is always rather like that of a much younger child. Still, her contact with reality is basically sound, and there is no evidence of psychosis."

Like many others, Jim had wondered whether Tina had faked the incidents. "Some motives for such faking are certainly present. Tina is highly conflicted internally and is relieved by creating stirs of activity so that conflicts can be avoided. She is also starved for loving attention, and would enjoy being the center of attention and seen as special. A strong coloring of notoriety wouldn't bother her at all, and would even fit in with her generally negative self-concept. Does she have the planfulness and sneakiness and ability to conceive complicated tricks (such as would seem to be required by the more amazing RSPK observations)? This part is harder to believe. Tina would not be above creating confusion and perhaps even pulling tricks to get attention, but she would not appear to be planful enough to figure out how to do complex chicanery. Some of the events observed would seem to require very complex chicanery, if they were contrived. On the other hand, could these be the results of someone who is honestly plagued with RSPK events that are as disturbing to her as they are to others? This certainly seems possible."

Tina was confused, Jim said, "about boundaries between the self and others and between the self and surroundings." The process of individuation where the child learns to distinguish itself from its surroundings had been disrupted for Tina.

As a result, the threshold for psychokinesis may have been lower for Tina than for other children. A similar confusion might be seen in Tina's relationship with others. Joan evidently thought little of her adopted daughter and Tina followed suit. Her identity was interwoven with Joan's and she was compelled to value herself the way her mother valued her.

Comparing my own observations with Jim's report, I could see that the movements of objects reflected three emotions: anger at her parents for not loving her enough, self-aspersion because she wasn't good enough to be loved, and the hope that someone would come to rescue and love her. The occurrences hurt her parents because their belongings were destroyed and their lives disrupted; the occurrences hurt Tina herself because things often hit her. But many of the occurrences were rewarding to Tina because witnesses such as her brother Craig, Bruce Claggett the electrician, and photographer Fred Shannon all appreciated the displays and let Tina know they regarded her as somebody special.

That same regard continued when Tina joined us in the lab. We had reached a major goal when she was able to induce the movement of chosen target objects and to do so in a scientific setting. This goal could not have been achieved without the aid of Steve and Jeannie, but Tina was the central figure, and we valued her contribution. My only regret was that I had no video record of the occurrences. This would have added to the evidence for RSPK and could have thrown light on the nature of the energy. I decided to make up for the deficiency as soon as possible.

My first opportunity came nine months later, in the last week of July 1985. After months of being tutored at home, Tina had returned to school with mixed results and was now on summer vacation. In December a story about her had appeared in *Reader's Digest,* making the other students resent and fear her; she was glad to be out of the classroom and back in North Carolina.

Jeannie was available to assist me, and the Psychical Research Foundation now had its own space, Spring Lake, a two-story log house near Durham, nestled among trees and overlooking a lake. Before the foundation moved in, Spring Lake had been a training center for the Patricia Hayes School of Inner Sense Development. I had met both Kelly Powers and Becca Zinn there. Patricia had moved her center to Georgia so the building was vacant.

According to local legend, the house dated back to the Prohibition era and had been a hunting lodge for the New York Mafia. The main room was commanded by a cavernous stone fireplace with Indian arrowheads and ax heads that had been found on the property and were set in the mortar. The house was dark and seemed gloomy at first, but the log structure and the natural setting soon made it feel cozy and homey.

To prepare for the next round of tests with Tina we placed a table with target objects between the living room and the dining room. There were thirty-seven objects, seven belonging to Tina and the rest mostly small household items. We chose the place because there was a grille for air circulation in the ceiling where I could install my video camera upstairs while Jeannie stayed downstairs with Tina.

We began by inviting friends and colleagues to Spring Lake for a "metal bending party." This seemed a good idea because the incidents at Spring Creek were preceded by Tina's report of metal bendings at her home. Jeannie brought several eating utensils and asked those present to choose what they felt they could bend. She had first tested the utensils for strength and rigidity. Encouraged by the ease with which Tina twisted the spoons and forks between her fingers, we looked forward to an impressive display of PK.

Our experience at Spring Creek told us not to expect anything to move while Tina was concentrating on a target. The incidents seemed to happen afterward when Tina was relaxing. Jeannie then led Tina through a hypnosis session similar to those in the first study. She asked Tina to stay focused on her body and to allow the objects to move free of fear or anxiety. She asked Tina to select three of the targets and to choose a location where she wanted each to land. Tina was to concentrate on an image of each target in the new location for fifteen minutes, after which there would be twenty-five minutes of conversation and unplanned activity away from the table. This was when we thought the objects might move.

There were no incidents the first day, and Tina discovered the camera toward the close of the session. When there were no incidents the second day either, I took the camera down. The third day, July 29, while Jeannie was with Tina, two objects moved soundlessly to the chosen locations. But because they moved without the usual falling or crashing sounds that would have enabled us to pinpoint their distance from Tina, we were unable to tell if the incidents were genuine. The following day there were two events when Tina was not supervised. That was it.

In contrast to the Spring Creek episodes, there was no real evidence of psychokinesis at Spring Lake. Tina seemed less motivated to perform. During the hypnosis sessions, she repeatedly said she wanted objects to move "quietly and softly" if at all. She was now fifteen, and her interests had changed. The enthusiasm she had earlier expressed for bringing her PK under voluntary control now centered around clothes and her social life back home. Her coordination had also improved, reducing her jerkiness and showing that she had more control of her body and perhaps less excess energy for psychokinesis. But her boiling point was still low. One time when Jeannie annoyed her, Tina swung at her. Jeannie saw it coming and ducked. I was standing nearby and received the blow instead. It broke my glasses.

# 19

# TRIGGERS AND CAUSES

As impressive as Tina's abilities were to me, they were still a puzzle whose pieces I hadn't been able to fit together. Searching for answers, I remembered an intriguing connection I had come across in the work of Michael Persinger. Persinger, a renowned neuropsychologist at Laurentian University in Ontario, has found that geomagnetic disturbances interfere with ESP. Beginning on March 1, 1984, and lasting for the three days that followed, a magnetic storm had swept through the earth's atmosphere. Tina's RSPK began March 2. The first incidents were malfunctions of the baby's heart monitor and other electrical installations in the house. Tina's confrontation with her father the night before may have been unleashed by the same powerful forces.

Magnetic flares from the sun are known to affect life on earth. Radio transmissions are commonly disrupted during an increase in solar activity. In 1989, magnetic storms above

Quebec caused a wide collapse of the power grid, leaving 6 million Canadians without electricity. Reports of automatic garage doors opening and closing on their own followed in the storm's wake, and sightings of the northern lights showed up as far south as Key West in Florida and Mexico's Yucatán Peninsula.

The human body is immersed in the earth's magnetic field, and the brain is sensitive to changes in this field. The disturbances are associated with sunspots, dark areas on the sun that are due to magnetic eruptions. But while geomagnetic flares seem to hinder ESP, they may be the spark that starts the RSPK engine. When Persinger examined the timing of the occurrences around Tina, he found that they began during an upswing of geomagnetic disturbances.

Persinger's discovery was not unexpected. I had previously studied all the published RSPK cases I could find where the evidence for RSPK seemed strong and where the dates of onset were reported. Of the thirty onset dates, twenty-two were during heightened magnetic disturbances. The likelihood that this arose by chance was three in one hundred. The study, which was done in the early 1970s, was coauthored by Livingston Gearhart, a professor of humanities at the State University of New York in Buffalo. Gearhart had found that uncommon animal migrations and other unusual behavior tended to occur on days of higher than average geomagnetic disturbances. He thought that RSPK might follow the same trend. Some years later Gearhart and Persinger repeated the study of geomagnetism and RSPK using a larger number of cases and reported a significant correlation.

Persinger's regular work focused on ways to treat epilepsy. He used epileptic rats to understand the disease and had found that the rats were more likely to have seizures on days with increasing disturbances in the earth's magnetic field. He believed the same might be true for people.

I had already suspected that the brains of RSPK agents generate the same kind of electromagnetic surges that bring on epileptic attacks. To test this theory I examined all the cases I could find where people from outside the family group had witnessed at least one occurrence that seemed beyond normal explanation. I restricted myself to cases that had been published in reputable journals and books and where the people could be identified. There were ninety-two; of these, twenty-two had symptoms that seemed suggestive of epilepsy. They ranged from a young man with grand mal, the type of epilepsy in which the whole body goes into convulsions, to people with milder symptoms that could be complex partial seizures (CPS). An additional twenty-seven individuals had other medical or psychological problems. The number of people with CPS or CPS-like complaints would probably have been higher if everyone had been tested by neurologists, which few of them had.

The connection between geomagnetic eruptions and RSPK was making sense. If RSPK and CPS were initiated by the same or similar brain processes, I thought they might be affected by the same environmental conditions. Before I met Tina and only knew that she might be the center of RSPK, I suspected she had CPS and suggested to the Resches that they take her to a neurologist. They did so in March before my arrival, with a follow-up in May. John Corrigan reported that her brain-wave record showed no epileptic spikes. But the exams demonstrated occasional muscle jerks, blinking, twisting, and incessant finger movements. Persinger analyzed the neurologist's reports and thought that Tina may have suffered from a mild form of Tourette's syndrome. Tourette's is characterized by tics, such as eye blinks and shoulder jerks, and by compulsions to curse and utter profanities. Like CPS, Tourette's tics and vocalizations are due to involuntary and recurrent electrical discharges of brain neurons.

Persinger found that adolescents with Tourette's are often hyperactive and show attention deficit. This was consistent with reports by Tina's teachers of constant movements and lack of concentration on her tasks, for which they insisted she take Ritalin. They and her parents also said Tina was verbally abusive. Temper tantrums, extreme mood swings, extreme anxiety, depression, irritability, and self-abusive behavior, such as scratching oneself, are common in Tourette's children. Tina showed the same behaviors.

Tina had an urge to express herself that she could not suppress. At home with Joan this often caused her to be "loud" and brought on demands for quiet, which released torrents of loud and foul language. This would lead to a slap on the face, or when Tina became too big for Joan to handle, a beating from John.

Communication with her mother was a one-way street for Tina. She was frustrated when her attempts to speak up for herself were met by a deaf ear. Other children can swallow their hurt, but that was not an option for Tina. Her brother Craig once asked her why she couldn't just shut up. No matter what Joan said, Craig advised, "Just don't say anything back."

For Tina, that was impossible. It wasn't right—it wasn't fair what Joan said to her. Verbal explosions and at least one physical attack on Joan were her ways of dealing with being rebuffed. Tina's urge to express herself even in the face of punishment was consistent with Persinger's diagnosis and was one of the pieces in the puzzle of her RSPK.

Many Tourette children do not attend school because of

difficulties with teachers and peers. Tina's disruptive behavior in class and constant harassment by the other children made Joan take her out of school when she was twelve. Home tutoring brought her into constant contact with her parents, who had no idea that her "mouthy" behavior might have a neurological basis. Instead, they tried to control her outbursts with punishments and the removal of privileges, including refusing to let her attend church or Girl Scouts meetings. When this didn't work, they locked her in her room or tried beating her into submission. None of this had the intended outcome, and it only intensified Tina's anger. With the anger came the conviction that her adoptive parents didn't love her, and that they didn't love her because she wasn't worthy of love. This must also be the reason, she thought, her birth mother had abandoned her in the first place.

Tourette tics frequently disappear when the child is asleep; similarly, Tina's RSPK was never displayed while she was asleep. The tics and aggressive vocalizations also often disappear when the child is away from home, but reappear when back. The excitement of being in a different environment apparently overrides Tourette's syndrome. As I knew, this too was true for Tina; there were no reports of RSPK at church or Scouts, nor during her first few days in North Carolina or during the trip to Florida.

I think Tina's RSPK may have been a form of Tourette's where the tics and explosive behavior occurred outside her body in the form of object movements and banging sounds. If electrical discharges in the brain could trigger CPS or CPS-like symptoms like Tourette's, as well as RSPK, I had to ask myself why the effects were confined to the body in most children with CPS or Tourette's but occurred in the environment for Tina. The most plausible explanation, I thought, would be different wiring in the brain neurons of people with and without RSPK. The cluster of neurons most likely to be involved could be in the brainstem, because this is where instructions pass from the brain to the rest of the body.

I suspected that an anomaly in Tina's brain stem diverted the signals away from her muscular system to external objects. The involvement of the brain stem was also suggested by the fact that Tina's RSPK was a daytime phenomenon. Structures in the brain stem control the circadian rhythm, the cycle of daytime versus nighttime functioning.

The autonomic nervous system was probably part of the process. This has two branches of neurons, the parasympathetic system, which dominates during sleep and relaxation, and the sympathetic system, which kicks in during physical activity and mental arousal. Since Tina's RSPK mostly occurred during the day and seemed to be associated with emotional arousal, this told me that her RSPK in all likelihood was a response by the sympathetic system.

Emotional arousal is processed by the limbic system, a network of structures below the cortex that we share with other species. This system also operates below the level of awareness. It includes the amygdala, which processes emotions, and the hippocampus, which accesses long-term memories. Since the RSPK seemed to express Tina's emotional memories, this pair of structures was probably involved as well.

When Tina had her third neurological examination in May 1984, she mentioned frequent headaches at the back of her head (in the occipital region where visual input is processed). The headaches were daily during the RSPK period but abated afterward. She also described persistent coldness and spells of daydreaming.

The neurologist thought Tina might have a lesion in the

left side of her upper brain stem in the area of the pons, the large bundle of nerve fibers connecting the two halves of the cerebellum, which coordinates muscular movement. He based the diagnosis on intermittent twitching of Tina's left eyelid, lower than normal saccade movements of her eyes when she gazed to the left, lower sensitivity to pain on the lower left side of her face, and other anomalies on the left side of the body. This was consistent with my expectation that aberrations in the brainstem may facilitate RSPK.

We had tested this idea during Tina's visit to North Carolina in October 1984. Toward the end of her stay, Steve Baumann brought her to his laboratory at the University of North Carolina, with Jeannie and me in tow. He used a standard test to look for anomalies in the upper brain stem, the BAEP test, which stands for "brain stem auditory evoked potentials." This is simply a hearing test where clicking sounds are fed into the ears one ear at a time and the electric responses to the clicks from the auditory nerve that serves the ear are recorded. Aside from hearing problems, the BAEP can detect multiple sclerosis and brain tumors in areas that are adjacent to the auditory pathway. Steve used scalp electrodes to record the responses from the two auditory nerves, much like an EEG examination.

Steve discovered abnormally fast transmissions of electrical signals from the pons area in Tina's brain stem. The pons, he said, may be involved in focused arousal where "attention is temporarily locked onto specific aspects of the environment," in Tina's case perhaps to objects that were emotionally significant to her and others. Steve said that the faster streams of electrical impulses may have amplified Tina's capacity to focus on objects.

Could the electrical impulses cause stationary objects to

move? This did not seem possible. There had to be another source of energy on which Tina drew that could cause objects to move. But I couldn't imagine what it might be.

I had come to a blind alley until I heard a talk by physicist Hal Puthoff at a conference at Princeton University. Hal was director of the Institute for Advanced Studies in Austin, Texas, a group of physicists and engineers who are attempting to extract energy from the vacuum of space. Hal had also studied remote viewing, a form of ESP, and was coauthor of a book about his experiments.

Hal's talk turned on a light in my head. According to modern physics, he said, objects are not only composed of energy and matter, they also contain information. Physicists no longer think that information is a one-way street from object to observer; it also goes the other way, from observer to object. An object is not a blank slate, but has been written on by people who have previously interacted with it. When we are exposed to an object, we are exposed to the previous writings.

This fit what I knew about RSPK. Put in the context of Tina, the moving objects she affected had been colored by other people such as her parents, Bruce Claggett, and Fred Shannon, and the investigation teams in her home and in North Carolina.

I had known Hal for many years, and after his talk I wrote him asking for more information on his work with this newly discovered source of energy. In his reply he said that what seems to be empty space is actually not empty, but is filled with an infinite sea of electromagnetic energy. Physicists call this force "zero-point energy" or ZPE because it remains active at absolute zero when other activity is stilled. Hal's group was exploring the ZPE as a source of energy for space travel.

The ZPE interacts with gravity, so if it can be extracted, space-craft would be able to travel as far as desired.

Gravity is the force that attracts objects to the earth near its surface. When a cup is dropped to the floor and shatters, gravity is to blame. Closely related to gravity, inertia is the force that causes stationary objects to remain at rest and moving objects to remain in motion. For example, Hal wrote, if you stand on a train at a station and it leaves with a jerk, the force of inertia may cause you to topple backward. Inertia is due to pressure from the ZPE. The ZPE has also been detected in the lab. Boundless and nonpolluting, it's the perfect fuel.

I was ready for the idea that RSPK might be due to harnessing the ZPE. In a lecture I gave the previous year in Germany, I said that RSPK may involve "transient suspensions of the earth's gravitational field . . . in proximity to the RSPK agent." The idea occurred to me after I had watched a TV clip from the Mir space station and seen things that were not fastened down float about in the cabin. Perhaps the objects near Tina had also escaped the pull of gravity.

Hal's goal was to extract energy from the ZPE using the technology of physics. He thought that people like Tina may do so inadvertently and without technical tools. The force is everywhere, connecting us to the farthest parts of the galaxy and to the coffee cup on the table. In science fiction, Hal pointed out, it is "the Force."

In Tina's case, once the objects were freed of gravity, they themselves may have contributed to the energy that made them move. The information they contained was emotional information, and the emotions were in conflict. In many of the incidents, two opposing emotions seemed to be at work: Tina's intense need to be accepted and her intense anger at being rejected. Tina desperately needed others, especially her mother, but she also craved to express herself and needed her mother to accept this. I speculated that the energy from these opposing emotions may have built up an energetic charge not only in Tina, but in the objects as well. I speculated that this charge was released by movement when the objects had been freed of gravity and inertia.

The process may have been initiated by electromagnetic bursts from brain neurons due to accumulated psychological and social stress. Tina's history, together with her neurological and psychological profiles, attests to the power and pervasiveness of the tensions in her life. The attention-seeking, sometimes aggressive character of the disturbances seemed to bear this out.

The energy would not have to be sustained for long periods of time but would be brief in the manner of seizurelike eruptions. Brief, involuntary, and recurrent discharges of energy were consistent with the spasmodic character of the movements and the explosive sounds.

The electromagnetic energy that may underlie RSPK is not the impersonal energy of traditional physics. RSPK energy has an informational side that includes people's emotions. As the term suggests, emotion entails motion. The motion can be "in the head," or it can take place in the external environment. Overt motion is usually accomplished by the body's muscular system but may also occur in the absence of this, as in Tina's RSPK.

Emotions can be complex, but they have a feature in common: they serve the survival and well-being of the individual, its group, and species. If we allow that animals lower on the scale of evolution also experience emotion, this would be true for them as well. But there are no reports of mysteriously moving objects around animals, nor around very young children. RSPK seems to be restricted to humans with mature brains.

The occurrences around Tina showed a feature I had seen in other RSPK cases I had studied. The number of object movements declined with increased distance from wherever the individuals displaying psychokinesis were at the time. Except for the Sunday while Tina was at church, there were eighty-seven incidents where I or the other witnesses knew Tina's position and the location of the objects before they moved. Using a tape measure, I had measured the distance between Tina and the starting position of each object. I then separated the objects into five-foot groupings according to how far each object was from Tina before it moved, that is, 1–5 feet from Tina, 6–10 feet, 11–15 feet, and so on. I had used the same procedure in other cases.

The distribution of the eighty-seven events showed a clear decline: 48, 18, 11, 5, 4, 0, and 1. The decline was statistically significant. To exclude the possibility that there were more movements of objects close to Tina simply because she threw them, I was careful to only include incidents that were vouched for by observers from outside the home.

My discovery of a decline was important because it suggested that Tina's RSPK resembled familiar kinds of energy. But the numbers were mute about the kind of energy that was involved. To shed light on the matter, I went to an expert on energy, William Joines, professor of electrical engineering at Duke University. Joines, who had collaborated in my earlier studies of RSPK, believed that RSPK is due to psychic energy or "psi waves" that can transform to electromagnetic energy, sonic energy, and other forms of known energy.

I first worked with Joines when the Psychical Research Foundation was a sponsored program at the Duke Department of Electrical Engineering. A tall, kindly, and soft-spoken man with a Southern accent, Joines wore glasses and had a vision problem that made him look at everything sideways. When he wanted to focus on an object, he had to move his face to the side as if he were seeing something beyond the material thing.

Hal's vacuum theory of RSPK enabled Joines to be specific about the energy that might be involved and therefore the type of decline to expect. If psi waves with an electromagnetic component were transmitted from Tina, they should spread out like light from a point source. They should also be attenuated from traveling through the space between her and the object. In technical terms, the decline should follow the "inverse function" and also the "exponential decay function." This in fact is what Joines found. When he applied a mathematical formula that incorporated both kinds of decline, the formula fit precisely the distribution of occurrences around Tina. Joines's analysis supported the ZPE theory of RSPK.

The incidents also showed focusing, the tendency for objects and areas to be repeatedly involved. For instance, the love seat and the phones in the Resch family room moved more often than other things that were equally close to Tina. Joines pointed out that psi waves with an electromagnetic component should concentrate in objects and areas. The love seat and telephones may have carried intense emotions for Tina and thereby led to a focusing on these objects. The love seat was her place in the family room, but she felt unloved by her family. The repeated disturbances of the phone and the screeches that interrupted conversation may have been Tina's way of saying that she had no real connection with people.

Our studies threw light on several factors that may have contributed to Tina's RSPK. According to Jim Carpenter, Tina did not make a sharp distinction between herself and her surroundings. She was prone to dissociate, which may have contributed to her alienation from people, and her poor depth perception made it difficult for her to manipulate things. RSPK may have been a form of overcompensation. She experienced deep tension in her relations to others and had an overpowering need to express herself, but was punished when she did, which increased the stress. The night before the occurrences began, her fight with John may have brought the stress to the breaking point. Tina's brain was already susceptible to Tourette-type discharges, and she had a brainstem anomaly that may have increased these discharges and focused them on significant objects. Finally, a geomagnetic storm may have tipped the scales. The puzzle behind Tina's psychokinesis was beginning to fall together and make sense to me. Now all that remained was what it would mean to Tina.

# 20

# NO ESCAPE

"**W**eirdo." "Freak." "Outsider." It seemed to Tina she had heard those words her entire life. Just before her sixteenth birthday, Tina couldn't listen anymore. She slit her wrists and was taken to a psychiatric ward for teens at the Medical College of Ohio.

In the past Tina had tried every ploy at her disposal to free herself from the Resches' control. She had fought them, blanked them out, run away from home, competed with her siblings, and finally disrupted their world with her RSPK. None of it had won them over to her side. The suicide attempt was just the latest in a long series of self-destructive behaviors.

Tina was released from the hospital on December 24, 1985. Before she went home, a hospital counselor made the mistake of telling the Resches they were Tina's biggest problem. The information only deepened the resentment each party felt for the other, and the blame level increased. Not only had Tina destroyed their belongings, their livelihood as foster parents, and John's health, but now they were being called bad parents.

Early on, Tina's adoption had appeared to be a success. Golden-haired and precocious, Tina quickly became "Daddy's girl," scrambling onto John's lap every night when he came home after work, helping him clear the yard of snow, admiring his tattoos. Then, almost overnight, it all stopped. Suddenly, Tina was out in the cold. The change in the Resches' affections was so abrupt, Tina was left reeling. From being the family darling, she was demoted to sleeping in a locked basement. All she could ask herself was, Why? Why didn't the Resches love her anymore? What had she done?

Confused and frightened, Tina could only assume that it had something to do with not measuring up to the Resches' own children. Joan was especially critical: Tina was messy, Tina was loud. Peggy and Pam, Kevin and Craig—her older children—hadn't behaved like that; they were good. Even Jack, the Resches' adopted son, behaved better than Tina.

The more she was nagged and punished, the more anxious she became. Childhood fears took on life-threatening proportions: fears of the dark, vampires, and being stabbed all made bedtime particularly horrific. Tina could not sleep without dozens of stuffed toys in the bed. One by one she surrounded herself with a cushioned barrier against both her real and imagined adversaries. The sheer number of animals she required became a danger in itself. One night Tina nearly suffocated when a teddy bear got too close to a night-light, caught fire, and filled her basement room with smoke. She escaped disaster by picking the door lock and running upstairs to tell her parents the house was on fire. The Resches took the toy animals and stored them in trash bags in the attic.

Life with the Resches went from bad to worse. Tina had trouble following the rules, and the rules in the house were rigid. If her bed wasn't made correctly before she left for school, she would come home to find the entire bed stripped—spread, covers, and sheets wadded up in the middle of the mattress. In her closet the hangers and clothes had to face a certain way, Joan's way. If one item was incompletely buttoned or carelessly placed, out came every article of clothing onto the floor. The same for clothing in the drawers. Anything that failed to pass Joan's inspection resulted in the entire contents of the drawer or chest being dumped to the floor to be refolded and replaced in the approved manner.

School was as bad as home. From the start, Tina was labeled "different," the underlying message being not "creative" or "special," but "bad." Her physical appearance didn't help matters either. Ignoring contemporary fashions, Joan insisted Tina wear, at least in public, clothing from an earlier decade. While the other girls wore straight-leg jeans and miniskirts, Tina had to wear bell-bottoms and skirts below the knee. As minor as these discomforts may have been from Joan's perspective, to Tina it was torture to stand out and be called Dork Girl. Joan's response to Tina's pleas to "fit in" was to tell her that what others did was their own concern; Tina wasn't them.

Joan may have believed she was helping Tina by taking her to counselors and acknowledging what they thought was hyperactivity and attention deficit disorder, or ADD. But along with her readiness to seek out professional help for Tina there was a personal hostility toward the girl that kept Joan from being genuinely caring or concerned. Her need to control Tina's behavior overrode any feelings she might have had to occasionally bend the rules or make allowances. An example was Joan's attitude toward sugar. Because of the possible link between ADD and sugar consumption, Joan went to the extreme of denying Tina any sweets or desserts whatsoever. Tina began to crave sugar to such a degree she would get up in the middle of the night and eat sugar straight from the bowl. At Tina's school it was customary for children with birthdays during the school year to celebrate with a party in the afternoon. Joan told the teachers to exclude Tina. While the other children ate cake, Tina sat in the hallway. She also had to stay in the hallway during Halloween, Easter, and Christmas festivities. The same strictness applied whenever Tina was invited to out-of-school functions: she wasn't allowed to go. Eventually the invitations stopped. Joan kept Tina home even when her own family wanted her to visit, only this time she used the excuse of Tina's bad behavior. Joan told cousins, aunts, and uncles that Tina was being punished and couldn't leave the house. The excuse became so frequent they, too, gave up and stopped asking to see the girl.

Tina began to wish she had never been adopted and even to wish she had never been born. The urge to find her "real" mother ran through her life like a burning red thread. She felt the Resches had never wanted her, and she dreamed of being accepted and loved by her biological family. Pestering Joan for the name of her mother was also a way in which she could get back at her without being overtly punished. But Joan knew how to fight back; no matter how much Tina begged or pleaded, she refused to share any information concerning Tina's birth mother. When Tina passed the breaking point, Joan found that the easiest route to peace was to ask John to give Tina a thrashing.

Hounded by both parents, Tina learned to blank out when she was scolded or beaten. Afterward she would have no memory of the confrontation, nor of anything else except that she felt relaxed. She also learned that a show of indifference when-ever Joan took away privileges such as Girl Scouts, church at-tendance, or wearing jewelry would soon make Joan lose interest in punishing her.

The week I spent with the Resches made clear the anger between Tina and her parents, but there was no evidence that Tina had been abused in any way. Yet later I was to learn that the same year Tina had left school to be tutored at home, her older brother Jack had begun to molest her in her room at night. Only twelve at the time, Tina had tried to tell Joan, who refused to believe her. To Joan, it was one more example of Tina's unacceptable behavior: now she was telling malicious lies about her brother.

With Joan turning her back on Jack's violation of his sister, Tina's sense of abandonment increased. By the time she turned fourteen, Tina accused Jack in front of Joan. Jack ad-mitted what he had done, and Joan grudgingly accepted the truth. But Joan never hinted to either Kelly or me that some-thing as traumatic as this had happened to her daughter. Tina herself kept the abuse a secret. But it was always under the sur-face. Together with her father's violence, it would affect her life choices for years to come.

In January 1986, the Resches sold the house on Blue Ash Road. The next few months with Tina were difficult, and Joan and John decided the only solution was to to put her back into foster care. At sixteen, Tina would normally have been placed in a group home, but nothing was available at that moment. Franklin County Children's Services told the Resches Tina would have to wait at a juvenile detention center until some-thing better came up.

Tina had no idea what Joan and John were planning, but

now that the house was sold, she also didn't want to live with her parents any longer. She had recently met a young man named James Bennett, who worked at a convenience store. James lived with his mother, Estella, and when he heard about Tina's battles with her parents, he offered Tina a place to stay. Tina accepted and went to live with the Bennetts in their Columbus apartment.

To the Resches, this was just one more example of Tina's out-of-control behavior. They decided she had to be detained for her own good. On a day while Tina was out of the apartment, a truant officer showed up at the Bennetts' door with papers for Tina to appear in court. Her parents were going to place her in the detention center, and they needed to go through the proper legal channels.

James drove Tina to the courthouse where she was to meet the Resches and a referee from the court. Columbus law allowed for parties in disputes of this nature to first meet with a referee before they reached actual court proceedings. Joan and John spoke to the referee first, describing the grief and embarrassment Tina had caused them over the years, and how they now wished to relinquish their parental rights. The referee asked Tina if there was anything she wanted to say, but before Tina could open her mouth, James broke in and announced that he and Tina were legally married. Tina was shocked into silence. Even the Resches were left speechless. At the same time, Tina wondered if she should just play along. Anything was better than the threat of juvenile hall.

The referee wanted proof of the marriage, which James claimed had taken place in Pensacola, Florida. James knew that the Ohio long-distance telephone services were down, making it impossible for the referee to call Florida. Tina was then asked to produce the marriage certificate. Taking her cue from James, she said it was packed away because she and James were planning to move, and besides, no one had said to bring it with her to court.

The Resches were livid. They knew the entire story was a lie, but had no way of proving it. Sixteen was the legal age for marriage in Ohio, so there was nothing they could say about Tina being too young. Because Tina had complied with the court order and had showed up on time, the referee gave her thirty days to produce a copy of the certificate, which would then be placed in her file.

Driving back home with James, Tina had a crisis of conscience. As much as she wanted to avoid life in what was essentially jail, she was filled with remorse for having lied in court. Despite her angry outbursts and difficulties obeying the strict rules laid down at home, Tina held to a strong moral code. Lying in court was wrong, and Tina felt bad for having done so.

James disagreed and a fierce argument ensued. James thought Tina was being stupid. Listen, he told her. If Tina married him now, they could divorce when she turned eighteen. It was either that, James said, or she could go live on the streets. Tina had run away enough times to know what street life was like, and she didn't want any part of it. But to get married, she needed her parents' signatures for the marriage license. Asking them for help was not something she looked forward to.

Just as Tina had expected, the Resches took the news badly. Joan cried as if her heart would break, and even John had tears in his eyes. Joan insisted that Tina was making a big mistake. Tina countered that if they didn't sign the papers she would walk out the door and they would never see her again.

"Don't you care that we're crying?" Joan asked.

"Why should I?" Tina replied. "I've been crying for years and nobody's cared. So it's your turn; cry and maybe you'll see how I've felt all these years."

There was no way out of the predicament. The Resches still believed the best place for Tina was the detention center, but to Tina the option was far worse than married life with James. Finally, the Resches signed the papers and Tina returned to James.

It was a jump from the frying pan to the fire. In place of any teenage fantasies Tina may have harbored about a white wedding and a caring husband, it was back to the courthouse for a cursory ceremony and marriage to a man Tina later described to me as "a monster." That night James reminded Tina of the bargain they had made. He told her that he owned her now and she had to do whatever he said for the next two years.

While they were married, James's tumultuous and abusive behavior sent Tina running to women's shelters and even to the hospital. When she came home, the fighting would start up again and the cycle would repeat itself: James becoming angry, Tina running, then coming back for more of the same. She was only seventeen years old.

In March 1987, John Resch succumbed to the last of his many heart attacks. A few weeks later, Tina's grandmother, the one person Tina knew loved her unconditionally and whom she called Tippy Toes, passed away as well. John left Tina $5,000, which James promptly took. Now that he had her money, James let Tina go seven months earlier than in his initial plan, and she divorced him.

With James out of her life, Tina took steps to find work and share living arrangements with friends. She began dating a young man she had met at church. The relationship had no real foundation and they soon began to drift apart, but not before Tina had become pregnant. Uncertain about her future but desperate for a family of her own, Tina decided against an abortion. She also decided not to ask the baby's father for child support or to tell him he had a child. On September 29, 1988, at the age of eighteen, Tina gave birth to a healthy baby girl. She named her Amber.

# 21

# AMBER

On June 28, 1990, I found a message in my college mailbox from Tina. She had phoned from Columbus and said, "Same thing that was happening in the laboratory is happening again."

I hadn't seen Tina for five years. Much in my life had changed during that time. Muriel and I were now divorced, and I had moved to Carrollton, Georgia, when Mike Arons, the chair of the Psychology Department at West Georgia College, had invited me to teach parapsychology. Mike and I had met a few years earlier at a parapsychology convention in Durham. My research and ideas were a natural fit with his progressive humanistic program, and we became good friends.

Carrollton is a small, friendly community filled with private lakes and heavily wooded properties. Some sixty miles west of Atlanta, it is far enough away from the big city to feel like a retreat, but not so rural as to lack amenities. It is here that I met and married Lydia, a psychotherapist originally from Hawaii who shared my interest in parapsychology.

Jeannie Lagle, the therapist who had worked with Tina using hypnosis, had also moved to Carrollton when her own marriage had ended. Having obtained her master's degree at West Georgia, Jeannie still knew people in the area, which made it a good place to come back to.

When I returned Tina's call, she said that two of Amber's toy balls had bounced around on their own, and pieces of silverware had bent by themselves in the drawer. Then unexplained fires started up in the bedroom, bathroom, and in Amber's crib. Tina was worried Amber might get hurt.

She told me she had married again, for Amber's sake as much as for hers. Larry Boyer, a kind man before marriage, became a wife-batterer afterward. A beating that had left Tina unconscious and badly bruised had forced her to have him arrested. Larry had promised to reform, Tina said, and she still felt attracted to him, but she knew it wouldn't work. She needed to put distance between them, and to be with people she trusted. I suggested she and Amber move to Carrollton. With Jeannie and me here, she would be with friends. The climate was milder than in Columbus, and the more relaxed lifestyle would be better for Amber than the city.

Tina had some idea about what life in Carrollton would be like. During one of her visits to North Carolina as a teenager, she had traveled with me to Carrollton to participate in a psychology conference Mike Arons was hosting at the college. Mike's wife and daughter, Sandrine, had even had a brush with Tina's RSPK the afternoon she'd visited their home.

Tina was a couple of years older than Sandrine, but the age difference hadn't prevented the girls from enjoying each other's company. Another girl, a college student, was also at the house. The three were busy conversing about everything from clothes to RSPK when Tina said her stomach hurt and that she was worried because "that's how things started." Sandrine was worried, too; her parents had nice things and she didn't want to stand by and watch them break. She told Tina that they should go outside.

Just as Tina was heading for the door, an ashtray that had been on the edge of the kitchen counter hit her in the back, causing her to cry out. Sandrine didn't see the ashtray fly, but that weird things were happening made her more anxious to get Tina outside. As the girls were going toward the glass door to the deck, Tina was hit by a small Mexican figurine. Again, Sandrine didn't see the figurine actually move, but she did see that it was lying on the ground. She put it back where it belonged, then it hit Tina a second time. It almost seemed as if something didn't want Tina to leave the house. After a painting and a silver mask fell down from the wall, Sandrine was relieved when her mother took over and sent Tina out to the swimming pool.

I reminded Tina she would be among friends in Carrollton. She said she would come for a visit to see if the move would work. The visit went well, and soon after she moved down with the baby. To start with, Tina and Amber alternately stayed with Jeannie and with Lydia and me. When Tina got an apartment of her own, we would baby-sit Amber during some weekends to give Tina a rest from motherhood. An active and inquisitive toddler, Amber would pull the tails of our two dogs, chase the cat, and get into our closets. One closet below the stairs she took for her own, calling it "my apartment." She kept some of her toys there and we added a little chair and table.

Amber was a charming girl and easy to care for, at least when her mother wasn't around. With Tina present, it was as if a switch were thrown in her little head. She got into con-stant trouble, opening the refrigerator, heading for the stairs to the basement, pushing a chair to the kitchen counter so she could climb up. Her behavior was not difficult to explain. Get-ting Tina to scold and punish her was Amber's way to engage her mother. When Amber was calm, Tina enjoyed the peace and paid little attention to her daughter. Then Amber would get into some mischief, Tina would scold her, and when this had no effect, run after and grab her, sometimes pulling down her pants and slapping her behind.

Amber never cried when she was punished. It seemed that the punishment had become Amber's way of knowing that her mother cared for her, and she sought it out. Tina was raising her child in the only mold she knew, her own. In front of my eyes, I saw Amber turn into another Tina. I knew that if Amber was to avoid her mother's torturous path, she needed a different upbringing. Carrollton Tech offered parenting classes, and Tina agreed to attend.

Tina turned her life around. She added nursing and com-puter courses to the parenting classes. She was able to get a rent-subsidized apartment not far from Adamson Square, the center of Carrollton. The brick house was one story and the three rooms were newly painted and well kept. Her backyard faced a public playground that Amber often used. When Tina and Amber moved in, their friends helped them furnish the place; Lydia and I contributed a couch.

To top it all off, she met and started dating David Herrin, another divorced parent. A friendly, good-looking young man, he held down two jobs, as a truck driver and a supervisor in a warehouse. He, too, had a three-year-old daughter, a playmate for Amber. Tina's friends told her how lucky she was.

Both Tina and David had light brown hair. David had a

short, trimmed beard. They seemed a good match, and for the six weeks they were together, David brought an element of stability to Tina's life.

After his divorce, David had rented a trailer about ten miles from Carrollton. Sometimes Tina and Amber would stay with him there, or else they would go to Tina's apartment in town. Tina often visited Jeannie to talk or to work on Jeannie's computer. David would then take care of Amber when he wasn't working. The arrangement worked well, I thought, until Tuesday, April 14, 1992.

I was in New York on business when I received a call from Lydia. "Amber has died."

I was stunned.

Lydia said that Amber had died the night before while Tina was visiting Jeannie and David Herrin was baby-sitting. I decided to go home immediately.

I was equally appalled when I got home and saw the headline in the *The Times Georgian* for April 16: "Mother, Boyfriend Charged in Girl's Death."

The story went on, "The mother of a three-year-old girl who died at Tanner Medical Center Tuesday night and the woman's boyfriend have been charged with murder. An autopsy showed Amber Bennett Boyer died of bleeding in the brain and swelling of the brain, according to Captain Mike Bradley of the Carrollton Police Department. Amber's pancreas was also bleeding and her head and face were badly bruised. 'It always seems worse when it involves children,' Bradley said, 'but this is some of the worst I've ever seen.'"

There was a picture of Amber in the newspaper with the smile I knew so well, lips slightly down, a smile that could also become a frown. Her blond hair was shorter and less wavy than when I had last seen her three weeks before, when Tina had called me with an emergency. She said she had lost her wallet with the money for rent and her food stamps. She only had food for a few more days, and if the rent was not paid by March 24, she and Amber and their furniture would be put out on the street. Could I help?

I had assisted Tina before when she needed money, but this time I thought David should be able to help. Tina said he was broke. I then suggested she call her caseworker at the Carrollton Department of Family and Children's Services, and Tina said she would.

Next time she called from a pay phone. Her telephone had been disconnected because she couldn't pay the bill. She said she had not been able to reach her caseworker and didn't know what to do about the rent and food. I phoned the caseworker, who said she would do what she could and asked me to bring Tina to see her.

I took Tina and Amber to two Family Services on Monday, March 23, the day before the rent was due and when the refrigerator was nearly empty. Tina received a generous supply of food but no cash, so I paid the rent. One of the food services was in the same building as Head Start, where Tina had intended to register Amber for day school in the fall. They told us that registration was the following Monday, and Tina said she would bring Amber back. This would be the first step in Amber's education and would free Tina for her own studies.

The crisis behind and the future looking good, I asked Amber where she wanted to go for lunch. She chose her favorite, McDonald's. Tina and David couldn't drive past a McDonald's without Amber standing up in her car seat crying out, "French fry, Mommy!" Now while Tina and I watched, Amber flung herself on the carousel and the other minirides, taking bites of hamburger in between. Mother and child were happy. A sign of improving family life and less stress for Amber was that she was finally free of diapers. I felt good for both of them.

When Tina called the following week, she said they were both fine. But now, two weeks later, Amber, so full of zest, lay bruised and dead.

# 22

# MURDER

On Tuesday, April 14, Tina had borrowed David's car and was visiting Jeannie. David was again baby-sitting Amber. He said he had fed Amber lunch, after which she felt drowsy and took a nap. When he tried to awaken her, she didn't respond. There was no phone in the trailer, so David rushed to a neighbor's house and tried to call Tina from there. But she had already left Jeannie's and was on her way to the trailer. She arrived ten minutes later. Tina called Jeannie, who said they needed to go straight to the hospital; she would meet them there.

Tina and David brought Amber to Tanner Medical Center at six-thirty that night. Amber was unconscious and was placed on life support. It was too late; she couldn't be revived and was pronounced dead.

The police questioned David and Tina most of Tuesday night. David said he hadn't hurt the girl, and Tina said she hadn't either. What she did say, though, was that the previous Thursday she had found her daughter "banged up" when she got home. David explained to her that the injuries were caused when Amber had fallen off the curb outside of Tina's apartment, busting a lip. Amber said the same. Then on Saturday, Amber had new injuries. Again, David said Amber had fallen, this time down the steps from his trailer, hitting her head and cutting her cheek on the gravel. As before, Tina asked Amber if this was true, and Amber said, yes, it was. Since Amber showed no fear of David, Tina believed he was telling the truth. As best she knew, he had never hurt Amber, nor had he ever laid hands on Tina herself.

Tina told the police she knew about the bruises from Thursday and Saturday, but she didn't think they were serious as Amber continued to be her usual lively self. While she had no reason to suspect David, her daughter had died while in his care. The child also had a new injury to her lips. Without any other explanation, Tina thought David must have killed her.

David, for his part, said he had never seen Tina injure Amber but had sometimes seen her slap the child. She must have hit Amber too hard earlier in the day, he said, causing her death several hours later. When the police asked David why he hadn't called an ambulance when he couldn't arouse the child, he said he was too confused and worried.

Throughout the night, the police continued to question David and Tina, noting that in all three of her interviews, the information Tina gave them remained the same. But by David's third interview early Wednesday morning, his story took a bizarre twist. The interview was conducted by Captain Bradley and Deputy Culver, monitored by Detective Thomas. They informed David that Amber's body showed signs of having been sodomized. What could he tell them about that?

David appeared shocked; he couldn't tell them anything. The police told David that it would be better for him to tell the truth. Amber had died not from the molestation, they said, but from being beaten. But they still needed to know if David had molested Amber. David kept insisting he could never do such a thing, but then, all of a sudden, he said it was true; he had sodomized Amber on two occasions, once at Tina's apartment while she was asleep, and once at his trailer. He also said that Amber hadn't cried, and that he had hit her once in the face.

Wednesday morning, the police charged David, and Tina as well, with murder and cruelty to children. The murder charge brought with it the threat of the death penalty.

The chance that David as well as Tina would be sent to the electric chair was not a remote possibility. Right from the beginning, two leaders of the county, District Attorney Pete Skandalakis and Sheriff Jack Bell, seized hold of the case in their bids for reelection. Skandalakis made no secret of his being in favor of the death penalty, a position shared by many in Carrollton.

The day of the funeral, the charges against Tina and David were reported in *The Times Georgian*. That Tina had been with Jeannie when Amber died was not mentioned, nor that she had been with Jeannie the two previous times when Amber had been hurt.

Sheriff Jack Bell, who was in charge of the Carrollton jail, announced his intention to run for reelection in the same issue of the paper. "I became the sheriff to make Carroll County a safe place to live for my children and my grandchildren to grow up here," Bell said.

He also commented on Amber's murder: "It was just one of the saddest things you ever want to see. Her little body was so bruised all over, you couldn't tell it was the same child."

The next several issues of the paper focused on child abuse. "Carroll County Child Abuse Stats Alarming," pronounced one headline. From 1987 to 1989, the article said, the number of child abuse cases in the county jumped almost 92 percent, as compared to just over 16 percent for all of Georgia.

A detective accompanied Tina to the funeral home for a private viewing before the actual service. Crying and scarcely aware of what was happening, Tina was brought up to the casket where a chair had been placed for her. She was allowed to sit down while the casket was fully opened, revealing Amber in her Easter dress and socks.

Something about the child's hair bothered Tina: the bangs were oddly combed. She reached out to smooth them down but was told she couldn't. The same thing happened when Tina began to straighten Amber's dress: "Leave it alone." Tina asked why. "Just don't," she was told. Tina began to cry harder, saying that Amber was cold and needed a blanket, and that she couldn't understand why her chest was so hard. Her questions were met with silence. A few moments more and it was time to go. As she was hurried out of the room, Tina quickly leaned down and kissed her daughter good-bye.

The next thing she knew she was sitting in a corner of a jail cell with a headache, banging her head against the wall and screaming. The noise brought two officers to the cell, and she was taken to another room where a chair was pulled from the wall and Tina was told to sit. If she didn't calm down, they said, she wouldn't be allowed to attend the funeral.

She was then driven back to the funeral home where she was instructed not to cry or get upset. Carrying a Bible, Tina sat to the side, hidden from view, when she heard someone begin to sing. Regardless of what she'd been told to do, Tina couldn't stop the tears. She was grabbed by the arms and taken back to the car.

Before the day was over, Tina saw Joan one last time; she had come down from Columbus for the funeral. Walking down a hallway, Joan and her oldest son, Kevin, were about to pass Tina without seeing her. "Mom!" Tina called out. Joan seemed startled. Together with Kevin, Joan and Tina went into a small room for a final visit. Still holding on to her Bible, Tina sank to the floor and put her head in Joan's lap. She couldn't stop crying. Kevin noticed the Bible and told her she was going to need it in the days to come. He then asked her if she had a lawyer. Tina didn't know the answer. "You're in a lot of trouble, kid," Kevin said.

Tina and David were to be tried separately. Neither could afford an attorney, so public defenders were appointed. Tina's lawyer seemed determined to put up a serious defense. But after several months on the case, he was suddenly dismissed. I was told that District Attorney Skandalakis had discovered that he was related to someone in Skandalakis's office and that it would be conflict of interest if they were on opposing sides in the case.

Spring passed, then summer. Jeannie, Mike Arons, and I visited Tina regularly in the Carroll County jail. This was not a good place to be. In September, Tina got the flu and asked for medicine to reduce the fever and relieve the pain. She received neither. After recuperating on her own, she was given an injection against the flu, now several days past. The same month Tina lost a filling from a tooth and got a bad toothache. When she asked to go to the dentist to have the filling replaced, she learned that the only available treatment was to have the tooth pulled. I spoke to Sheriff Bell, saying I was willing to pay a dentist. Bell said he couldn't change the rules. Tina lost her tooth; it was just the beginning of a long period of sheer torment.

On Monday, September 21, Tina found that her T-shirts and socks were gone, evidently taken by another prisoner. She reported the theft to the guards, who made a search of the other female inmates' cells. Tina's clothing didn't turn up, but a quantity of drugs did. The women were furious at Tina, threatening to beat her up, so the guards took her to the only place in the jail where the other prisoners couldn't get at her, solitary confinement.

Tina asked for her belongings, but the guards had left them in her old cell, with the result that everything else was stolen, including her toilet articles, her money, writing paper, envelopes, and stamps. Even her photographs of Amber were taken.

The solitary confinement cell was near the showers used by the male prisoners. One of them, a trustee who worked the night shift from five to five, woke her up at four-thirty one morning. Making crude sexual suggestions, he opened the trapdoor to her cell and placed his penis in the opening. This went on for the next three days, until Tina was transferred to a cell in the women's wing. Afraid of reprisals, Tina hadn't reported the trustee, but she now told the hall lady, who informed the guards. The man was questioned, but nothing was done, and he was still allowed access to the hallway outside Tina's cell. There he got his revenge by waking her up at night, banging on her door at all hours and screaming obscenities. The guards ignored him with the same disinterest they showed in Tina.

Tina didn't look good during my weekly visits. She had lost a great deal of weight and seemed deeply depressed. She said she wasn't sleeping well, even when her tormentor left her alone, and that she was having flashbacks and nightmares about Amber's death. She felt she needed to go to the hospital.

When I saw Tina's health worsening, I wrote to Sheriff Bell and asked for permission to see her for counseling. The visitors' cubicles, placed right next to each other, made speaking difficult. I could see Tina well enough through the glass pane, but we had to shout to be heard through the metal grille below the glass. Frequent interruptions and lack of privacy made any real communication impossible. Since then, phones have been installed in the visiting section of the jail.

Bell said he couldn't authorize the sessions and suggested I phone Dewey Smith, the chief judge of the Carroll Superior Court, for permission. Judge Smith told me to speak to Judge William Lee, who was in charge of Tina's case. Lee directed me to Dr. Phil Austin, the physician who looked after the inmates, and Austin said I needed a court order from Judge Smith. I didn't call Smith again.

About this time, the guards became worried about Tina's mental state, and she was taken to the mental health clinic in Carrollton for evaluation. The therapist on duty said Tina needed medication for her depression and sleep disorder. The jail made an appointment with a physician, then canceled it without explanation. At this point, I wrote a long letter to Judge Smith telling him about the jail's inhumane treatment of Tina and asked him to intervene. After this, Tina's tormentor was sent away, her treatment became less harsh, she saw a physician and received medication for her depression and insomnia.

By now Tina had been in jail for nearly six months without an attorney to look after her interests, let alone set a trial date. I reminded Judge Smith of this in my letter and also phoned

Judge Lee, as he would appoint her public defender. Lee said that the matter was on his mind, and that the delay was because he wanted to get Tina the best defense possible. Finally, at the end of October, Lee appointed Jimmy Berry as Tina's public defender. I wrote Berry to let him know that I would assist him and Tina as best I could.

Berry had passed the bar exam in 1971. After a few years in real estate, he had turned to criminal law. He had defended a large number of people accused of murder and had a high success rate. I was relieved that Tina's defense was in such capable hands.

# 23

# UNSOLVED MYSTERIES

In February 1993, I received a call from Cindy Bowles, a researcher for *Unsolved Mysteries*, the television documentary series covering unsolved crimes as well as psychic phenomena. Several of my investigations had been featured on the show, and Bowles asked if I had anything more that might be of interest to their viewers. I said I had explored various cases of recurrent spontaneous psychokinesis, but that I had lost touch with the families. The single exception was Tina Resch, and she was in jail.

Bowles called back a few days later to say that jail might not be an obstacle and that the director of the proposed segment, Jim Lindsay, wanted to talk to Tina. I doubted that her attorney, Jimmy Berry, would allow Tina to talk in public about flying objects. Even if he gave permission, the jail certainly would not. I was mistaken. Attorney Berry said he would not be opposed if the show was restricted to the occurrences in

1984 and if Tina was referred to as Tina Resch, not as Christina Boyer, her married name. Berry told me to call District Attorney Skandalakis for his approval. Skandalakis said it was okay with him if it was okay with Sheriff Bell, as he was running the jail. When I contacted Bell, he, too, said Lindsay could interview Tina.

I supposed that Skandalakis and Bell were favorably disposed to *Unsolved Mysteries* because the program often collaborated with the police. The series had helped to bring in a number of escaped murderers when their pictures were displayed on the show. In the meantime I had spoken to Tina, and she said she would participate if her exposure on the program was not going to damage her case in court. I said that Berry didn't think it would.

The meeting in the jail was set for Tuesday, March 2. The day before, I had shown Lindsay my photos and news clippings about the RSPK incidents and answered his questions about my experiences in the Resch home. Lindsay was short and intense with dark brown hair and a bulldog face. He asked his questions in rapid succession. There was little causal talk, though I did learn he was married and had two children. He said he wanted to get back to California by Friday, his tenth wedding anniversary.

We were to meet Berry for dinner at Jimmy the Greek's, a restaurant on Marietta Square, a few miles north of Atlanta. Berry's secretary, Kathy Allen, recommended the restaurant and suggested we use a separate dining room where we wouldn't be interrupted. Berry was widely known, she said, and people might come up to the table to chat.

Tina had asked me to speak to Berry about her trial. Although he had been her lawyer for more than four months, she had yet to hear from him. After choosing rack of lamb and a glass of red wine, I brought up the subject of the trial. Berry sipped on a glass of ice water and told me that her case would come to trial in three to six months, but it was up to the prosecutor and the judge to set the time, not him. He said that he had applied for a detective to talk to witnesses and make investigations. I mentioned the neurological studies that had shown anomalies in Tina's brain and asked if he wanted to see a paper that Persinger and I had written. Berry didn't reply but looked at me as if I should have known better, and I didn't ask again. He was more loquacious when the talk turned to his children. A single parent with sole custody of his son and daughter, Berry took an evident pride in his children's achievements. His son, James Jr., was an amateur wrestler and had won several trophies. He also liked to watch *Unsolved Mysteries*. I offered to send the boy some articles about my investigations, but Berry quickly said James was going into law and there would be "no deviation."

The next day Lindsay and I went to the jail shortly after two, met Sheriff Bell, and then saw Tina. Before we went in, a guard said we were not to give her anything. We were then left without further supervision, and Tina told Lindsay about the incidents in her home, about going to church and being confirmed, and her fear of being possessed. Lindsay asked her about Amber's death. Tina said that she hadn't been present and didn't know what had happened. All she could think was that David must have killed her.

Tina brought up the trial delay. I told her that Berry said she would go to court in three to six months. She was dismayed; she thought her case would come up in April. Lindsay advised her to send Berry a letter, with a copy to the judge, asking to be told at least once a month how her case stood. He said she should send Berry the names of any witnesses who could testify that she had never hurt Amber. Her letter should also tell him about the days preceding Amber's death. He said that if Berry didn't speak to the witnesses or use the information Tina gave him, this could be grounds for an appeal if she was convicted.

The interview over, Lindsay and I were guided to the office of Major Gorman, Sheriff Bell's assistant, to discuss the time and place for filming Tina's interview. Lindsay asked for a room that didn't look like a jail cell, and Gorman said he could use the chapel. As soon as we left, Tina was searched for contraband, even though we had followed the jail's instructions not to give her anything.

The next week, on March 8, 1993, Tina followed Lindsay's advice and wrote her letter to Jimmy Berry: "I heard from Bill Roll that I won't be going to court for another 3–6 months. This came as quite a shock. I was hoping to go next month. . . .

"I was also informed that if I were to receive bail, it would be high. I am not a threat to anyone and I have no intentions of running. I am not guilty, and no matter what I'm faced with, I intend to see this through . . . I have been in jail 11 months, 327 days to be exact. Is there any possibility of receiving a lower bond? Also could you please explain why I haven't been to court. . . .

"Lastly could you send me a letter once a month to inform me of any developments in my case, such as court dates? . . . I need to hear any news from you instead of through others second hand. I hope you can understand."

There was no copying machine in the jail that Tina could use, and she sent the letter to me so I could make copies before sending it on to Berry. He did not reply, according to Tina.

❋         ❋         ❋

Filming was set for Friday, March 26. Lindsay and the film crew arrived at the jail by nine-thirty and spent the next hour converting the chapel to a living room and setting up the camera and lights. Tina replaced her prison uniform with a dark blue dress I had bought the day before, and Lindsay had her sit in front of the piano as if she were at home. The interview took ninety minutes, and Tina was calm and well-spoken. Lindsay seemed satisfied. After we wrapped up, Lindsay took me to the Ramada Inn in Carrollton, where the film crew was staying, and interviewed me about my time in the Resch home.

The documentary aired on May 18, 1993. In addition to myself, Joan Resch, Bruce Claggett, Mike Harden, and Fred Shannon told of their experiences. The interviews were interspersed with simulations of the events, professional actors taking our places. The show was entertaining and close to the facts. The actor who represented me had a British accent similar to mine and the same mannerisms.

After the show's debut, some viewers were interested enough in the story to write to Tina. One of them was John Riggle, a retired TV repairman living in Houston, Texas. Tina wrote back that she was in jail, accused of murdering her child. Her reply was totally unexpected, and Riggle said he wanted to help. He was retired, a widower, and had time on his hands, and he believed Tina was innocent. "I don't know what other people choose to call it," he said, "inspiration, intuition, hunches, or even ESP, but it chose that moment to kick in, and somehow I knew she couldn't possibly be guilty. She was pleading for someone to help her." Riggle offered to be that someone. He asked Tina to send him a letter authorizing him to obtain information pertaining to her case. She did so on October 28, 1993, naming twenty-two individuals who knew her, the same list she had given Berry.

Riggle came to Carrollton and turned out to be somewhat of an expert on police procedure and legal matters. He told me, "While I was still in Texas, I had the privilege of being instructed in proper police procedures and investigative techniques by Sargent Roy G. House of the Houston Police Department Major Crimes Division and Internal Affairs Division, and by Sargent T. E. Merritt of the Harris County Sheriff's Department Training Division." He added that he was appalled by the amateurism of the police, sheriff's deputies, as well as District Attorney Skandalakis. He was accustomed to deal with Harris County, Texas, District Attorney Johnny Holmes, whose competence, he said, was beyond question.

"When I arrived in Carrollton," Riggle said, "the first thing I did was meet with Tina. . . . Tina had several documents in her possession in the jail and I obtained all of them from her. Next I went to the West Georgia University [sic] library and made copies of every newspaper article published about Tina and her daughter and David. In the first seventy-six days following Amber's murder, there were seventy-eight articles about the murder." Riggle continued, "I have never seen such a media blitz. The county was literally whipped into a frenzy by this. No responsible police, sheriff, or district attorney would ever make all the statements made by the police, sheriff, and district attorney to the press. It could only mean that they had seized this case as the sensational case they needed to get themselves reelected."

Alongside the articles reporting on Tina's case, Riggle discovered that even though Sheriff Bell and District Attorney Skandalakis were outspent three to one by their political opponents, Bell and Skandalakis had been reelected. "They didn't care who they hurt or how much harm they did to do it. They chose Tina to be their victim when David battered and murdered her three-year-old daughter. She was a woman, was handy, a damn Yankee, had few friends locally, in fact few people locally even knew her, and she had no money to hire a lawyer who would truly defend her. She was literally a made-to-order victim for their purposes."

A year earlier, on November 29, 1992, Atlanta businessman Fred Tokars's wife, Sara, had died from a shotgun blast to the head. The murder took place in front of their two sons, Rick and Mike. Eddie Lawrence, a business partner of Tokars's, had hired a hit man, who forced Sara Tokars and the boys into her car and shot her from behind. The motivation for the crime was obvious: Sara Tokars had threatened to reveal her husband's shady business dealings, and Fred Tokars had bought a $1.75-million insurance policy on her life.

Lawrence pleaded guilty to hiring the hit man and testified against Tokars in exchange for a reduced prison sentence. Tokars was a former Atlanta lawyer and part-time traffic court judge, and he had the money to hire top attorneys. They included Jimmy Berry, who was also Tina's attorney. The Tokars case was big, far more important in terms of income to Berry and media attention than an impecunious woman in a county jail. One suspects that given the choice between working to the best of his ability for Tina or Tokars, Berry must have put the bulk of his time toward defending Tokars.

John Riggle was outraged by Berry's apparently slack attitude regarding Tina, and he went to his office to tell him just that. "I did not get a good impression from him at all," he told me. "Berry seemed to me to be only interested in the Fred Tokars case. Supposedly he is one of the best lawyers in Georgia." As far as Riggle could tell, Berry had merely submitted some thirty or so motions to the court, and all but two or three were routine, and he had conferred with the Cobb County medical examiner, Dr. Burton, as to the accuracy of the autopsy.

After Riggle left Berry's office, Berry probably didn't have a good impression of Riggle either. Like a modern Don Quixote fighting Tina's legal windmills, Riggle wanted Berry to consider that there might be causes for Amber's death other than those given on the death certificate. The one he thought most feasible was rat poisoning. Knowing that Amber had liked to snack on dry cereal, Riggle wondered if she had seen a box of the poison pellets, mistaken them for cereal, then nibbled enough to fall sick and die.

Berry found the idea absurd.

Fed up with Berry's unwillingness to listen, Riggle thought that he himself could do a better job of guiding Tina through a trial. Riggle went to Judge Lee with an amicus curiae (friend of the court) plea, which is legalese for someone who is permitted to advise a judge about legal matters that affect a case. Riggle argued that the case against Tina should be dismissed because of the excessively long time, more than two years, she had been incarcerated without a trial. If this motion was denied, Riggle argued that Tina be allowed out of jail on a personal bond until the trial. He used eight pages for his two amicus curiae motions and brought them to Lee's office June 1, 1994. Lee did not take long to consider the matter. He dismissed both motions the next day. Lee noted that Riggle was not a lawyer and that all motions on Tina's behalf should be submitted by Berry. Lee pointed out that he had appointed Berry, "an able lawyer who has much experience in criminal and death penalty cases," to represent her.

Berry may have been distracted during the year he had

been Tina's attorney. But I thought he might have more time after the Tokars trial. Fred Tokars was convicted April 8, 1994, for kidnapping and murder for hire, as well as for money laundering and racketeering. He was sentenced to life in prison. Thanks to Berry and his other lawyers, he escaped the electric chair. I thought Berry was still Tina's best hope.

# 24

# SILENT JUSTICE

**"W**hy have I not heard from you? Why have you not put in a demand for a trial? Is there no time limit how long they can keep me here without a trial? I have given you a list of witnesses, why have you not questioned them? Do you intend to plea bargain? If you do, I need to discuss this with you."

Tina's questions filled a letter she sent to Jimmy Berry on July 14, 1994, a year and four months after her fruitless attempts to reach him by phone and letter. Five days later, Mike Arons and I followed up with a letter of our own.

> *Frankly, it is hard for us to imagine that 27 months in jail with no trial date yet set expresses the principle of a speedy trial. It is equally hard for us to imagine that Ms. Boyer is enjoying the right to be considered innocent until proven guilty in a court of law.*
>
> *One matter which is the most frustrating to Ms. Boyer*

*and to ourselves is that she has been left in the dark con-*
*cerning any explanation . . . she has complained that dur-*
*ing all the time you were assigned to her case she has seen*
*you personally for at most two hours. When she has tried*
*on any number of occasions to reach you by phone you*
*were not there and never returned her calls. This frustra-*
*tion is intensified by our realization that none of the*
*witnesses on her behalf, whose names she gave you—*
*including our own—has yet been contacted let alone*
*interviewed by you or your staff . . . by contrast, the prose-*
*cution's witnesses have long ago been interviewed.*

*Ms. Boyer has recognized you are busy. We have coun-*
*seled patience. I think we have all now reached our limit*
*on this.*

*We are fully convinced of Christina Boyer's innocence*
*of the charges leveled against her. We are far less con-*
*vinced of the motives, competency, and adequacy of the*
*Carroll County Police and Judicial and Penal systems.*
*We would like to be convinced of your compassion, good*
*faith, dedication and strategy.*

Berry didn't reply.

Finally, three months later, on October 14, Berry went to
see Tina to tell her about his strategy. The trial was to begin in
less than three weeks, on Monday, October 31. To avoid any
prejudice from a Carrollton jury, the small town of Rome, fifty
miles north of Carrollton, had been chosen for the trial. But
Berry wasn't interested in any of that. Instead, he told Tina
that he had spoken to District Attorney Skandalakis not about
going to trial, but about accepting a plea bargain. Skandalakis
had been amenable; he would trade the death sentence for a
sentence of life in prison if Tina would plead guilty to Amber's

murder. Berry told her to consult her friends before making up her mind, but that he recommended that she accept the deal.

Mike and I were stunned. Mike phoned Berry to express our dismay and went to see him at his office in Marietta with a three-and-a-half-page, densely typed statement listing the reasons we could not advise Tina to accept the plea bargain.

> *We cannot understand, and frankly this shakes our confidence in you, why you waited until such a late date—after two years and only weeks before the trial date—to express to Ms. Boyer your plea recommendation. We feel the case should be fully investigated with her innocence and not probability of conviction in mind. We have a hard time understanding how a person against whom no premeditation is charged, where the evidence is circumstantial, where the defendant has no previous record of any kind, and where another person (Mr. Herrin) has admittedly caused the child serious injuries during the critical period of time, can be subject in your eyes to a sentence of death.*
>
> *In fact Mr. Herrin's statement to the police, admitting sodomizing Amber, admitting hitting Amber, admitting being with her most of the weekend, suggests that if the injuries were physically inflicted it was he, not Ms. Boyer, who was responsible for the child's injuries. She was not there any of that time. David acknowledges this. Jeannie Lagle can testify to this. Did you know that David Herrin was fired the very day that this happened? Have you looked into the good possibility that he was frustrated and angry enough to do such things?*
>
> *We would appreciate it if you go over all the attached material with a fresh eye. We would have to be convinced*

*by you that Ms. Boyer is guilty or that the evidence was so
overwhelming that she might actually receive a death sentence before we could support a plea for life in prison.
However, we could support a much lesser charge, such as
negligence, because Ms. Boyer in fact did not bring
Amber to the hospital to have her injuries checked.*

Mike turned to the selection of the jury, something he was
familiar with from having arranged a course at West Georgia
College on the psychological aspects of jury selection. His
consultant for the course was Millard Farmer, a prominent Atlanta attorney for criminal cases. In his statement to Berry,
Mike wrote: "It is obvious that the nature of the jury is crucial
to a fair trial and that you, as her attorney, have considerable
control over this. We would like to know what procedure you
intend to follow in choosing a jury." Mike added a lengthy series of questions for potential jurors, including questions about
physical punishment of children and about injuries that are serious enough to take a child to the hospital.

Berry was not impressed. He showed Mike the autopsy photos of Amber's damaged face and body. It was inconceivable,
he said, that a jury would let Tina go after seeing the pictures.

On October 20, Mike, John Riggle, and I saw Tina at the jail
and counseled her against the plea bargain. Everyone, we said,
including the police, agreed that Amber's injuries had all occurred while Tina was visiting Jeannie and Amber was alone
with David. Although Mike and I both thought that Tina had
been negligent by not seeking medical attention for Amber's
cuts and bruises, we could not imagine this would lead a jury
to sentence her to death.

I phoned Berry when I returned home. As usual I couldn't

reach him, but left a message on his answering machine. "Mr. Berry, this is Dr. Roll. I have come from a meeting at the jail with Dr. Arons and Mr. Riggle. We have been speaking to Christina, and Christina has decided to go through with the trial with an innocent plea. She does not wish to accept the plea bargain arrangement that you have conveyed from the prosecutor. She and her friends expect you to do your very best in presenting her case to the jury at the trial. We know that you have many other important matters to attend to, but we respectfully suggest that it is high time that you turn your full attention to the defense and the very best defense that you can mount for Ms. Boyer."

For the first time, Berry returned my call. He didn't identify himself, but I recognized the voice.

"Did you hear it?" I asked, referring to my phone message.

He said he had, then asked me what I based by recommendation on.

"Well, partially on the conversation we [I should have said Mike Arons] had with you the other day, and partially on the discussion Dr. Arons had with another lawyer, a friend of his, a sort of private consultation." I didn't say that the other lawyer was Millard Farmer, who was known to Berry.

"Well, why don't y'all get this lawyer?" Berry demanded. "Because I can tell you what will happen." In Berry's opinion, if Mike, John, and I continued to interfere, we were going to put Tina in the electric chair. If that happened, Berry was not going to be responsible, and he was going to say so on record.

I tried to stay level-headed as Berry went on to tell me that I should "see the handwriting on the wall." "Crap" like John Riggle's theory that Amber had eaten rat poison was "complete bull" according to a medical expert. The evidence spoke for itself: Amber had been beaten over a several-day time period.

The photographs from her autopsy revealed tissue damage and bruises of various ages. He insisted Tina could not fight the photographs. When she received the death penalty, it wasn't going to be because of him. He'd done everything he could to save Tina's life while Mike and I had done everything we could to destroy it. And that, he said, was something that would be on our consciences, not his.

"All right, Mr. Berry," I said, seeing we were getting nowhere. "Can I ask you a couple of questions?"

He said I could ask but he wasn't going to answer because he was "thoroughly hacked off."

I tried anyway. "Is there any appeal from the death penalty?"

Berry just about exploded. What did I want to worry about an appeal for? "If she gets convicted," he said, "she gets convicted."

I started to speak, but Berry cut in, repeating, "She is gonna be convicted—"

This time I cut in, loudly. "What do you recommend, Mr. Berry?"

When he said he'd already given his recommendation to Mike, I said, "It's a plea bargain—is there any appeal from that or is Tina going to be stuck with something she's never done?"

It was clear that Berry wasn't listening anymore, so I switched topics and asked if he had read the police report.

Berry reacted as if I'd lost my mind; of course he'd read the report.

"Well, what about Herrin?" I asked when I could get a word in, but Berry brushed me off; he didn't "give a rat's ass" about Herrin. I pointed out that according to Amber's autopsy, her anus was enlarged by several centimeters.

"So what!" he exclaimed. "The child has been beat to death!"

I asked how he thought a three-year-old could be sodomized without being beaten.

"People sodomize children without beating them."

Realizing we were talking in circles, I tried bringing the conversation back to the police report. I said that the report stated that David Herrin had been alone with Amber when she was injured.

Berry was dismissive; Amber's bruises had taken place over a long period of time, not just in an hour.

"They didn't take place over a long period of time," I argued.

"Yes, sir, they did."

"I was with the girl three weeks before. She was fine."

Berry groaned. "I've done everything I can," he said. He was going to do his best on the case; he was going to put up the evidence and we would just have to see what happened. He repeated, "I've done everything I can do."

"I don't think you have taken care of Tina," I said. "You have not spoken to her. You have not seen her. It's been impossible for her to get in touch with you. You have been on the case for two years, and then two weeks before the thing—"

Berry interrupted to say that he wasn't responsible for when a district attorney said, "Okay, I will accept a plea." It wasn't up to him.

"That's an impossible plea," I said. I told Berry that Mike and I expected to see an expert defense. "We expect you to question the—" I was going to say "witnesses," but Berry hung up.

Immediately afterward, Berry must have spoken to Tina. The next day, October 21, she wrote to Mike, Jeannie, John Riggle, and me, saying that she had agreed to the plea bargain.

*I know that my decision to go ahead Monday with the offered plea may seem like I'm giving up. Please try to understand that I'm scared. At least this way I know I'll get out some day. Please support me in this. One of my biggest fears is that everyone will just forget about me. I know how crazy this sounds to you all. But I need your love and support in this. Believe me when I say this has been the hardest decision of my life. It isn't easy knowing I'm signing away my life for the next 4 plus years. But I feel it's the safest thing to do. I wish so badly that things were different. But they're not, so I simply must accept it and go on.*

*I'm going to go to college while I'm there and make the most out of the time. . . . At least when I come out I'll have an education behind me and I'll be able to support myself.*

*Court is Monday at 9 A.M. My mother is flying in Monday morning at 7:25 A.M. My lawyer is picking her up. But I don't know how she'll make it back to the airport at 5:11 when her plane takes off. . . . So if she should need someone that day, will one of you look out for her please? . . .*

*Please, if you can, come to court with me. It'll be so much easier knowing you all will be there and support me. I've thought long and hard (in the time I was given) about this decision and even though it's not great, it's one I can live with. . . .*

*These two and a half years have been the worst years of my life. Without you all I know I never would have made it this far. There were so many times I felt like giving up. Just knowing that I had you all here behind me has kept me going. Your weekly visits and phone calls have given me the strength that otherwise I believe I wouldn't have had. Please stand by me and don't forget about me.*

Attorney Millard Farmer had told Mike that it was next to impossible to win an appeal after a plea bargain. If Tina accepted, it would be the end of her legal recourse. At the same time, he gave Mike a glimmer of hope. If Tina could take a lie detector test and it supported her innocence, Berry would surely change his mind and take her to trial for a real defense. The problem was time. It was already Friday, and Tina was to be in court Monday morning at nine.

# 25

# THE PLEA

It was Sunday, October 23, the day before Tina was to be in court to accept the plea bargain. On Millard Farmer's recommendation, Mike had spent two days trying to get in touch with W. A. Robinson, a court-qualified expert witness in polygraph or lie detection interrogation. Farmer had called Robinson "the best." Fortunately, for Tina's sake and on such short notice, he was willing to come out to Carrollton during the weekend.

A tall, mild-mannered, and self-confident man with graying hair, Robinson had been conducting forensic investigations since 1964. The Police Officers Standard Training Council had certified him as an instructor. When we informed Jimmy Berry that we wanted him to test Tina, Berry agreed, saying he would notify the jail to let them know we would be there Sunday afternoon.

We arrived at the jail on time, but no one had heard from

Berry nor could he be reached by phone. It was now up to the jail whether they would let us in or not. While Robinson, Mike, John Riggle, and I nervously waited outside for a decision, Robinson explained his procedure. He would ask Tina several questions while she was connected to the polygraph. The machine was designed to pick up signs of anxiety that may be due to lying. It had four channels and a recorder to trace her responses on a roll of graph paper. The machine would register her breathing, her heart rate, blood pressure, and perspiration. If her responses increased when she answered a question, Robinson said, this could mean she was lying. Robinson would use two types of questions, "relevant questions" and "control questions." The relevant questions would be about Amber's death. The control questions would be about irrelevant issues Robinson expected Tina to answer with a lie, a reaction anyone can have to a question that is, for instance, embarrassing but unimportant.

At about 5:30 P.M., the jail finally agreed to allow Robinson inside to test Tina. Ninety minutes later he came back out and gave us an account of the test and its results. "The first control question I used was 'In the first twenty years of your life, other than what you've told me about, which is your husband and mother, did you physically hurt anyone?' That was a fair control," he said. "Some response but not a whole lot. The second control question I used on her was 'In the first twenty years of your life, did you ever lie to any authority?' Which she had told me no, she never had. She also told me no to the other one, other than husband and mother.

"The relevant question, the very first one, was 'Did you inflict the wound that caused Amber's death?' Of course, the answer to that was no, and of course the polygraph showed that she was truthful on that question. My second relevant one was

'Did David tell you on Monday night—this is the Monday night prior to Amber's death—that the Family and Children's Services would take Amber if you took her to the hospital?' She answered yes to that, and it showed she was telling the truth. And then the next relevant question was 'Did you not take Amber to the hospital because you were afraid that Family and Children's Services would take her?' She answered yes to that and that showed she was truthful, too. So that's the reason she did not take her to the hospital."

Robinson said, "Someone has got her convinced that she is guilty of murder because she didn't take the child to the hospital. That's what's in her mind, that's what she thinks she is, that she's guilty of murder because she didn't take the child to the hospital."

He returned to the control question, "'The first twenty years of your life, did you ever lie to any authority?' After my third test that I had run on her, I came back and confronted her with that question and said, 'Why did you lie to me about that?' Then she admits that she went to the authorities and lied to them. She was age twelve. And then they planned to send her to a detention center for lying. So I know the test was working. She's not guilty. The only thing she might be guilty of is bad judgment."

We asked Robinson if a polygraph test could be used as evidence in court. He said it can if the prosecution and the defense both agree. If there is no agreement, a polygraph examiner can still be an effective witness, because his profession would be known to the jury on the witness stand even though he couldn't say outright that his judgment was based on a polygraph examination. He said he would be willing to be a witness for Tina.

Robinson had told Tina that the test showed she was innocent. "You better think about that tonight before you plead," Robinson said to Tina.

The Carroll County Court House was built between 1928 and 1929. A Greek Revival structure two stories high and made from light pink sandstone, the building is a short walk from Adamson Square, the center of Carrollton. A perpetual flame in front of the courthouse honors the Carroll County veterans of World Wars I and II. To the right, outside a sleek modern addition, a statue of a Confederate soldier stands atop a marble column in remembrance of the fallen in the Civil War.

Steps at the center of the courthouse lead up to a pair of massive bronze doors. Above the doors is a clock that always reads a quarter to six. The doors are locked and a spiderweb across them proves it. You enter through a door on the side.

The first floor of the courthouse is occupied by administrative offices. The two courtrooms are on the second floor. They are furnished in dark and somber oak. I have spent a few days in one as a juror.

We had been told that Tina's plea bargain would be in state superior court where Judge William Lee was presiding. I arrived at nine in the morning with Mike and John. Judge Lee came fifteen minutes later. Mike Thomas, the detective who had been in charge of the investigation of Amber's death, came at 9:23, then left. He returned at 9:30 with a large box of papers. Several visitors appeared at the same time, including Michael Flinn, the attorney who had prepared the deed to my house.

At 9:45, Judge Lee announced that he was going into a jury room and that the press should come along. I was at a loss about what to do when Flinn came up and said I should follow Lee. I lost track of the judge but joined a small group who seemed to know where they were headed. Suddenly a short, black-robed figure appeared on my right. It was Judge Lee and he wanted to know where I was going. I said that I was a friend of Ms. Boyer's and that I planned to attend her hearing.

"No, you are not," Lee said.

I supposed Berry had told him not to let me in since I might persuade Tina to reject the plea bargain. I would certainly have tried to do so, especially now that I had the results of the polygraph test.

Flinn must have seen the encounter, for he directed me to the other courtroom, where he would meet me later. He then went to the jury room where Lee would rule on the plea bargain.

Flinn returned at 10:20 and said that Tina had pleaded guilty to the murder of Amber and cruelty to children and that she had been sentenced to life in prison plus twenty years.

Joan did not show up for the hearing.

The next day, a smiling Tina and Amber greeted the readers of the *Atlanta Constitution*. The color photo, taken in December 1990, was at the center of an article by Bill Torpy: "Telekinetic Mom Averts Trial." It shared the front page with an announcement of the peace treaty between Israel and Jordan.

Inside the paper was another article accompanied by Fred Shannon's famous photo of the flying phone and a story about the different opinions about the poltergeist incidents. The headline said, "Tina Boyer's Tragic Trip Ends." Beneath this was "From celebrity to cellblock." Tina was quoted as saying, "I'm not guilty of beating her. I'm guilty of not taking her to the hospital."

Writing about Tina and David Herrin, Torpy said, "The case against them was never clear-cut." He quoted District Attorney Skandalakis: "Each one said the other must have done it." Skandalakis told the reporters that he didn't know "who delivered the blows."

But that was never in doubt. It was clear from the outset that David was alone with Amber when she died and that the injuries she'd received during the preceding days had also occurred when he was alone with the child. The police never questioned this.

Torpy's article said that Berry was "holding a packet of horrific photos showing Amber's battered and swollen face" and saying, "We couldn't have beat these."

When Tina left home to marry James Bennett back in 1986, one of the first things she did was buy herself a black, tight-fitting suit on the installment plan. She loved the suit and she was proud of the achievement. Then she wore the suit home for a visit with Joan. The buttons to the jacket popped open and Joan lit right in: Tina looked like a slut, just like her real mother. Tina had heard it all before: "No wonder your mother didn't want you." "I wish we never would have adopted you." "Your mother was a whore, a prostitute." Tina wondered if this was the same mother Joan claimed to know nothing about, or was it just another way to pick at unhealed wounds?

After Amber was born, Joan made a surprising revelation. She admitted to Tina that she had been jealous of her. When Tina had been very young, Joan said, she had been jealous of the close relationship Tina had shared with John. The statement was so startling Tina forgot to ask why. In the past, Tina had learned the best way to get information out of Joan was to keep her mouth shut, but this time Joan didn't say any more. All Tina could think was that this had to be the reason behind John's sudden coldness and brutality toward her—Joan couldn't

stand being left out and here John was so obviously fond of his
adopted daughter.

Tina knew about jealousy. In his report on Tina's psychological profile, Jim Carpenter wrote, "She experiences a lot of
painful jealousy, probably of the odd flood of foster siblings
with which she has had to cope. She sees her mother as per-
petually busy and unavailable. She carries a lot of silent inner
pain at this perceived neglect. This simmers into depression
and helplessness, relieved a bit by wishful fantasy."

Tina's insecurities and vulnerability made her an "easy target" at home as well as school. Jack's sexual assaults, Joan's
mental torture, and John's beatings—each family member attacked Tina from his or her own perspective. Tina was suffo-
cating, and the psychokinesis was an unwitting attempt to
break out. It didn't work and it couldn't work because Tina
carried Joan's critical voice inside her head no matter what she
did to block it out. Even when they were apart, Joan went
wherever Tina went. There was a direct, almost inevitable
road from home to prison. The same emotional tensions and
burdens Tina felt as a child made her select partners who repeated the behavior of her parents. Dating David Herrin was
part of a lifelong pattern.

Herrin was tried after Tina's plea bargain. But since Tina had
already admitted to the murder of Amber, there was no need
to charge him as well. Tina was called as a witness at David's
trial. With the same lack of foresight that made her wear the
black suit home to Joan, Tina came to court in a light, blowzy
summer dress. Herrin's defense couldn't have done better if
they had told Tina to wear the dress. Her outfit went right with
their evidence.

While she was living in Carrollton, Tina was always short

on cash, and she had done some things to earn money that Herrin's defense exploited to the full. A local individual known to the police for his homemade adult videos had paid Tina to perform on tape. The videos were shown in court.

For Tina, it was bad enough to be seen compromising herself on film, dredging up all the old embarrassment of the "lamp incident," now with an even more self-destructive bent, but there were also a few seconds of tape showing Amber running into the room. On the tape, Tina is seen jumping up and shooing her daughter out of the room, followed by the sound of slapping. Tina was mortified; not once had she thought the videos would be seen by anyone other than the person who had taped them.

Despite the defense's tactics to show Tina in the worst possible light, Herrin was sentenced to twenty years in prison for cruelty to children. With the sentence, though, came the possibility of parole and an early release. Tina wasn't so lucky. The videos and her inappropriate courtroom attire stayed in the public mind, further ruining any chances she might have had for future leniency and parole. Only twenty-five years old, Tina was going to spend the rest of her life in prison.

# EPILOGUE

**W**as there a link between the earlier poltergeist activity and Amber's death? Perhaps not in a direct sense, but Tina's damaged psyche prevented her from making good choices for either herself or her child. Tina should have taken Amber to a hospital so her injuries could be examined. But her failure to do so does not amount to murder or even to child cruelty.

Amber was not the only victim. Tina was a victim as well, and the perpetrators were David Herrin, Peter Skandalakis, and Jim Berry. Herrin can be excused because he tried to save his own neck; Skandalakis can be excused because it was his job to get a conviction, whatever the facts. But Berry cannot be excused because it was his duty to do his best to show a jury that Tina was innocent. In my opinion, he had evidence to accomplish this.

Berry's advice that Tina accept the plea sent her to prison

with little chance of parole. The Georgia Board of Pardons and Parole saw the photos of Amber and accepted Tina's admission of murder and cruelty to her child at face value.

About the time Amber was born, someone sent Tina a clipping from *The Skeptical Inquirer* where James Randi retracted an offer he had made to write a second article, this one about the testimonies of electrician Bruce Claggett and photographer Fred Shannon. Randi said he would have explained in this article how Tina could have turned on the switches in Claggett's presence and made the love seat move out while Shannon was watching. But there was no longer any need, Randi said, to explain how Tina had tricked the two men, because he had already shown that she "was a publicity-seeking teenager who used simple deception and considerable guile" to make up the story about moving objects.

Reflecting on his experiences, Claggett told me, "On the one hand, I don't believe generally in supernatural forces or strange powers. On the other hand, I know for a fact that those things happened while I was there and that switches untouched by hands were moved and tape disappeared. I'd stake my bottom dollar and reputation on that. I guess the answer I've reached for myself is simply that there was some sort of force doing things that I couldn't account for."

Fred Shannon recently sent Tina a photograph he had taken back in March 1984 of her and her parents. She was shocked by the way her father looked: "Maybe because he's dead I have forgotten his 'looks.' When I got the picture, for a moment I was scared. The look on my father's face was the squinted, mean-eyed look I'd been so familiar with growing up. He was angry in that picture and being made to tolerate something he didn't wish to do."

Tina had hoped to take college courses in prison, so she could be prepared for a job when she got out, but college courses are not offered to "lifers," who are not expected to be released. She still dreams about her home and family: "I dream about the house on Blue Ash a lot. They're never good dreams either and I always find myself thinking—when I wake up—that I wish I could go and bulldoze that house to the ground. Like somehow that would make me feel better. Crazy, huh?"

Tina never saw her mother again; Joan died in 2000. Her adoptive siblings want nothing to do with her. In 2002, a habeas corpus plea requesting a trial for Tina was rejected. David Herrin is currently serving his twenty-year sentence for cruelty to children. He may be released at any time.

The goal of investigations like mine is sometimes misunderstood. It was not my purpose to gather evidence of strange phenomena, in Tina's instance the movements of objects without tangible contact, but to discover their cause.

Most scientists regard RSPK as impossible and research to study it a waste of time. For my part, I cannot deny what I have witnessed near Tina: movement of objects with which she had no tangible contact. This does not mean that the phenomena cannot be explained, only that they cannot be explained away. For me, RSPK has opened a new chapter in the book of human nature. A large portion of that chapter is due to Tina, to her parents, and to Steve Baumann and Jeannie Lagle.

I have been working on Tina's story for twenty years, and still I find much about her mysterious: her origins; the full extent of her abilities; the circumstances surrounding the death of her child. But one thing is certain. For a time Tina had the power to directly affect the physical world. I am convinced that this power is still to be found in the depths of her mind.

# NOTES

## CHAPTER 1

In 1995, on the fiftieth anniversary of the liberation of Denmark from Nazi Germany, the town of Birkerød published a book by William Roll, *Forsinket Forår (Delayed Spring)*, about his life during the occupation.

The articles by H. H. Price have been reprinted in *Philosophical Interactions with Parapsychology: The Major Writings by H. H. Price on Parapsychology and Survival* by Frank Dilley, Palgrave Macmillan, 1995.

Roll received the M.Litt. degree from Oxford for his thesis, "Theory and Experiment in Psychical Research." It was published by Arno Press, New York, 1975.

Two articles were written about the occurrences in Seaford: "The Seaford disturbances" by J. G. Pratt and Roll in the *Journal of Parapsychology*, 1958, and "Some physical and psychological aspects of a series of poltergeist phenomena" by Roll in the *Journal of the American Society for Psychical Research*, 1968.

Roll's book, *The Poltergeist*, was published in 1972 by New American Library, followed by later editions in the United States and by Italian, German, and Japanese translations.

## CHAPTER 2

Mike Harden's report "Strange happenings unnerve family" was published on March 6, 1984, in the *Columbus Dispatch* together with a photo of a flying phone by news photographer Fred Shannon. Other articles by Harden followed on May 7, 8, and 9. May 7 stories, often with Shannon's photo, appeared in the *Durham Morning Herald* (North Carolina), the *Arizona Daily Star*, the *Ohio Messenger* (Athens), the *Boston Globe* (Massachusetts), and the *Kitchener-Waterloo Record* (Ontario, Canada). On March 8, the *Durham Morning Herald*, the *Arizona Daily Star*, and *The Daily Progress* (Virginia) had additional accounts of the events. Other stories appeared in the national and international press.

The article "Another Amityville?" came out in the New Jersey *Trenton Times* on March 7.

On March 16, Harden's column in the *Dispatch*, told of a plethora of absurd suggestions he had received about the events and how to get rid of them.

Roll and Stump's "The Olive Hill poltergeist" was published in *Proceedings of the Parapsychological Association*, 1969, and in Chapter 11 of *The Poltergeist*.

## CHAPTER 7

Fred Shannon's photo of the telephone handpiece flying

past Tina appeared with Mike Harden's report in the *Dispatch* on March 6, 1984, and in many of the other news stories.

## CHAPTER 8

The Resches' insurance claim was reported in the *Dispatch* on March 11, 1984.

## CHAPTER 9

Paul Kurtz, chairman of the Committee for the Scientific Investigation of Claims of the Paranormal, was quoted on March 9, 1984, in the *Dispatch* (on March 10 in the *Cape Cod Times*) as saying that the country had probably been "bamboozled" and that he would send the magician James Randi and two scientists to investigate the suspected hoax.

On March 10 the *Columbus Citizen-Journal* reported that a TV news crew had filmed Tina pulling down a lamp.

On March 11 the *Dispatch* ran articles by Harden and Steve Berry, and a column by editor Luke Feck titled "We can't explain it but must report it."

## CHAPTER 10

On March 12 an article by Harden in the *Dispatch* announced the arrival of William Roll and Kelly Powers in the Resch home.

## CHAPTER 11

A March 13 column by Harden stated, "Things quiet at Resch home," and reporter Steve Berry quoted James Randi as saying that while people who report paranormal phenomena are like believers in Santa Claus and the Tooth Fairy, but he was still coming to Columbus with an open mind. The *Columbus Citizen-Journal* said that Steven Shore, an astronomer at Case Western Reserve, would accompany Randi, and quoted both men as being highly skeptical of the occurrences.

On March 14, Harden told of Randi's arrival at the Resch home and of Mrs. Resch's refusal to let him in. A photo shows Randi, Shore, and Roll in the Resch driveway. The event was also reported in the *Columbus Citizen-Journal*. The *Northland News* (Columbus) interviewed Harden about his reaction to the response by the public and the media to his reports.

## CHAPTER 14

On March 15, Harden wrote about some of the incidents Roll said he had witnessed, adding that Tina would be going with Roll to North Carolina. Harden quoted Randi as saying that "everything we have" suggested a hoax.

On March 16 the *Columbus Citizen-Journal* reported on Randi's and Roll's separate news conferences and opinions about the occurrences, and Joe Dirck's column was titled "The Resch case boils down to simply a matter of faith."

## CHAPTER 15

On March 22 the *Columbus Citizen-Journal* said that Tina's stay in Durham had been devoted to counseling rather than research. An article in the *Raleigh News and Observer* (North Carolina) discussed the incidents and Tina's stay in the Roll home.

On March 26 an interview with Roll appeared in the *Dayton Journal-Herald* dealing with the psychological and physical aspects of the occurrences.

"Becca Zinn tells of the events she witnessed in her book *Stardust* (Providence Books, Chapel Hill, N.C.). On pages 45 and 47–50 she relates her experiences with Tina as a "lesson about fear." She reports: "There was a greyness around me. My skin felt clammy, my stomach slightly nauseous. I felt a thick, heavy energy in the air.""

On April 14 the *Charlotte Observer* and the *Enterprise* (North Carolina) covered a news conference in Chapel Hill during which Roll discussed Tina's stay in North Carolina, including incidents he and psychotherapist Rebecca Zinn had observed. The articles also reported that Tina had broken a leg and returned to Columbus.

On April 29, *The Atlanta Journal-Constitution* interviewed Roll about the occurrences and about his other research.

On May 6 in the *Winston-Salem Journal* (North Carolina) ran a general interview with Roll about his investigations and theories of psychic phenomena.

## CHAPTER 16

The Summer 1984 issue of *Skeptical Inquirer* magazine had a two-page story by Paul Kurtz with a pair of photos: Shannon's photo of the phone flying past Tina, and a photo of Kurtz showing a phone in the air that Kurtz had just thrown.

Randi's paper "The Columbus Poltergeist Case: Part I: Flying phones, photos, and fakery" ran in the Spring 1985 issue of *Skeptical Inquirer*. Part II, in which Randi promised to examine the accounts by Fred Shannon and Bruce Claggett, never appeared.

Paul Kurtz's *A Skeptic's Handbook of Parapsychology*, which came out in 1985, included comments by Kurtz about the Resch incidents. The account is replete with errors. Kurtz said that "[Roll] maintains that he observed a picture and the picture-hook fall to the floor." Roll had said that he was in another room with Tina when this happened. Kurtz stated that "no one could testify to having seen an object first standing at rest and then take off." Lee Arnold said that on one occasion she was sitting on the couch looking at Tina when the phone on a table next to Tina flew to the couch. In another incident, Shannon said that the small couch, with its hideaway bed, suddenly slid about eighteen inches toward Tina, who was sitting on the arm of a recliner several feet away. Shannon snapped a photo of the incident. Speaking of this photo, Kurtz wrote, "In one case a sofa seems to be rising in the air. People on the scene swore that it was a case of paranormal manifestation. A close inspection of the photograph, however, clearly shows Tina's foot under the couch and apparently responsible for lifting it." Kurtz seems to have confused this photo with one Shannon had taken earlier, which showed Tina standing by the couch with one foot partway underneath. Kurtz continued: "Another photograph of a moving chandelier shows a hand striking it—though it is not clear if the hand is Tina's or that of a collaborator." The hand belonged to someone wearing a white T-shirt. Craig's T-shirt was white, while Tina wore a red T-shirt. Craig and Tina appeared in the same T-shirts in other photos. Shannon did not claim that he saw and photographed the lamp swinging by itself. While reconstructing an incident Craig had told him about, he had asked Craig to set the lamp in motion so he could get a picture. Shannon snapped the photo after Craig had removed his hand. Shannon then took another photo of Craig as he steadied the lamp.

Kurtz's last examples of "chicanery" came from an interview with Tina by Joel Achenbach in *The Buffalo Magazine* (on Oct. 28, 1984). Kurtz said the reporter visited Tina in the hospital after she had broken her leg. He did not. Achenbach saw her when she was bedridden in Roll's home and in his presence. Kurtz said that the reporter saw her "hurl" her hospital wristband and a bottle of nail polish through the room. During the interview, Tina was pulling at the plastic wristband, which she still wore, until it snapped off and fell to the floor. A little later she was playing with a bottle of nail polish, which also fell to the floor. Achenbach mentioned the two incidents but did not suggest Tina had tried to trick him.

Roll's "The question of RSPK vs. fraud in the case of Tina Resch" came out in the Proceedings of Presented Papers, the Parapsychological Association, 1993.

## CHAPTER 17

A paper chronicling Steven Baumann's PK experiments with Tina, "Preliminary results from the use of two novel detectors for psychokinesis" by Baumann, Lagle, and Roll, appeared in *Research in Parapsychology, 1985*. Tina was asked to affect two types of PK targets: a neuron from a marine snail and a piezoelectric crystal. The two systems were mounted side-by-side on a vibration-damping table; a computer collected and analyzed the data. The outcome of the neuron tests was highly significant, but a statistical problem prevented an adequate evaluation. The crystal tests used two crystals, an experimental crystal and a nearby control crystal. Tina was instructed to affect only the experimental crystal. Both were affected, which could be due to unfocused PK or to PK on the table.

## CHAPTER 18

The occurrences at Spring Creek Institute, are discussed in "Hypnotic Suggestion and RSPK," by Lagle, Roll, and Baumann, which came out in *Research in Parapsychology, 1986*.

The article in *Reader's Digest* by Claire Safran, "Poltergeist? Or Only a Teen-Ager?," appeared in December 1984.

In August 1985, Patricia Hayes invited Tina to attend a weeklong workshop for psychic development at Spring Lake South in Roswell, Georgia, in the hope that Tina's participation would bring back her PK. Tina was accompanied by Doris Koob, a research associate at the Psychical Research Foundation. There was no evidence for PK, but several of the participants commented favorably on the psychic readings Tina gave during the workshop.

Also in August, B. K. Kantamani ("Kanta") gave Tina a series of ESP card tests at the Institute for Parapsychology in Durham. They showed no evidence of ESP.

Jim Carpenter's "Projective Testing on Tina Resch" came out in the Proceedings of Presented Papers, the Parapsychological Association, 1993.

The paper chronicling the occurrences at Spring Creek Institute, "Hypnotic Suggestion and RSPK," by Lagle, Roll, and Baumann, was published in *Research in Parapsychology, 1986*.

## CHAPTER 19

Roll and Livingston Gearhart's "Geomagnetic perturbations and RSPK" was published in *Research in Parapsychology, 1973*.

An article by Gearhart and Michael Persinger, "Geophysical variables and behavior: XXXIII. Onsets of historical and contemporary poltergeist episodes occurred with sudden increases in geomagnetic activity," appeared in *Perceptual and Motor Skills* in 1986.

Persinger's "Enhancement of limbic seizures by nocturnal application of experimental magnetic fields that simulate the magnitude and the morphology of increases in geomagnetic activity" came out in the *International Journal of Neuroscience* in 1996.

Roll's "Poltergeists" in Benjamin Wolman's 1977 *Handbook of Parapsychology* included a survey of 92 RSPK agents, a large proportion of whom showed epileptic symptoms.

The suggestion that the brainstem may be involved in RSPK was made in Elson Montagno and Roll's "Psi and the upper brain stem," *Research in Parapsychology, 1983.*

Baumann summarized his brainstem examination of Tina in "An overview with examples including a study of an RSPK subject," Proceedings of Presented Papers, the Parapsychological Association, 1995. The paper also had a summary of a three-day study conducted in September 1993 at a neurophysiological facility in Galveston, Texas, where Baumann was working at the time and where Roll brought Tina. Tina had reported spontaneous fires at her home, so a PK task in which she attempted to affect the temperature of a thermistor was included. At the same time an MEG was placed over her head and hands to test for magnoencephalographic changes. Tina was unable to affect the thermistor, and there were no abnormalities in the MEG. Baumann also did an MRI (magnetic resonance imaging) test and an EEG record covering nineteen sites on her scalp. The EEG showed brain wave slowing and supported the diagnosis of ADD.

The data from Baumann's examination of Tina's brainstem and a discussion of the neurological processes that may have contributed to her RSPK were discussed by Baumann and Roll in 1988 in an unpublished report, "Upper brainstem abnormalities in an RSPK subject."

Hal Puthoff's ideas about zero-point energy and RSPK were discussed by Roll in "Poltergeists, electromagnetism and consciousness," *Journal of Scientific Exploration*, Spring 2003.

Roll's address in honor of Hans Bender, "Poltergeist and space-time: A contemplation on Hans Bender's ideas about RSPK," appeared in Proceedings of Presented Papers, the Parapsychological Association, 2000.

William Joines's "A wave theory of psi energy" came out in *Research in Parapsychology*, 1974.

Persinger's proposal that Tina was suffering from a Tourette-type disorder appeared in "Potential neurofunctional correlates of the Tina Resch 1984 poltergeist episode," by Persinger and Roll, Proceedings of Presented Papers, Parapsychological Association, 1993.

"The question of RSPK vs. fraud in the case of Tina Resch" by Roll was published in Proceedings of Presented Papers, Parapsychological Association, 1993.

## CHAPTER 21

On April 17, 1992, *The Times-Georgian* reported on its front page that Tina and David Herrin had been denied bond. On the same page, Sheriff Jack Bell brought up Amber's death in his bid for re-election.

On April 18, *The Times-Georgian* announced Amber's funeral the same day and the contributions people in Carrollton had made, including the casket and cemetery plot.

On April 26, the article, "Carroll Co. child abuse stats 'alarming'" appeared in *The Times-Georgian*, followed by related stories on April 28 and 29. The paper later ran letters to the editor and an editorial.

An October 17 headline in *The Times-Georgian* read, "No lawyer named yet for woman." Gerald Word, a Carrollton lawyer, was quoted as saying that Tina's lack of representation constituted "a breakdown of due process of law." He added that it would be hard to find a qualified defense lawyer because of the "incredible number of hours" required to prepare for a trial. He said, "You literally have to close down your practice for a couple of months to get ready." Word added that Judge William Lee had asked him to help find a lawyer for Tina and that he, Word, was negotiating with a lawyer in Marietta, a suburb of Atlanta. Shortly afterward, Lee appointed Jim Berry, whose office was in Marietta, to be Tina's public defender.

## CHAPTER 23

A report by Detective-Lieutenant Mike Thomas dated April 14, 8:30 p.m., reads: "According to Dr. Watson, E.R. doctor on duty, Amber had been sodomized recently and . . . over a period of several weeks. Dr. Watson stated the opening of the anus measured approximately 3 to 4 cm across and there were signs of internal tearing, so in his opinion Amber had been sodomized." A report by Thomas at 11:30 p.m. states that after receiving Miranda warnings, "David gave a taped statement in reference to Christina and Amber and the events leading up to Amber's death. David said Amber did appear to fall more when she was alone with him and did seem to bruise more. When David was asked the same question—if the autopsy shows the injuries which caused Amber's death were received within the past three or four days, would it be fair to say that either you, Christina or both were responsible for the injuries? — David's response was 'yes' because Amber was not with anyone else, nor has been with anyone else in the past two months. David was also asked about a [toilet] tissue found in the trash which had a large amount of blood and also about what appeared to be blood in Amber's underwear. David said the blood on the tissue was from Amber's mouth, cuts which Amber had reopened, and the blood inside the underwear must have dripped from Amber's mouth. David also admitted, not on tape, that he had in fact sodomized Amber twice, once on Friday 041092 [i.e., April 10, 1992] at 102D Davis Homes [Tina's apartment] and once on Sunday 041092 at his residence, 46 Martin Rd." In a police report by Captain Mike Bradley, dated April 15, 1992, at about 7 a.m., Bradley says, "I asked where Christina was at these times and [David] said she was asleep. I asked David if Amber had bled and he stated that he did not notice any bleeding. I asked him if Amber cried and he said no. David then stated that he was not responsible for all the injuries on Amber. That he had only hit her once in the face with his hand. David stated that he had seen Christina hit Amber before. When I tried to question David further about the hitting and asked if he would give me a taped statement he stated that he wanted to talk to a lawyer first. Interview was concluded at that time."

## CHAPTER 24

On October 24, *The Times-Georgian* announced, "Boyer pleads guilty, gets life plus 20." Skandalakis was quoted as saying that a pathologist concluded that the bruises on Amber were inflicted over several days, and Jim Berry said that a private pathologist drew the same conclusion. Berry added that it was in Tina's best interest to plead, because of the severity of the injuries and because she should have known the child needed medical attention. He thought that a jury would have held Tina responsible for the death, "even if she did not actually inflict the injuries." The paper added that Berry was part of the Fred Tokars defense team. Berry said that a polygraph test indicated Tina was being truthful, and that he felt "she did not inflict the fatal injuries." He said he wanted the polygraph results included in Tina's record so the board of pardons and parole could consider it when she came up for parole.

On February 2, 1995, *The Times-Georgian* covered the first two days of Herrin's trial. The paper quoted Dr. William Watson, the emergency room doctor who treated Amber the night she died, as saying the child had been injured for at least three days. The jury was shown a videotape by James Sacandy that showed Sacandy, another man, and Tina watching pornographic tapes and Amber repeatedly running in from the next room. On one tape, Tina is heard to admonish her child, followed by what sounds like three slaps out of camera range.

On February 4, 1995, *The Times-Georgian* headline read, "Herrin guilty on cruelty only, gets 20-year sentence." David's relatives "reacted with relief as not-guilty verdicts were read on each of the murder charges against him; with shock as the judge stated 'guilty' on cruelty to children, then tears of sorrow as he was sentenced to 20 years." The paper said that Skandalakis "had originally intended to seek the death penalty but later reconsidered." Scandalakis added, "A murder conviction could have brought a life sentence for Herrin."

In its May 29, 1999, story "Parole denied for woman convicted in child's death," *The Times-Georgian* quoted parole board chairman Walter Ray: "Words can't begin to describe the pain and suffering that this child endured at the hands of her mother." He added, "If there has ever been a crime that demands a long sentence, this is it." Assistant District Attorney Anne Allen, speaking of the autopsy photos, said, "It was so incredibly horrible," adding that she had sought to block the parole bid. The paper said that the parole board would not consider parole for Tina again until April 2007.

# ACKNOWLEDGMENTS

This book rests on the shoulders of many individuals. In the first place Tina Resch, now Christina Boyer, who is the center of the book. Also her adoptive parents, John and Joan Resch, both deceased, in whose home in Columbus, Ohio, it all began and who asked me to investigate and said I could bring an assistant.

The many others who told us about their experiences in the Resch home include reporter Mike Harden and news photographer Fred Shannon of the *Columbus Dispatch*. Special thanks to Fred Shannon for allowing us to use his photos. And to electrician Bruce Claggett, who came to the home to repair what he thought was an electrical problem and instead was met by an unknown force.

Friends and relatives of the Resches, who came to give moral support and help clean up spilled food and broken glass, witnessed the events and told us of their experiences.

They include three of the Resches' grown children, Craig, Peggy, and Pam; Joyce Beaumont, a friend of Pam; Kathy Geoff of Franklin County Children's Services; Lee Arnold, Tina's case worker at FCCS; Barbara Hughes, a friend of the family, her husband Ted, and foster son, John Edward; and Lisa, one of the Resches' foster children, who was six years old and the youngest witness we spoke to. Chris Tinnerillo, Tina's Girl Scout leader, told us about the girl when she was away from home.

Tertius Roll, then a student at nearby Denison University, came by for a social visit and was corralled by his father into making a video record of the incidents; and Bill Cacciolfi, a sergeant at Wright Air Force base, who attempted "thoughtography" tests with Tina.

We are grateful to Kelly Powers, who donated his time so he could counsel Tina and help in the investigation in Columbus and also in Florida; to Mary Rossi of Orlando, Florida, who reportedly had psychokinetic powers and who tried to help Tina bring hers under conscious control; and to Emmy Chetkin, who shared her home in Florida with our group.

Thanks to Muriel Roll, who allowed Tina to stay in the Roll home in Durham, North Carolina, in spite of fear for the porcelain that lined the walls; to Dr. Richard Broughton, who tried to evoke Tina's psychokinetic abilities at the Institute for Parapsychology; and to Patricia Hayes, who attempted the same by inviting Tina to a workshop for psychic development. Doris Koop was Tina's companion and wrote a report about the session.

We are thankful to Jeannie Lagle (now Dollar) for counseling Tina and assisting in the research at Spring Creek Institute in Chapel Hill, North Carolina. At that time the incidents had died down, but Lagle used a special form of hypnosis that may have brought on a resumption and made it possible to explore the phenomena at the institute. Thanks also to Dr. Stephen Baumann, then associated with the University of North Carolina and with Spring Creek, who made it possible to investigate the phenomena there.

We are grateful to Dr. Jim Carpenter, a psychotherapist in Chapel Hill, for giving Tina the Rorschach and Thematic Apperception Tests, and for his report of moving objects when Tina visited his office. Thanks also to Farrell Carpenter for her account of the incidents in her father's office; to Dr. Becca Zinn, also a psychotherapist in Chapel Hill, for counseling Tina and for her description of incidents in her office, her home, and her car; and to Sandrine Arons, who told us of incidents when Tina visited the Arons home in Carrollton, Georgia.

# INDEX

*The names of the two clergymen and the children have been altered.*

Printed in the United States
By Bookmasters